MW01013099

*Palgrave Macmillan Studies in Family and Intimate Life*

Series Editors: **David Morgan**, University of Manchester, UK, **Lynn Jamieson**, University of Edinburgh, UK and **Graham Allan**, Keele University, UK.

*Titles include*:

Graham Allan, Graham Crow and Sheila Hawker
STEPFAMILIES

Harry Blatterer
EVERYDAY FRIENDSHIPS
Intimacy and Freedom in a Complex World

Julie Brownlie
ORDINARY RELATIONSHIPS
A Sociological Study of Emotions, Reflexivity and Culture

Ann Buchanan and Anna Rotkirch
FERTILITY RATES AND POPULATION DECLINE
No Time for Children?

Deborah Chambers
SOCIAL MEDIA AND PERSONAL RELATIONSHIPS
Online Intimacies and Networked Friendship

Robbie Duschinsky and Leon Antonio Rocha (*editors*)
FOUCAULT, THE FAMILY AND POLITICS

Jacqui Gabb
RESEARCHING INTIMACY IN FAMILIES

Jacqui Gabb and Janet Fink
COUPLE RELATIONSHIPS IN THE 21ST CENTURY

Dimitra Hartas
PARENTING, FAMILY POLICY AND CHILDREN'S WELL-BEING IN AN UNEQUAL SOCIETY
A New Culture War for Parents

Stephen Hicks
LESBIAN, GAY AND QUEER PARENTING
Families, Intimacies, Genealogies

Clare Holdsworth
FAMILY AND INTIMATE MOBILITIES

Janet Holland and Rosalind Edwards (*editors*)
UNDERSTANDING FAMILIES OVER TIME
Research and Policy

Mary Holmes
DISTANCE RELATIONSHIPS
Intimacy and Emotions amongst Academics and Their Partners in Dual-Locations

Rachel Hurdley
HOME, MATERIALITY, MEMORY AND BELONGING
Keeping Culture

Lynn Jamieson and Roona Simpson
LIVING ALONE
Globalization, Identity and Belonging

Lynn Jamieson, Ruth Lewis and Roona Simpson (*editors*)
RESEARCHING FAMILIES AND RELATIONSHIPS
Reflections on Process

Carmen Lau Clayton
BRITISH CHINESE FAMILIES
Parenting, Relationships and Childhoods

Lara McKenzie
AGE-DISSIMILAR COUPLES AND ROMANTIC RELATIONSHIPS
Ageless Love?

David Morgan
RETHINKING FAMILY PRACTICES

Petra Nordqvist and Carol Smart
RELATIVE STRANGERS
Family Life, Genes and Donor Conception

Julie M. Parsons
GENDER, CLASS AND FOOD
Families, Bodies and Health

Gillian Ranson
FATHERING, MASCULINITY AND THE EMBODIMENT OF CARE

Róisín Ryan-Flood
LESBIAN MOTHERHOOD
Gender, Families and Sexual Citizenship

Tam Sanger and Yvette Taylor (*editors*)
MAPPING INTIMACIES
Relations, Exchanges, Affects

Lisa Smyth
THE DEMANDS OF MOTHERHOOD
Agents, Roles and Recognitions

Vilna Bashi Treitler (*editor*)
RACE IN TRANSNATIONAL AND TRANSRACIAL ADOPTION

Katherine Twamley
LOVE, MARRIAGE AND INTIMACY AMONG GUJARATI INDIANS
A Suitable Match

**Palgrave Macmillan Studies in Family and Intimate Life**
**Series Standing Order ISBN HBK: 978–0–230–51748–6**
**PBK: 978–0–230–24924–0**
(*outside North America only*)

You can receive future titles in this series as they are published by placing a standing order.
Please contact your bookseller or, in case of difficulty, write to us at the address below with
your name and address, the title of the series and one of the ISBNs quoted above.

Customer Services Department, Macmillan Distribution Ltd, Houndmills, Basingstoke,
Hampshire RG21 6XS, England

# Fathering, Masculinity and the Embodiment of Care

Gillian Ranson
*University of Calgary, Canada*

First published 2015 by
PALGRAVE MACMILLAN

Palgrave Macmillan in the UK is an imprint of Macmillan Publishers Limited, registered in England, company number 785998, of Houndmills, Basingstoke, Hampshire RG21 6XS.

Palgrave Macmillan in the US is a division of St Martin's Press LLC, 175 Fifth Avenue, New York, NY 10010.

Palgrave Macmillan is the global academic imprint of the above companies and has companies and representatives throughout the world.

Palgrave® and Macmillan® are registered trademarks in the United States, the United Kingdom, Europe and other countries.

ISBN 978–1–137–45588–8

This book is printed on paper suitable for recycling and made from fully managed and sustained forest sources. Logging, pulping and manufacturing processes are expected to conform to the environmental regulations of the country of origin.

Library of Congress Cataloging-in-Publication Data

Ranson, Gillian.
Fathering, masculinity and the embodiment of care / Gillian Ranson.
pages cm. — (Palgrave Macmillan studies in family and intimate life)
ISBN 978–1–137–45588–8 (hardback)
1. Fatherhood.   2. Masculinity.   3. Caregivers.   4. Men—Identity.
I. Title.
HQ756.R36 2015
306.874'2—dc23                                                    2015019829

Typeset by MPS Limited, Chennai, India.

# Contents

# Acknowledgements

This book is about fathers, and I am deeply indebted to the fathers who made it possible, either by their direct participation in my research, or through their own writing about the care of young children. In the former group, 13 fathers met with me in their homes on several occasions, and 21 others participated in solo interviews. I am very grateful for the time they were willing to give, and for their thoughtful reflections on caregiving. I also learned a great deal from the second group of fathers – 28 memoir writers and bloggers – whom I did not meet or talk to, but whom I came to know as fathers as I read their work.

I owe a debt of another kind to sociologist Andrea Doucet, whose research I draw on heavily in the chapters to follow. Andrea's work on fathering and embodiment is groundbreaking; it is the foundation on which any scholar interested in the area must build. She is a generous and supportive Canadian colleague, and I hope I have done her justice here. Another Canadian supporter is sociologist Glenda Wall, whose collegiality and friendship, in the course of many conference sessions and other get-togethers, I have very much appreciated.

In my own department, I reserve special and heartfelt thanks for my friend and colleague Liza McCoy. Over the years in which I have been working on the research described in the book, Liza has been an invaluable sounding board. As the book took shape, she read and commented on drafts of every chapter. As a highly skilled photographer (which I am not) she also guided my choice of photographs to accompany the text of Chapter 2, and prepared the photographs for submission. I deeply appreciate her help and encouragement. I would also like to thank my kind and supportive department head, Erin Gibbs Van Brunschot, whose willingness to adjust my teaching responsibilities gave me time I badly needed to get the writing done.

Finally, with trumpet fanfares and other family rituals of celebration, I acknowledge the sustaining love and support of Matt and Caro, who don't need to be told what they mean to me.

# Part I
# Setting the Scene

## Introduction

This is a book about men and caregiving – specifically the kind of direct, hands-on care that many fathers are now providing to babies and very young children. This kind of caregiving is a distinctive form of work, and it is usually mothers, not fathers, who are recognized as doing most of it. The reasons why this is the case are embedded in understandings about how men, as fathers, should think and behave (particularly in relation to the mothers with whom, in most families, they live). So this book is about masculinity as much as it is about a particular kind of work – the physical, engaged and embodied work of caring for children.

What does a study of men's caregiving as *embodied* involve, and why is such a focus important? What's involved, in a nutshell, is an examination of what it is that fathers are actually *doing*, in the time they are engaged with their babies – the tactics they develop to hold them or feed them or wash them or play with them, and the bodily capacities they bring to their caregiving tasks. In this book, I also examine how fathers *experience* this caregiving – how they talk about it, what it means to them. My intention is not to valorize them for doing what legions of women have done and continue to do, but rather to show that this work, whether it is done by women or men, consists of a set of bodily practices that can be learned – and learned, furthermore, by men as well as women. As to why this focus is important, I argue that it is because fathers' embodied caregiving has important consequences. As I shall show, men can, if they choose, become competent in its practices. And in the process of acquiring this competence, they change, in ways that are deeply significant for their relationships with their children and their partners, and, some would argue, for the wider world.

How this particular book came to be written is a story that draws on the voices of fathers (and mothers too) whose words I have been hearing and reading and thinking about for several years, mostly in the context of my research on Canadian families and the division of caring work. The first of these projects (described in Ranson, 2010) examined this division by couples who were clearly going 'against the grain' of stereotypical understandings of mothering and fathering work, and (by definition) involved fathers who were doing a much greater amount of hands-on, direct caregiving to young children than is usually the case. Their assured performance of this work showed me that gender did not have to be a factor in the allocation of caregiving labour. It tended to have other consequences as well: a sense of confidence in their abilities, a sense of closeness with their children, and equitable relationships with their partners. Sam, one of the fathers in that study, had taken leave from his paid employment to be a solo caregiver to both his children when they were babies, and had been deeply involved in their care as they grew. He commented: 'Just that hands-on, like literally hands-on ... it's something that sort of shapes you, for the life of your child ... and just sort of innerly as well' (Ranson, 2010: 182).

Outcomes like those Sam and other fathers in the study described seemed to have their beginnings in fathers' early and direct involvement in childcare. So my next research step was to look more closely at fathers who were committing to this early involvement – namely, fathers taking advantage of Canada's relatively generous provisions for shared parental leave to care for babies in their first year of life. As part of a project that I describe in more detail later in the book, I paid multiple visits to a group of fathers who were at home providing just this kind of care. I thought I would be talking to them in general terms about the experience of the leave, their engagement with this new kind of work, and, possibly, changes in their thinking about their paid employment. But because I was seeing them regularly, and *watching* them as they looked after their babies, I began to realize the extent to which this care was embodied. Their interactions with their babies were physical – they were not 'caring' in the abstract. And this physical engagement seemed to matter.

It certainly seemed to matter to the fathers involved in it. Like Sam, they were coming to know their children in ways most often associated with mothers, and to experience the attachment that came with that knowledge. My observations, and our conversations, were added to other stories I came across in the course of my research, and that stayed with me. One was sociologist Barbara Katz Rothman's moving testimony to her own husband's capacity for care – care that he learned through years of 'nursing earaches, bellyaches, changing diapers, calming night terrors, holding pans for vomit, taking out splinters, washing bloody wounds.' He had 'grown accustomed to the sheer physicality of the body, the sights and sounds and smells' – and in the process became a man who knew how to care, in a physical, engaged way, for others as well (Rothman, 1989: 227).

Another came from the writer Michael Chabon, a father of four children, who reproduced from his own experience an account of the 'daily work' of caring for children, and its effects, in terms very similar to Rothman's:

> [A]bove all, there is intimacy in your contact with their bodies, with their shit and piss, sweat and vomit, with their stubbled kneecaps and dimpled knuckles, with the rips in their underpants as you fold them, with their hair against your lips as you kiss the tops of their heads, with the bones of their shoulders ... Lucky me, that I should be permitted the luxury of choosing to find the intimacy inherent in this work that is thrust upon so many women. Lucky me.
>
> (Chabon, 2009: 18–19)

I also found food for thought in a chapter I read (in an anthology of writing about men's bodies) by the philosopher (and father) Maurice Hamington. In the chapter, entitled 'A Father's Touch,' Hamington looked beyond the personal to envisage what the broader consequences of fathers' caregiving could be. He used his own experience of the bodily dimension of caring for his daughter – reading to her while she was sitting on his lap, or going through the routine of washing her hair – to build a case for fathers' caring embodiment as the basis for a 'moral revolution.' Hamington writes that when he is washing his daughter's hair – touching her gently, protecting her eyes, working round her ears and so on – 'something more than the given task passes between us' (Hamington, 2001: 278). Through interactions like these, '[c]hildren can know their father's body and touch as accessible, kind and caring, just as tradition has allowed this understanding of women's bodies' (p. 275). What fathers learn, in their turn, is the 'caring moral orientation' more often acquired by women, because they are the ones who have done most of the caring. Fathers, he writes, have often been 'socialized to suppress their bodies' relational tuning.' So they have much to gain from a closer engagement with their children's care. 'If involved, embodied acts of caring become an integral part of the experience of fatherhood, then a new element is introduced into what these fathers bring to encounters with the world' (p. 276).[1]

Hamington's recognition of the effect of children on their fathers is picked up by many studies whose focus is on fatherhood more generally. There is a growing body of research literature, from scholars in many countries, who have investigated, from many angles and disciplinary perspectives, the changes in men over the transition to fatherhood, the type and degree of involvement they have with their children, and the effects of this involvement on their understanding of fatherhood, and their sense of themselves as men. The resounding conclusion is that fatherhood matters to men, almost always in positive ways. In the US, for example, a study by Palkovitz (2002) of men who described themselves as 'involved' fathers suggested that fatherhood stimulated a 'settling down' process, made them more giving, and caused them to assume fathering as a key responsibility. In Canada, a major research study of 215 fathers, representing diverse groups in seven cluster sites across the country, produced similar findings. The authors note: '[Fathers] become more other oriented, emotionally aware and attentive, more careful about time choices related to work and family, and overall more confident and self-assured. These positive benefits in turn have implications for more healthy relationships with children and parenting partners' (Daly et al., 2012: 1422. See also Daly et al., 2009; Ashbourne et al., 2011).

In the Canadian study, the researchers offer glimpses of embodied caregiving in the accounts of the fathers they interviewed. Ashbourne et al. (2011) note:

> One father describes his experience of his own frustration in response to his son's 'whining': 'When I get too frustrated I start singing … and when I start singing, he sings with me, he doesn't cry. And that makes me laugh and simmer down, and then I'm singing and he stops whining, and that helps me relax even more.' (p. 76)

Another new father was asked at what point he really felt like a father:

> Honestly, might sound funny, but it's when I changed that first diaper … my son was having gastro problems, helping him, that's when I felt like I was a father, not when my child first came out, when he was first born, I mean the doctors were doing everything … when I

stepped in and started doing stuff when my child was at home ... that's when I started to feel like a father. (p. 78)

The *embodiment* of fathers' caregiving evident in these excerpts is not taken further in the study. And in most other studies of fathering, it does not appear at all. Fathers' caregiving is generally considered in the context of the gendered division of household labour, or of broader gender differences in parenting. Fathers' bodies are not the focus (Doucet, 2006b).

But if the embodiment of caregiving is absent from the literature on fathering, research on embodiment 'deals only sparsely with how bodies matter in fathering' (Doucet, 2006b: 697). In studies of embodiment, as Morgan (1993/2002) notes, 'a somewhat one-dimensional picture of men and their bodies emerges, one over-concerned with hardness, aggression and heterosexual performance, a kind of "over-phallusized" picture ... ' (p. 407). Why is this the case? One answer is that perceptions of men's bodies fit with dominant understandings of masculinity. According to Connell (2005), 'true masculinity' is thought to *proceed* from men's bodies, either because it is inherent in them, or because it expresses something about them. In other words,

[e]ither the body drives and directs action (e.g. men are naturally more aggressive than women; rape results from uncontrollable lust or an innate urge to violence), or the body sets limits to action (e.g. men naturally do not take care of infants; homosexuality is unnatural and therefore confined to a perverse minority).

(Connell, 2005: 45)

To change this picture of masculinity is to change perceptions of men's bodies also. For Connell, this requires *re-embodiment* for men, 'a search for different ways of using, feeling and showing male bodies.' He adds:

Re-embodiment is involved, for instance, in changing the division of labour in early child care. As well as the institutional changes required, this has an important bodily dimension. Baby work is very tactile, from getting the milk in, to wiping the shit up, to rocking a small person to sleep. To engage with this experience is to develop capacities of male bodies other than those developed in war, sport or industrial labour. It is also to experience other pleasures.

(Connell, 2005: 233)

Of course, fathers' bodies are not the only ones implicated in the activities Connell describes. Lupton (2012) uses the concept of *interembodiment* to capture the relational dimension of embodiment – the fact that 'apparently individuated and autonomous bodies are actually experienced at the phenomenological level as intertwined' (Lupton, 2012: 39). Drawing on the work of Tahhan (2008), she describes the 'skinship' that develops through this intertwining, and the intimate relationships between infants and their carers that follow from it. Though mothers and infants have been the focus of much of the discussion of interembodiment, Lupton notes that fathers too can experience its pleasures, as they too engage in embodied caring work. She calls for more research to 'document and theorize the changing ways in which carers think and feel about the tiny bodies they care for, the practices in which carers engage and how they negotiate the strong emotions engendered by this caring' (Lupton, 2012: 48).

I was introduced to Lupton's conceptualization in a 2013 theoretical study by Canadian sociologist Andrea Doucet, whom I cited earlier, and who (as I will show in the next chapter) is the scholar widely recognized as having done the most to bring the separate research streams of fathering and embodiment together. In a series of studies, she interviewed more than 200 caregiving fathers. In their narratives she was able to hear the 'ethic of care' described by Hamington, and she too noted the moral transformation caregiving could produce. But it was 'the *weight of embodiment*' within the fathers' accounts of their caregiving that emerged as 'one of the stronger themes' in the research (Doucet, 2013: 288, emphasis in original). This was not what she was expecting. She notes that she did not set out to study the body; it never appeared in interview guides and she never asked any of her interviewees to speak about it. Yet it came up again and again. Fathers talked about their discomfort in 'female-dominated childrearing venues' (like playgroups); they emphasized the 'masculine and physical' quality of their caregiving, demonstrated through play with babies and sports with older children; single fathers, in particular, described the occasional uneasiness they experienced as their daughters entered adolescence, when public displays of physical affection could be misconstrued (Doucet, 2006b, 2013).

Doucet's research has been groundbreaking in making the embodied character of fathers' caregiving visible. She has shown how, as subjects embodied in time and space, they are aware of their own, male bodies and the way they are perceived by others. This is especially true in the 'estrogen-filled worlds' (Doucet 2006b) through which, as children's caregivers, they are often required to move. A father, rather than a mother, attending to children in certain community contexts (like a moms' and tots' playgroup) brings issues of intersubjective embodiment very much to the fore. More recently, Doucet has revisited her earlier work in the light of new materialist scholarship that has led to a significant theoretical reframing (Doucet, 2013). She has moved from a focus on *inter-actions* to what she calls '*intra-actions*' – the intricately intertwined connections between bodies that take into account not only bodies and their social settings, but also subjects as themselves embodied (p.294). It is a reframing that 'brings the body into full view' (p. 297). Doucet draws on Lupton's work as she calls on scholars to think in new ways about how bodies are part of 'this old and still critically important story of gender and care work'. This rethinking, for Doucet, would involve 'recognizing that care involves temporal, spatial and fluctuating embodied entanglements – mind, muscle, flesh, breasts, lungs, hormones, hugs, physical play, arms, hands, face, neck, touching, holding on, letting go – and emotions of unbridled joy and unexpected grief'. It would involve exploring, as Lupton describes it, the 'inseparability of bodies' that are joined by caring work (Doucet, 2013: 300).

I will be taking up Doucet's research in more detail in later chapters. Here, I will note that I too am interested in 'intra-actions', and the 'entanglements' of embodied care. My particular focus is on the mundane and daily things that fathers are doing for their babies – the cuddling, diaper changing, bathing and soothing that, in Lupton's (2012) terms, are practices by which fathers experience interembodiment. I want to understand what they learn to do, and what they make of what they are doing. I am also extending Doucet's work by looking more closely at the period in fathers' caregiving – their children's infancy – when she suggests that involvement may be subject to the greatest gender challenge.

My research for this book began with the project I noted earlier, on Canadian fathers who were taking parental leave to care for babies. It was this project that sensitized me to the issue of embodiment in caregiving, and what that embodied experience meant for fathers. From this point the research grew in several directions. My recruitment of current leave-takers serendipitously put me in touch with a father who had taken leave in the past, and was keen to talk about his experience. I realized that he represented a group of fathers from whom I could learn a great deal, and I set out to locate and interview more of them.

As my interest in fathers' caregiving grew, I sought out men's memoirs about fathering, to add to my background knowledge. This is a burgeoning genre, and much of it, consciously designed to entertain a general audience, did not speak to my interests. But I was lucky enough, early in my reading, to discover two memoirs[2] that were rich with descriptions of fathers' caregiving labour, combined with thoughtful reflections on fathering as practice and identity. Much later, I discovered the sociologist Arthur Frank's praise of published memoirs as valuable sources for the analysis of stories, but by then I had come to the same conclusion. I soon realized that memoirs, as 'the revised reflections of especially articulate individuals' (Frank, 2012a: 41) could serve as far more than background reading; they were valuable data sources in their own right. With persistence, and much sifting, I located others to include in this study.

Some of the memoirs I came across had begun life as blogs written by fathers. Recognizing this, aware of blogs as another burgeoning field of 'self-writing,' and open now to other sources of fathers' stories, I began to explore the world of fathers' blogs. As with the memoirs, I found a great number that did not address my research interests. But some bloggers surprised me by their evocative descriptions of daily life with children, and their self-reflections as fathers. Many were explicit in their intention to reframe conventional understandings of fathers and fathering, and to position themselves as competent caregivers deeply engaged with their families. I realized that the blog format of short journal-like entries, often with photographs, covering an extended period, could give me insights into fathering that I would not find anywhere else. So I added fathers' blogs to my data sources.

I wanted to study fathers' embodied caregiving as observable practice, and I had the field notes and photographs from my visits to fathers at home with babies to address this interest. I also wanted to study fathers' embodied caregiving as *lived experience*. And while this focus poses many methodological and epistemological challenges,[3] the use of three different sources of fathers' accounts – interviews, memoirs and blogs – allowed me to uncover many commonalities and provide rich detail on fathers' experiences in many settings. The addition of memoirs and blogs also allowed me to extend my geographic range. My Canadian interviewees are joined by memoir writers and bloggers from the US, the UK and Australia. They are, as I will discuss in more detail in later chapters, a strategically chosen set of men who are far from representative of all fathers. But their inestimable research value lies in their ability to describe a phenomenon that has received scant scholarly attention up to now. Their stories are at the heart of this book.

## Outline of the book

In the next chapter, I establish the scholarly context in which my research is located. In examining the separate streams of literature which bear, at least indirectly, on my work – literature covering fathering, caregiving and embodiment – I am consciously painting a very broad backdrop, which I hope will illuminate the space in which research on fathers' embodied caregiving might fit. Then, having provided the backdrop, I outline the theoretical and methodological framework guiding the research I will be describing.

Part II introduces the Canadian fathers who participated in my research in person. In Chapter 2, I draw on my visits to the fathers who were at home caring for babies, to consider embodied caregiving as observable practice. From my observations, and our conversations, I develop an outline of routine caregiving practices that I intend as an informal benchmark for what other fathers, similarly situated, would be doing. In that sense my benchmark is also a proxy, standing in as a description of the work of *most* similarly situated[4] fathers at home caring for babies.

In Chapter 3 I move from a focus on practice to a focus on lived experience – my second research goal. Here I introduce the fathers I interviewed who had taken parental leave some time in the past to care for babies, either in company with mothers, or as solo caregivers. Here too, there are descriptions of embodied practice, but these emerge in the context of broader discussions about the meaning of the caregiving experience. Fathers' understandings of their experience link to understandings about fathering more generally, and help set up my analysis of fathering and masculinity.

Part III introduces the fathers who contributed to my research through their writing. In Chapter 4, I draw on a series of memoirs by fathers chosen because their writers obviously recognized themselves as providers of engaged, embodied care to very young children, and reflected on themselves as fathers in the light of their caregiving. My choice of memoirs allows me to extend the range of contexts – both geographic and domestic – in which fathers' caregiving takes place, and adds nuance to the discussion of fathering and masculinity.

Chapter 5, on fathers' blogs, allows me to continue the discussion opened up by my analysis of the memoirs. The blogs offer insights into the daily lives of a larger group of fathers, all of whom have, or have had, the kind of embodied caregiving experience I am exploring. Like the memoir writers, they are deeply involved as fathers, and committed to sharing the work of caregiving over the long term. They too expand the discussion of fathering and masculinity.

As its title suggests, I use Part IV for 'joining the threads.' The concluding chapter will pull together the images of, and ideas about, fathers' embodied caregiving outlined in the earlier chapters, and explore the implications of the work that are both theoretical and political.

# 1
# Research Context

As I established in the introduction, the subject of fathers' embodied caregiving has received little scholarly attention up to now. So literature which bears directly on the research I will be describing in this book is scant. But several areas of existing research bear on it indirectly, and would be enriched by its inclusion. As a study of fathers' caregiving, it could add to a burgeoning literature on fathering, as identity and practice. In its focus on men as hands-on caregivers, it could extend research on caregiving as body work, and the circumstances in which men engage in it. Finally, and most directly, it could be a significant addition to research on embodiment – and men's bodies in particular. More importantly, it has the potential not only to add to these existing areas of research, but to act as a nexus bringing them all together. In the sections that follow, I fill in the broader research context, as a means of shading in the background and making space for what needs to be in the foreground. I end the chapter with a discussion of the theoretical and methodological assumptions that guide my research.

## Fathering

There is now a growing body of research studies examining men as fathers, and a consensus, as the introduction to Part 1 also noted, that fatherhood makes a positive difference to men. The nature of the difference is theorized in many ways. For example, Palkovitz argues, from a developmental psychology perspective, that fatherhood is directly linked to men's adult development. He writes:

> When men have found a way to embrace the responsibilities of fatherhood, and yet at the same time see their inadequacies, a

developmental pull is exerted. The relationships they have with their children seem to compel men to make themselves people who are more mature and responsible than they think they currently are. Thus, when men embrace involved fatherhood as something worth investing in, it has developmental consequences. Specifically, men's thoughts, feelings and behaviors are characterized by qualitative and long-lasting change associated with the experiences of fathering.

(Palkovitz, 2002: 59)

Another way of connecting involved and committed fathering with men's adult development, as Palkovitz and others (for example Snarey, 1993; Dowd, 2000; Marsiglio and Roy, 2012; Pratt et al., 2012) point out, is to see it as the attainment of *generativity*. Generativity is one of the final stages in the developmental psychologist Erik H. Erikson's model of psychosocial development. It is conceptualized as 'a form of adult caring focused on helping future generations thrive'; for many adult men the 'first and most central generative experience is linked to caring for their first-born children' (Marsiglio and Roy, 2012: 20). Generative fathering is social, rather than biological. While those who write about it use different terms[1] to describe it, they are generally agreed that it involves close, hands-on engagement with children on an ongoing basis.

There are other theoretical explanations for the effects of fatherhood on men. Eggebeen et al. (2013) add role theory (framing fatherhood as a status with particular expectations); identity theory (framing fatherhood as producing a change in the order of roles contributing to a man's identity); and life course theory (with its core tenet of linked lives connecting fathers to children across the life course) as perspectives informing the issue. In a summary of empirical research, they note effects of fatherhood on men's psychological wellbeing, physical health, social connections and working life. Not all effects are positive, and some fathers (notably white, middle-class, well-educated ones) are better positioned to reap the benefits. However, the authors conclude from the 'accumulating body of research' in their review that

when men become actively involved in the lives of their children there can be marked improvements in their health, work lives and wellbeing. In addition, the transforming effects of fatherhood on men potentially have the benefit of strengthening their family ties and enriching their communities.

(Eggebeen et al., 2013: 352)

If fathering in general is beneficial for men, there is now strong empirical evidence to suggest that they are also spending more time on it. Time use research in many countries shows that the direct care provided by fathers to their children (however it is defined and measured) is steadily increasing. In Canada, for example, time use data from several Statistics Canada surveys indicate that, though still less involved than women in primary child care (defined by such direct involvement as reading to children, taking them to the park, helping them with homework, or driving them to activities), men have significantly increased their participation.[2] Comparison of UK and US time use data sets spanning a 30-year period from 1975 revealed similar increases in fathers' child care in both countries (Sullivan, 2010; see also Sayer et al. [2004], Fisher et al. [2007], Bianchi et al. [2006] for the US). Craig and Mullan (2012) compared time use data for Australian fathers between 1992 and 2006, and found increases both in the time they spent on childcare, and in their participation in 'hands-on routine care' (Craig and Mullan, 2012: 172). Survey research from European and Nordic countries (for example Holter, 2007, 2012; Halrynjo, 2009) offers further support for these trends as does cross-generational biographical research (for example Brannen and Nilsen, 2006; Mooney et al., 2013) and other qualitative studies (for example Gatrell, 2005; Ranson, 2010; Kaufman, 2013).

Shifts in fathers' caregiving are also accompanied by other signs of change – notably shifts at the level of popular discourse and ideology (Sullivan, 2004, 2006). Scholars are generally agreed that the dominant image of the breadwinner father has gradually been modified (if not entirely replaced) by cultural images of a father who is also expected to be 'involved' with his children. Pleck's 1987 version captures many of the image changes, which persist to the present day:

> This new father differs from older images of involved fatherhood in several key respects: he is present at the birth; he is involved with his children as infants, not just when they are older; he participates in the actual day-to-day work of child care, and not just play; he is involved with his daughters as much as his sons.
>
> (Pleck, 1987: 93)

Studies that explore men's *talk* about fathering, notably with respect to their own intentions as fathers-to-be, reflect the changing cultural and discursive environment. Research in the UK (for example Henwood and Proctor, 2003; Williams, 2008; Finn and Henwood, 2009), Sweden (for example Johansson and Klinth, 2008), Canada (for example Fox,

2009), the US (for example Marsiglio et al., 2000) and Australia (for example Lupton and Barclay, 1997) makes this clear. As Henwood and Proctor noted of their study of first-time fathers:

> Our interviewees delineated with great consistency and in considerable detail the qualities of the new model of fatherhood (*presence, involvement, putting children's needs first, approachability, nurturing* and *caring*) that they could draw upon to represent what it means to be a modern father. This model of the caring, participative father not only gave them a sense of what fathers can provide and why fatherhood should be valued. It also enabled them to validate the desires they perceived in themselves for intimacy and emotional connection with others, and to see themselves as different and liberated from the constraints operating on their own fathers who, as a consequence, were not able to benefit from being full family members.
>
> (Henwood and Proctor, 2003: 350, emphasis in original)

But these changing cultural images have not entirely replaced the image of the father as financial provider. The fact that these images are to some extent antithetical raises questions, evident in a wide range of research studies, about how men make sense of them, and how expectations are balanced in the practices of daily life. Most of the studies already mentioned have shown that the expectation that fathers would *also* be financial providers (even if not sole breadwinners) frequently conflicted with their intentions to be caregivers to their children as well – a conflict apparent both in their talk and in their practice. For example a study by Miller (2010, 2011a, 2011b), of first-time UK fathers and mothers found a tendency for men to default to the traditional once paternal leave ended and the realities of the men's working lives took over. This tendency also appeared in Fox's (2009) study of Canadian first-time parents. Fathers may envisage their caring activities 'fitted in' around the paid work that continues to be their primary focus (Miller, 2012: 44), and may be selective about which aspects of caregiving they will take on (Dermott, 2008).

Fathers' attempts to accommodate contemporary, progressive images of 'new' fathering with more conventional (and more patriarchal) expectations about breadwinning also take place in particular economic, political and cultural contexts which influence both their talk and their practice. Differences in welfare regimes and public policy and their latent effects on fathers' participation in caregiving have been demonstrated in several national contexts (for example Gillies, 2009 on the UK; Marsiglio and Roy, 2012 on the US; Pocock, 2005 on Australia). These differences, along with (often corresponding) differences in public discourse about fathering and masculinity have been linked to the time fathers actually spend in childcare, as international comparative time use studies by Hook and Wolfe (2012) and Craig and Mullan (2011) have shown. Other researchers have noted the way public policy in specific national contexts links to cultural understandings of fathering and masculinity (for example Plantin et al., 2003), men's narratives of fathering (Eerola and Mykkanen, 2013) and to men's take-up of family-oriented programs in specific national (Björk, 2013) or organizational settings (Fox et al., 2009; Gregory and Milner, 2011; Burnett et al., 2013).

For example, in a multi-national survey of fathers' use of parental leave, O'Brien (2009) documented the importance of extended leave duration, combined with high income replacement, as critical variables influencing men's leave take-up. O'Brien et al. (2007), in another multi-national study, found that the experience of taking parental leave was associated with greater paternal investment in children and family life. Brandth and Kvande have also considered the way Norwegian fathers negotiate the amount and kind of leave they take, and the impact on men's fathering practices of time at home with infants; couples' collaborative (re)construction of the masculinity of leave-taking fathers; the effects of flexible work on fathers' leave time at home; and the implications of policies that do, or do not, set aside leave time specifically for fathers (Brandth and Kvande, 1998, 2001, 2002, 2003, 2009; Kvande 2005. See also Seward et al., 2006a and 2006b; Wall, 2014). Other scholars have examined the impact of work-family policies (like the availability of paid time off from work) on gender relations in families. Research in the UK and France (Gregory and Milner, 2008, 2011) and the Nordic countries (Lammi-Taskula, 2006) supports the suggestion that the *availability* of leave provisions and other workplace initiatives at least creates the possibility for more equitable sharing of household responsibilities through couple negotiation. It appears still to be the case, however, that fathers are far less likely than mothers to take advantage of such initiatives as a means to increase their share of family work. In the particular case of sharing parental leave, McKay and Doucet (2010) suggest one possible reason: fathers are inclined to defer to mothers, who are considered to be the 'owners' of the leave.

Within these diverse national policy and cultural contexts, differences in class, education, sexual orientation, employment status and family circumstances are also critical in shaping men's talk and practice with respect to fathering. For example, Raley et al. (2012) found US fathers provided more solo childcare when their wives were employed, took more responsibility for children when their wives' working hours were longer, and provided more routine care when their wives' earnings were higher. (See also Chesley, 2011).The study by Norman et al. (2014) of UK fathers found that mothers' employment hours were a more important predictor of fathers' involvement in toddlers' caregiving than fathers' own work schedules. These findings suggest, as does Holter's (2012) assessment of 'active' fathers in Norway, that material factors rather than gender ideology may be behind some of the observed change. Sullivan's (2010) comparison of fathers' time use in the UK and US, noted earlier, also found a strongly positive connection between fathers' education level and the time they spent in child care. (See also Craig and Mullan, 2011). Not surprisingly, then, a wide array of factors can be shown to shape fathers' 'identificatory positionings' – as fathers, and as men (Coltart and Henwood, 2012: 36). Researchers from many countries note the considerable complexity and fluidity apparent in men's accounts and behaviour, as they engaged with competing expectations about fathering against a backdrop of practical demands, constraints, predispositions and choices. (See for example Ranson, 2001, 2010; Doucet, 2004a and b, 2006a and b; Singley and Hynes, 2005; Braun et al., 2011; Magaraggia, 2013; Shwalb et al., 2013; Shirani et al., 2012a and b; Dolan, 2014). It is also important to note that, though the expectations fathers must balance are competing, they are nonetheless framed in Eurocentric, middle-class, heteronormative, able-bodied terms that impose extra challenges on fathers who do not fit this mould (Kilkey and Clarke, 2010; Ball and Daly, 2012a; Giesler, 2012; Marsiglio and Roy, 2012). And all this is to say nothing of the challenges facing fathers whose children are themselves challenged in some way, or who are classified as having 'special needs' (McNeill, 2007).

## Fathering, masculinity and caregiving

Fathering identities are inextricably tied to understandings of masculinity; changing cultural images of fathers, and changing fathering practices, have the potential to trouble conventional constructions of masculinity as well. This possibility derives from the understanding, most clearly articulated by Connell (1987, 2009) and now widely taken up in scholarly research, that masculinities are multiple in form; they are 'configurations of practice that are accomplished in social action and, therefore, can differ according to the gender relations in a particular social setting' (Connell and Messerschmidt, 2005: 836). Particular forms of masculinity tend to be hegemonic[3] or dominant[4] in different settings. While there is no template for what hegemonic or socially admired versions of masculinity might look like in any given context, configurations of masculine practice that involve hands-on caregiving to very young children are likely to challenge most versions, as Connell (2005) cited in the introduction, has noted. Doucet's question in this context is a good one: 'Since there is a strong connection between hegemonic masculinity and the devaluation of the feminine, what happens to dominant or hegemonic conceptions of masculinities when men are heavily invested in caring, one of the most female-dominated and feminine-defined areas of social life?' (Doucet, 2006a: 237).

As Ball and Daly comment, even to mention *men* and *care* in the same phrase serves to 'evoke a disruption in our dominant ways of thinking about gender' (Ball and Daly, 2012b: 225). But the extent, and effect, of this disruption is the subject of considerable theoretical debate. Some argue that there will be little transformation in dominant understandings of masculinity if, for men also strongly identified with paid work, 'involved fathering' comes to be seen as a sort of optional extra that leaves those dominant understandings more or less intact. In other words, the possibility exists that 'new fatherhood discourse can license the western(ized) middle-class father to enjoy parenting, while class and gender privilege allow him the resources to negotiate himself out of the majority of the labour and give him the free time and mobility needed to acquire publicly accorded status and recognition' (Henwood and Procter, 2003: 340). Dermott (2008) found that the fathers in her UK study were committed to what she called 'intimate fatherhood' – emotionally close relationships with their children, achieved through spending time together. But this could be time spent reading, or playing, or talking – it did not need to involve the routine tasks of daily care. Brandth and Kvande (1998) speculate that fathers involved in direct caregiving are men with little left to gain in the public world; '[c]are and intimacy with children can be seen as new territories to be conquered' (p. 309). (See also Gillies, 2009; Shows and Gerstel, 2009; Gottzen and Kremer-Sadlik, 2012). There may be little transformation also if fathers' push to play a more significant role in their children's lives is because they are trying to 'assert power over women in situations where male authority has been weakened' (Gatrell, 2007:368; see also Smart and Neale, 1999). Transformation will also be limited if 'change' stops at the level of discourse – if men 'talk the talk' but do not necessarily 'walk the walk' of transformed fathering in practice (Backett, 1987; Plantin et al., 2003).

Other research is more hopeful about the possibility of gender trans-formation. From this perspective, one possible outcome of changes in fathering could be the disruption of unproblematic binary understand-ings of family gender roles, and a blurring of the differences between fathering and mothering as parents who equitably share care become 'functionally interchangeable' (Ranson, 2010; see also Doucet, 2006a; Johansson, 2011; Rehel, 2014). As Hanlon notes, men's power is limited, and masculinities change, when men 'recognize and embrace affective relations; when care needs and inherent vulnerability are recognized and when the need and responsibility to care for others are embraced' (Hanlon, 2012: 26).

At the heart of the debate are the understandings of 'care' and 'caregiving' that are brought to bear when fathers' involvement with their children comes under scrutiny. In much of the foregoing dis-cussion, 'involvement' has been taken unproblematically (by me, and by the researchers I have cited) to mean some combination of time spent and engagement in 'routine care.' But this interpretation glosses important scholarly contributions that speak to the problems of definition and empirical measurement of two such amorphous concepts as 'involvement' and 'caring' (Day and Lamb, 2004). There is also, obviously, a political dimension to the debate. An analysis of paternal involvement widely cited in the North American literature on fathering divides it into three dimensions: engagement or direct paternal involvement with the child; accessibility or availability to the child, and *responsibility* – 'the role [the] father takes in making sure the child is taken care of and arranging for resources to be avail-able to the child' (Pleck and Stueve, 2001: 211; see also Lamb et al., 1985; Pleck and Masciadrelli, 2004). Research utilizing these divisions has tended to show fathers as least involved in the area of responsibil-ity. British feminists have understood 'caring' in broad terms as 'car-ing for' and 'caring about,' and have pointed out that, while fathers take responsibility for caring *about* children and others, it is mothers who do the bulk of the caring *for* (Rummery and Fine, 2012; see also Tronto, 1998; Himmelweit, 1999; Ungerson, 2005). An alternative view, put forward by several male scholars of fatherhood in the US, is that caring *for* children is not limited to the hands-on direct care traditionally provided by mothers; comparing fathers to mothers only in terms of what mothers do is to view fathering from a 'deficit per-spective' that ignores the unique contributions fathers make (Hawkins et al., 1993; Hawkins and Dollahite, 1997; Palkovitz, 1997). Seen from this perspective, '[f]athers are not mothers, and shouldn't try to be'

(Hawkins and Dollahite, 1997: 13) – though they should certainly be both 'caring' and 'involved.' This perspective suggests an essentialist view of fathering (and mothering) at odds with a feminist vision of equitable parental sharing of *all* dimensions of caring work, however it is defined. Pro-feminist male scholars also object to the essentialist position. Kimmel, for example, writes: 'The notion that men should be exempt from housework and child care, which should be left to their wives, is, of course, insulting to women. But it's also insulting to men because it assumes that the caring and nurturing of life itself cannot be men's province...' (Kimmel, 2012: 262). Clearly both perspectives have implications for how masculinities might be (re)constructed.

The essentialist perspective does not disrupt the gender binary that differentiates fathering from mothering, though it does call for some reframing of conventional understandings of masculinity.[5] But (to return to the question posed earlier by Doucet) what happens when fathers clearly trouble the binary by doing the work that mothers typically do? US scholars of the 1980s (such as Ruddick, 1982; Risman, 1986, 1987; Ehrensaft, 1987) concluded that, in such circumstances, fathers were 'mothering.' From this perspective, the work remains gendered, and caregiving fathers are viewed as border-crossers into maternal terrain – border-crossers, furthermore, who may still struggle with the identity issues that go along with practices still bearing the 'mothering' label.

As I noted earlier, more recent scholarship suggests another outcome: the blurring of boundaries between mothering and fathering (and their potential reconstruction as de-gendered 'parenting') as the practices conventionally attached to each come increasingly to be shared. This was a key conclusion of my study, cited earlier (Ranson, 2010), of couples contravening conventional expectations about the distribution of caring and earning work. Rehel (2014), who studied fathers who take parental leave, and Solomon (2014) who studied stay-at-home fathers, came to similar conclusions.[6] From a quantitative perspective, the essentialist view is also rejected by scholars like Fagan et al. (2014), who, on the basis of an extensive review of empirical research articles 'struggle[d] to find solid evidence for the argument that the dimensions of fathers' and mothers' parenting behaviors are conceptually unique' (Fagan et al., 2014: 390).

The stay-at-home caregiving fathers in Doucet's research did not consider themselves mothers, and were not putting their masculinity on the line through the caregiving work they were doing. Rather, in Doucet's terms, they were 'actively reconstructing masculinities to include aspects of traditional feminine characteristics.' But the recon-struction was not smooth; narratives of the men she interviewed were 'filled with visible and inchoate contradictions, which tell how fathers are both determined to distance themselves from the feminine but are also, in practice, radically revisioning masculine care and ultimately our understandings of masculinities' (Doucet, 2006a: 237).

## Men's bodies, caregiving and embodiment

The revisioning that is needed, of both care and masculinities, must begin with the recognition that the hands-on care of very young chil-dren that is my focus here is embodied. As I noted in the introduction, men's caring work is usually framed in the context of the gendered division of labour in families. Research in this vein seldom considers the embodied nature of the work of caring for children – and certainly not when men are doing the caregiving. Research that does focus on the material, embodied, messy reality of caregiving work is usually done in the context of caregiving as paid employment – a field from which men are mostly absent.[7] Explanations for *why* they are absent come down once again to 'normative assumptions in relation to gender, bodies, spatial regulation – and dirt' (Twigg et al., 2011). Twigg et al. cite Isaksen (2002) as arguing that '"masculine dignity" is much more dependent on fantasies of the body as closed and bounded, and consequently men find care work psychically challenging and fearful.' They add:

> Many of the positive cultural associations of body work, including touch as comforting or healing, are also seen as feminine, drawing on deeply entrenched patterns in relation to motherhood. Body work ... also borders on the ambiguous territory of sexuality. Hegemonic masculinity constructs men as sexually predatory (Connell 1995 [2005]), and this means that limits are often placed on their access to bodies, both female and male...
>
> (Twigg et al., 2011: 178)[8]

Men's bodies do come under scholarly scrutiny in contexts other than caregiving. Writing during the explosion of interest in bodies and embodiment during the 1990s, Featherstone and Turner (1995) noted the 'emerging literature on men and men's bodies' which they attrib-uted in part to 'the feminist challenge to conventional and naturalistic views of sexuality' (Featherstone and Turner, 1995: 1). Research on gay men, especially in the context of AIDS, and other studies of men's health were a growing part of this literature (see for example Connell et al., 1993; Ariss et al., 1995; Watson, 1998; Chapple and Ziebland, 2002). More common though were studies of men and embodiment, usually from a critical, pro-feminist perspective, which 'focused mainly on hyper masculine displays of bodies' (Doucet, 2006b: 696). Studies of men's bodies in sport (for example Messner, 1990; Young et al., 1994; Wacquant, 1995) were examples in this vein. So were studies of men's and boys' violence (Messerschmidt, 1999). But as Twigg (2000) noted, 'Focusing on issues of violence, aggression, war, sexuality (especially gay sexuality), this new gendered perception has, however, been slow to move as Morgan (1993) advocated beyond a "narrow, over-phallusised picture of man" to encompass the bodies of not just athletes and soldiers but dons and bishops also' (Twigg, 2000: 10).[9]

Since Twigg's 2000 assessment, there has been some change in the focus on men's bodies. The 'hyper masculine displays' noted by Doucet have not disappeared from the research (see for example Thiel, 2007; Beissel et al., 2014). But they are accompanied now by studies of men who are not soldiers or athletes (Riach and Cutcher, 2014) and of men whose bodily displays are not construed as reflecting conventional understandings of masculinity (Monaghan, 2005; Atkinson, 2008). That said, fathers as embodied caregivers are still not part of this more nuanced research picture. Men's engagement in early infant care requires *re-embodiment* – in Connell's (2005) terms, cited in the introduction, 'a search for different ways of using, feeling and showing male bodies.'

## Fathers, caregiving and embodiment: theoretical and methodological issues

To consider fathers' caregiving as *embodied*, as I wish to do, involves starting with a focus on everyday details – the holding and feeding and washing and soothing which is what daily life with babies is all about. The focus is on what fathers are doing, and how they experience what they are doing; 'doing' and 'experiencing' are key. Fathers here are not abstract figures, but physically present, engaged in a particular kind of physical activity, and bringing particular physical resources to bear on it. At the same time, their caregiving takes place in a broader social context in which ideas and beliefs about fathers circulate. These ideas and beliefs inevitably shape both the 'doing' and the 'experiencing.'

How could such a study fit with current theorizing and research on bodies and embodiment in the social sciences? According to Shilling

(2003), the field has been dominated by three major approaches. The first of these he calls 'social constructionist analyses of the ordered body.' Such analyses take the body as 'an object which is produced and regulated by political, normative and discursive regimes' (Shilling, 2003: 203). Foucault is key among several postmodern theorists central to this approach. Works such as *Discipline and Punish* (1977) and *The History of Sexuality* (1978) are especially relevant; Foucault's view that regimes of discipline and repression, involving 'ever more subtle and implicit techniques' of regulation, produce 'docile bodies,' has been widely taken up (Turner, 2012: 68).

The second approach cited by Shilling incorporates 'phenomenological and action-oriented studies of the "lived body."' Here the critical influence is the phenomenology of Merleau-Ponty, with the critical text being *The Phenomenology of Perception* (1962). Citing this text, Shilling notes: 'For Merleau-Ponty ... embodied subjects develop direction and purpose on the basis of the *practical* engagements they have with their surroundings and through the *intentionality* they develop as a result of the situatedness of embodied existence' (Shilling, 2003: 204). The focus of this approach is on what Shilling, citing Frank (1991) calls 'the body's own experience of its embodiment.' The emphasis is on the 'determining rather than determined nature of our embodiment,' and on 'the universal bodily basis of meaning and knowledge' (Shilling, 2003: 204).

The third approach identified by Shilling encompasses 'structuration theories of the body.' He notes that in the broader field of social theorizing, structuration theories (like that of Giddens [1991] for example) developed to overcome the divisions between structure and agency and other dualisms that were fracturing the theoretical field. Similarly, structuration theories of the body seek to bridge the distinction between bodies as objects and bodies as subjects, by acknowledging that while bodies could act on and transform social structures, so in turn they (and their practices) are shaped by the structures with which they interact. The work of Bourdieu (for example 1984; 1990) has been particularly influential in this approach.

Bourdieu's link between the actor and the social world begins with the concept of *habitus*. This he describes as a system of embodied dispositions, or tendencies to act in a particular way. These dispositions, shaped by class, gender and culture, are learned from the social context into which individuals are born and in which they live. They come to generate, below the level of consciousness, 'all the "reasonable," "common-sense" behaviours ... which are likely to be positively sanctioned because they are objectively adjusted to the logic characteristic of a particular field' (Bourdieu,1990: 55–56). The *field* is a particular social environment (Turner, 2012: 69). It is the space, the 'pitch or board' (to use Bourdieu's sporting metaphor), on which a particular 'game' is played (Bourdieu, 1990: 67) *Habitus* in this sense can be understood as the player's 'feel for the game.' Bodies, for Bourdieu, are also the source of *capital* – sometimes, as Frank (1991: 68) notes, referred to specifically as *physical* capital. Capital refers to 'the set of actually usable resources and powers – economic capital, cultural capital and also social capital' (Bourdieu, 1984: 114) on which individuals can draw in order to position themselves in any social milieu.

Shilling acknowledges that there have been multiple responses to these three approaches, which in isolation can only ever be partial accounts of embodiment and the place of the body in social life. Of these responses, the one which speaks to my research is to see each as 'providing different resources for the pursuit of different analytical tasks' (Shilling, 2003: 207). Nettleton and Watson, citing Turner (1992), call this 'methodological pragmatism' – allowing the 'nature of the problem and the level of explanation required' to help determine theoretical orientation and method (Nettleton and Watson, 1998: 9). Their choice (in a collection of readings illuminating 'the body in everyday life') is to focus on the phenomenological approach, but to draw also from scholars who have developed the approach in ways that address some of its limitations.

Four scholars, in particular, have provided direction for my work on fathers as embodied caregivers. The first is the British sociologist Nick Crossley. Crossley is committed to Merleau-Ponty's phenomenology, claiming that Merleau-Ponty understands the body as 'an effective agent, and thereby, as the very basis for human subjectivity' (Crossley, 1995a: 44–45). According to Crossley, Merleau-Ponty also considers embodied subjectivity to be intersubjective – and it is intersubjectivity that does not occur in a historical or institutional vacuum. But Crossley's theorizing does not stop with Merleau-Ponty (though it is always his starting point). He draws on others – including Goffman (Crossley, 1995b), Foucault (Crossley, 1996), Bourdieu (Crossley, 2001) and Mauss (Crossley, 2007) to move beyond his starting point into new and theoretically useful reformulations. From Mauss (1950/1979) he draws the concept of 'body techniques' – ways in which we know how to use our bodies. Body techniques may have a historical or cultural basis; from Mauss's observations, for example, English and French soldiers march differently, and women and men walk differently. But the critical issue for Crossley (and for Mauss) is that body techniques 'embody knowledge and understanding ... Swimming is a form of practical understanding in its own right, as is holding a baby, using a screwdriver, writing a letter or a list, applying lipstick etc. To study body techniques is to elucidate this level of practical understanding' (Crossley, 2007: 86).

The second is the French sociologist Loïc Wacquant, whose ethnographic study of boxers (1995; see also 2004) draws directly on Bourdieu's concept of capital. In a vivid account of the training and lifestyle regimes boxers undertake in hopes of achieving success in the ring, Wacquant demonstrates the need to see boxers as

> holders of and even *entrepreneurs in bodily capital* of a particular kind; and the boxing gym in which they spend much of their waking time as a social machinery designed to convert this 'abstract' bodily capital into *pugilistic capital*, that is, to impart to the fighter's body a set of abilities and tendencies liable to produce value in the field of professional boxing in the form of recognition, titles and income streams.
>
> (Wacquant, 1995: 66–67, emphasis in original)

It is *body work* that converts the bodily capital boxers bring to the gym – their size and strength, their body build and capacity for speed, the shape of their fists – to the pugilistic capital they need for the ring.

The third is another British sociologist, Lee F. Monaghan (2002), who completed an ethnographic study of 'bouncers' at UK night clubs. Citing Wacquant's study, Monaghan also draws on the concept of *body capital* to show the extent to which bouncers' bodies – their weight, height and general physical appearance – convert to job qualifications for the potentially violent and dangerous work they do. Monaghan, like Crossley (2007), also draws on Mauss's concept of *body techniques* to suggest that techniques like fighting ability are an added component of bouncers' body capital.

Boxers and bouncers may seem far removed from a study of fathers' caregiving. But I suggest that fathers' ways of handling babies, and the physical routines they establish, are all 'techniques' that they learn. They build on fathers' bodily capital in just the same way that Wacquant's pugs or Monaghan's bouncers incorporated their bodily capital into the bodily labour in which they engaged. But where the pugs and bouncers were reproducing conventional understandings of masculinity in the course of their body work, fathers caring for babies are challenging stereotypes – and in Connell's terms becoming *re-embodied*.

With this framing of fathers' embodied caregiving in place, I turn to my fourth scholarly influence – Andrea Doucet (2006a, b;

2009a, b; 2013), whose extensive and influential research on fathers and embodied caregiving has already been noted. In her earlier work, in the tradition of much of the contemporary theorizing on the sociology of the body just outlined, Doucet drew on Merleau-Ponty (1962), Goffman (1963, 1972) and Bourdieu (1977, 1990) to analyze the accounts of fathers in an array of studies, which collectively examined men's experiences of caring for children. Working from Shilling's (2003) categorization of the varieties of this contemporary theorizing, described earlier, Doucet positioned herself as 'somewhere between ... "phenomenological and action-oriented studies of the lived body" and "structuration theories of the body"' (Doucet, 2006b: 699). She was 'interested in how bodies are experienced,' and at the same time considered that 'embodied subjects both "create their social milieu" and "are simultaneously shaped by the impact their social location exerts on their bodies"' (Doucet, 2006b: 699, citing Shilling, 2003: 206).

Doucet used fathers' accounts to illuminate some dimensions of the 'lived experience' of giving care. She noted how fathers themselves described this care as embodied – for example, in their use of play to engage with their children. And she also showed how, as subjects embodied in time and space, they were aware of their own, male bodies and the way they were perceived by others – especially true in the 'estrogen-filled worlds' (Doucet 2006b) through which, as children's caregivers, they were often required to move. As I noted in the introduction to Part I, it was this effect of embodiment in space – the 'intersections between embodiment, time and social spaces' – that was Doucet's particular early interest.

In this early research Doucet recognized that the 'estrogen-filled worlds' through which caregiving fathers must move might, over time, become less-estrogen filled, as more fathers became involved in their children's care at an earlier stage. She cited fathers' increased uptake of parental leave in Canada as a good example of this changing trend. It 'could arguably lead to greater fathering competence and confidence with infants' (Doucet, 2009a: 115–116). But she also raised the possibility of challenges to fathers' care of infants, as biological differences emerging from mothers' experience of pregnancy, childbirth and breastfeeding are used to support deeply held beliefs about the gender-differentiated nature of caregiving. Drawing on Bourdieu's concept of *habitus,* she concluded that this differentiation was largely the result of the gendered habitus of '"growing up as a girl" or "growing up as a guy,"' which was 'informed by deeply ingrained assumptions about gendered embodiment and about women as primary caregivers and men as secondary caregivers.' Doucet noted that '[t]here are certainly

variations in how this plays out across class, ethnicity, age and generation, and there is increasing evidence that these norms and ideologies
are changing over time.' She enumerated several categories of parents
for whom caregiving might be less gender-differentiated – including
'parents of adopted children, . . couples who deeply challenge any gender differentiation in parenting, ... fathers who take most or all of the
family's entitlement to parental leave, ... gay fathers, as well as ... single
heterosexual fathers who are parenting without the steady presence of a
mother'(Doucet, 2009b: 91). Nevertheless, she concluded, 'beneath the
surfaces of everyday practices, there is still a constant pull back to those
primary assumptions' (Doucet, 2009a: 113). This pull back, for Doucet,
was particularly critical during the first year of a baby's life:

> [W]hile each stage of parenting brings its own demands and gendered
> challenges, this early phase of parenting is one where the biological
> and social differences between women and men are magnified so
> that they can take on enormous dimensions. It is also the phase of
> parenting that can entrench women and men into long-standing
> gender differences in their parenting and employment opportunities.
> (Doucet, 2009b: 93)

It is just this period of fathers' caregiving that is my primary focus in
this research. As increasing numbers of fathers are undertaking infant
care – through parental leave provisions, from ideological commitment,
or as a result of changing economic or domestic circumstances – it is
important to understand how they manage it, and the difference it
might make, to them and to others. I hope this focus will clarify the
extent to which gender differences have an impact at this early stage
of caregiving.

While drawing on Doucet's earlier work in the ways just described, I
am also building on her more recent theorizing (Doucet, 2013), which,
as noted in the introduction to Part I, takes a more materialist view of
bodies and embodiment, and provides a different way to understand
fathers' caregiving. It allows her to view her earlier interviews through
a new lens. She writes:

> It is . . . clear that infants and children of all ages demand emotional
> and embodied responses from the women and men who are in close
> and constant proximity to those bodies. A key finding from my work
> across the past decade, and one that I articulate in slightly different
> terms through new materialist lenses, is how caring for children

has radical transformative and generative changes for men and that these changes are deeply emotional and embodied.

(Doucet, 2013: 297)

Doucet (2009b, 2013) also notes the potential for change in the gendered habitus of 'growing up as a guy', as fathers take on the embodied care of babies and children – activities that legions of mothers also engage in. In Connell's (2005) terms, they are experiencing *re-embodiment*. The process by which it happens – the physical, cognitive and emotional learning they must do to become competent caregivers – is well worth studying. So, more importantly, are the consequences, for fathers' understandings of themselves as men, and as fathers, of engaging in this caregiving work in the first place.

The work of these four scholars helps me to develop two theoretical understandings that are fundamental to my project. The first is that the embodied techniques fathers employ to care for their babies are *learned*. Competence is acquired through practice, in the course of ongoing engagement with the babies being cared for. Men who acquire this competence do so as embodied subjects, who bring particular physical capital to their caregiving, and who learn the skills – the 'body techniques' – necessary for the work. When it comes to engaged, hands-on care of babies, most fathers – certainly most of the fathers included in this research – are starting from scratch. To borrow from Wacquant, they are *apprentices*.[10] By appropriating a term more commonly used in the context of paid employment,[11] I am signalling that caregiving is a kind of skilled work, a kind moreover that *requires* an apprenticeship, but that, once acquired, remains in the repertoire, and can be performed on an ongoing basis in other contexts.

The apprenticeship analogy is particularly apt when applied to fathers taking parental leave (the situation of many of the fathers interviewed in person for this project). For the men who are eligible to take it (not all men are) and who choose to do so it represents an extended break from paid employment which many have never experienced before. At the same time it exposes them, especially if they are taking the leave to be solo caregivers, to a new form of work – traditionally performed by women, invisible, time-consuming, intensely demanding, and performed in a space in which fathers seldom spend solo time. Over the course of the leave, they learn to do something most have never done before, and invariably they are changed in the process.

This change links to the second theoretical understanding, relating to gender. When fathers become competent providers of care to very young children – thereby breaching conventional gender expectations – they become different kinds of fathers. They don't become mothers, but they become much more like mothers in their knowledge of their children, their attachment to them, and their willingness to take responsibility as co-parents rather than as helpers (Doucet, 2006a; Rehel, 2014). In the language of scholars like Connell (2005) or West and Zimmerman (1987), they are constructing a different kind of masculinity through new configurations of practice; they are 'doing gender' differently. In the language of Bourdieu, they have entered a field traditionally the terrain of women; their engagement in this field, through the practices of caregiving, disrupts the gendered habitus that would otherwise dispose them to behave in more conventionally masculine ways. (See also Doucet, 2009a and b, 2013). As Wacquant (2014) reminds us, Bourdieu's 'late specification' of habitus (Bourdieu, 2000) allows for just this malleability; habitus may 'change constantly as a function of new experiences' (Wacquant, 2014: 7).

These theoretical understandings underpin my focus, in this research, on fathers' caregiving as lived experience, and also as (observable) practice. Methodologically, such an approach poses some challenges. The observation of (fathers') bodies enacting care is subject to both ethical and practical limitations. 'Lived experience' is similarly difficult to access empirically – unless, as was the case with Wacquant and Monaghan, the researcher's own body is part of the research. Wacquant (1995) in his study of boxers, used participant observation (or, as he called it, 'observant participation' – he was himself a self-described apprentice boxer), along with interviews, and analysis of 'specialist publications, reports from the boxing press, and the (auto)biographies of champions and renowned trainers' (p. 66). Monaghan (2002) similarly used participant observation to study the world of 'bouncers' – as he put it, 'I became a bouncer in order to study their world' (p. 336).

Without this personal engagement, however, as Frank (2012b) points out, 'there is a problem writing about embodiment in a way that avoids substituting something else as the stand-in for bodies.' Instead, most social scientific studies 'turn to what social scientists are good at analyzing' – the 'texts (both written and conversational' and the 'images (both of bodies and on bodies' that, along with other objects of scrutiny, 'stand in' for the bodies themselves (p. 390).

Doucet was also aware of this dilemma. She notes that, while she was interested in how bodies were experienced, she also took into account in her research that 'experience and subjectivities are not completely accessible to researchers.' Her epistemological approach instead was to use her rich interview material from caregiving fathers to focus on 'how these embodied experiences or subjectivities are *narrated* within research processes' (Doucet, 2006b: 699, emphasis in original; see also Doucet and Mauthner, 2008; Doucet, 2008).

My intention, as noted earlier, was to explore what fathers *do* as they care for their babies, and how they *experience* this doing. I too was aware of the dilemma posed by Frank. Some of the doing I was able to observe, through multiple home visits to a core group of 13 fathers and their babies. I also recorded some of my observations photographically, to provide visual representations of fathers' bodily engagement with their babies. To understand how fathers *experience* their caregiving, I have drawn on the 'texts (both written and conversational)' to which Frank referred. I begin with the material I recorded with caregiving fathers – conversations with the 13 home-based caregivers just mentioned, and semi-structured interviews about caring for babies with another 21 fathers who had taken parental leave at some time in the past. I also draw on the written material volunteered by other fathers who have wanted to make their caregiving experiences public. Specifically, I examine a selection of eight book-length memoirs by fathers. I also analyze a series of 20 online blogs written by fathers, which focus specifically on their experiences of caring for young children.

These three different data sources raise different methodological questions. Rather than address them all here, I take them up in sequence, at the point in the book where each source is introduced. So issues of method and analysis relating to my observations of, and conversations with, fathers appear in the introduction to Part II. Those relating to the selection and analysis of memoirs and blogs appear in the introduction to Part III. Here, however, two more general issues need to be addressed. First, out of commitment to the principle of reflexivity in research, I consider how I, as a *person*, may have shaped the research that appears in later chapters. Second, I describe, in less personal terms, my general approach to the material I gathered.

Doucet writes that in studying fathers' lives she has felt like an anthropologist observing a culture that, though it is her own, she can know only in part. As she points out, 'I was not raised a boy, do not have a male body, do not relate to men in the ways that men can and do, and I have never thought of myself as a father, nor have I been treated like one' (Doucet, 2006a: 13). As an older, highly educated, middle-class white woman, and an academic, I might seem similarly far removed from the caregiving fathers who are the focus of this research. Many of the men I interviewed in person were not much older than my own children, who were in their early 30s when I completed the research. To most of those I met in person, I must have seemed a grandmotherly figure – and that clearly would have affected what they chose to reveal and conceal in their conversations with me. Yet there were also affinities between us, revealed through my explicit focus on the hands-on, embodied caregiving that has traditionally been work done by mothers. Though (in Wacquant's terms) I was hardly an 'observant participant,' the bond I had with all the fathers I talked to and whose words I read was that I was a mother, who vividly remembered her own experiences of caring for infants and young children. These memories are deeply embodied. To this day, I can feel the shape of a sleepy baby in her preferred position – lying against my shoulder, with her head tucked into my neck, grasping with one set of fingers the thumb of the hand I have wrapped around her. I know what it's like to change dirty diapers, to feel a forehead that is worryingly warmer than it should be, to listen for sounds of a baby waking from sleep, to clean up the mess made by a baby starting on solid foods. Thirty years on, I have a clear sense of what all that meant, in my own life. Incrementally, day by day, it entrenched and strengthened my connection to my children.

By the time I started this research, I had also spent time with many fathers whose experiences seemed to match mine. So I brought some clear assumptions to my present work – about the effect of embodied caregiving work, its meaning for relationships with children, and the transformative effect on personal identity that is perhaps the most powerful outcome. My assumptions shaped what I was looking for – but I would argue that this was no bad thing. What I was looking for – the practices of embodied caregiving, and signs of its significance – was just what my experience would predispose me to recognize. I knew it when I saw (or heard, or read) it. And having found it, I wanted to lay it out for all to see.

This is the link to the second issue – my general approach to the material I gathered. I was always aware that, in examining fathers' caregiving as embodied, I was tackling a topic that had received little previous scholarly attention. So simply demonstrating its existence seemed to be an important first step. I felt I was mapping a little-known phenomenon, which needed to be described before it could be deconstructed. My approach throughout, then, could best be described as ethnographic; there is certainly critical analysis of the material I gathered, but there is considerable description as well.

My approach is also phenomenological, and this too has implications. To focus on lived experience is to focus more directly on the individual, and rather less on the social. And while I appreciate that every father's embodied caregiving takes place in a distinctive social context, which clearly affects how it is done and how it is experienced, here I am much more concerned with *what* than with *how* or *why*. I borrow from Doucet (2009b: 80) the analogy of the camera lens to establish that I am using a zoom lens rather than a wide-angle one. This means there is less detail on social context than a wide-angle approach would require.

Instead, I am looking very closely at a select group of individual fathers. One by one, in the ways I have described above, they are sharing their lived experience. As I hope the following chapters will show, much can be learned from zooming in.

# Part II
# Seeing and Hearing Fathers

## Introduction

In the two chapters that follow, I introduce the 34 fathers who participated in my research in person. What they all shared was the experience of looking after infants and very young children, most of them as
solo daytime caregivers while their partners worked full-time in paid
employment. Thirty of them were either currently on formal parental
leave, or had taken such leave in the past.[1]

My original intention, as I noted in the introduction to Part I, was
to focus on the potential of parental leave for securing fathers' early
involvement with their babies, and, in the process, to find out how this
time at home went for them. My plan was to recruit fathers currently
on, or about to take leave, and to visit them at regular intervals while
they were at home. With this goal in mind, I made presentations to
childbirth education classes attended by couples, which were offered by
the provincial health authority at several hospital sites. I left descriptive
flyers with the childbirth educators running the classes, for distribution
to other classes, and sent flyers to a midwifery clinic whose directors
undertook to make them available to clients. Flyers were posted in the
post-partum waiting rooms of two hospitals. I also posted a call for participants on the well-known online classified advertisement site Kijiji.
As it turned out, all these strategies helped me locate eligible and willing
participants.

I began my visits, and in the process, as I also noted earlier, my
research focus began to shift as I became aware of the *embodied* nature
of the caregiving I was observing. That awareness expanded my criteria
for inclusion of participants in the research; if embodied caregiving was
now my focus, *any* father caring at home alone for a baby or toddler

33

would be eligible. In the end, 13 fathers participated in this phase of the research, which is described in Chapter 2. They were living at the time of the visits in two urban centres in the province of Alberta. Nine were currently on parental leaves anticipated to last between two and nine months; two had resigned from their paid employment at the end of a parental leave to become full-time caregivers. Two others were not eligible for formal parental leave; one had taken unpaid leave when his first child was born, and then, when she was a year old, resigned from his paid employment to become her full-time caregiver; the other was technically doing part-time home-based contract work, but in effect had been a full-time caregiver from the time his baby was three months old. In this group, fathers' average age was 36, with a range from 32 to 47. Nine were university graduates; two had trades training; and two had no formal qualifications after high school. All were partnered with women in professional jobs.

The research took an unanticipated turn when I was approached by a father who had taken a parental leave some years in the past, and been told about my research by a friend – presumably someone alerted by one of the recruiting strategies just described. I realized that fathers like him would be a welcome extension of my pool of informants – it was proving quite a challenge to locate fathers currently on leave – and would have had experiences that would enrich the material I was already gathering. I amended my information flyer to establish past leave-takers as eligible, and was also able to secure the co-operation of two major employers, one in the public sector, one in the private; both employers circulated information about my research to employee fathers who had taken parental leave in the recent past. Ultimately I was able to interview a total of 21 fathers, who are introduced in Chapter 3. These fathers were living in two urban centres in Alberta, and two in Ontario. In this group, the average age of the 20 for whom this information was available was 38, with a range from 29 to 48. Of the 20 for whom information on education and training was gathered, 13 had university degrees, five had trades training, and two had some post-secondary education. All but two[2] had taken formal parental leaves ranging from two months to the full nine months; seven had taken leave for each of two children. On average, and taking into account the unpaid leave time several also reported, they had spent about five months at home with each of a total of 28 babies. All were back at work by the time I interviewed them, mostly in professional jobs. On average I spent about an hour with each father – in person in 16 cases, by phone in five. Information from both groups of fathers was gathered between September, 2010 and October, 2013. Descriptions of all the fathers introduced in Part II are provided in the Appendix.

I have noted that my overall approach in this research was ethnographic; I was interested in mapping a little-known phenomenon – fathers' embodied caregiving – both as observable practice and as lived experience. The two groups of fathers I have just described allowed me to focus on each of these dimensions more or less in turn.

The group of 13 whom I visited multiple times were the source of my observations. The time I spent with each of these fathers ranged from about two and a half hours in one long visit with one father, to more than three hours for most other fathers – over several (usually three) visits. In every case, these visits were preceded by a joint interview with both father and mother, partly so that I could introduce myself to the partner who would not be participating in subsequent visits, and partly to get the perspective of both partners on the decision to have the father spend time as a caregiver.

It is important to note at the outset that there were limits to the observation I could actually undertake. Though I paid multiple visits to the fathers, I didn't feel I could stay for much longer than an hour at a time. And depending on the hour, there wasn't always a lot to see. Visits were timed in the hope that babies would be awake, and therefore needing *some* care. But babies' nap times are famously unpredictable, at least in the early months, and they didn't always co-operate with my schedule. Sometimes a baby slept in a crib upstairs while her father and I chatted. (Sometimes, though, the baby slept in a baby carrier on his father's chest, or cradled in the crook of one arm, and provided a lovely example of embodied caregiving.) Because I wanted to observe fathers as solo caregivers, I also visited during the day, when most of the mothers were at work. So I missed the often much more tense and difficult nighttime caregiving. I never saw a father bathing a baby, and because I visited them at home, I never saw fathers packing diaper bags and taking babies on outings or errands – though from their accounts they did all these things. But I did see plenty of good examples of fathers doing what needed to be done for babies routinely during the day.

The visits also lent themselves to some rich conversations. With each father's permission, I carried a digital voice recorder around with me during every visit, to capture our talk and to remind me later what had gone on. In most cases, I also took pictures of father-baby interactions, to provide a visual record of fathers' practices as well. After each visit, I listened to the audio file, transcribed key excerpts, and made field notes. Finally, with an explicit focus on fathers' body capital and body techniques as they cared for their little ones, my relatively straightfor-ward analytic strategy was to do multiple readings of all my notes, and make a list of what I saw and heard about in both areas. I also noted (here exclusively from accounts, not observations) the effects of their caregiving on fathers' own bodies. In the end, I was able to compile, partly from observing them, partly from their own descriptions, the outline of fathers' embodied caregiving presented in Chapter 2.

As hands-on caregivers, these fathers were so to speak in the thick of things. I was present, in their homes, watching them with their babies, while we talked, and focusing, as I have just noted, on what they were doing. To allow me to explore in more detail the *experience* of caregiving from a father's perspective, I draw on the second set of fathers, the 21 who had taken parental leave from their paid employment at some time in the past to care for babies in their first year of life, and whom I inter-viewed when they were back at work.[3] These fathers, unlike the group I visited at home, had left this very early caregiving behind. So the focus of the interviews was less on the day-to-day doings that were such a big part of my conversations with the fathers I visited. The fathers I inter-viewed were remembering their early caregiving from more of a dis-tance. But they were also in a position to describe what followed from it, and, sometimes years later, to contextualize their early experiences in a broader sweep of family life and fathering. The interviews were semi-structured, and conversational in tone. They took place in fathers' homes, at their workplaces, or in convenient coffee shops. I asked about how the leave was negotiated, both with employers and partners, what they remembered of the leave time itself, and what it had been like for them. The interviews were all recorded, and transcribed in full.

One analytic option would have been to consider the interviewees as a sample, and to code the transcripts for cross-cutting themes. And indeed, using the software program HyperResearch™, this was my first approach. But inevitably, this method glosses over what is distinctive and interesting about each interviewee. In this case, above all it glossed over a critical distinction between the leave-taking fathers – the domes-tic circumstances shaping their leave, notably the presence or absence of the mother. Those who were at home with their babies' mothers had experiences that were sometimes surprising, and that disrupted gen-dered stereotypes of infant caregiving. Those who were solo caregivers were different again – and again had distinctive stories to tell. In short, all the interviewees had much more to reveal as cases than as a sample. So, bearing in mind Zussman's (2004) outline of what 'works best' in qualitative research, I chose to work with the cases, and took up an approach that was more opportunistic than systematic, and geared to specify rather than generalize (Zussman, 2004: 352).

My analysis was also informed by the work of Holstein and Gubrium (1994, 1997, 2008) who call for ways of talking about the social world that balance naturalistic 'descriptions of reality' with attention to the way such descriptions are constructed. This constructionist awareness 'lead[s] the analyst to look for what informants are "doing with words" in the interview' (Holstein and Gubrium, 2008: 389). My strategy was to read the interviews naturalistically, for descriptions of what people were doing, but also to read them as accounts or particular framings of those doings. This is a delicate balancing act. As I have described elsewhere:

> To give interviews only a literal reading is to miss many of the nuances in accounts framed by interviewees with a particular purpose or audience in mind. But to read them only as accounts, as carefully crafted stories detached from the 'real world', is to ironicize what people say in a way I find disrespectful; in research, as in life, we do sometimes have to be able to take people 'at their word'.
>
> (Ranson, 2010: 36)

I did, however, always bear in mind that the interviews were also accounts, stories told to me that could have been told differently under different circumstances and to a different audience. The results of this approach appear in Chapter 3.

# 2
# 'Everything but Breastfeeding'

In Chapter 1, and in the introduction to Part II, I outlined an approach to the examination of fathers' caregiving as embodied practice – as a series of activities to which they bring particular body capital, and which requires them to learn new body techniques. Here, I put this approach into practice by looking at what fathers are doing from their perspective, as engaged, embodied subjects. As a basis for this exercise, I draw on my visits with 13 fathers, who had taken leave from, or who had given up full-time employment in order to care for babies.

At the time I first met them, these men were differently placed in terms of their experience as caregivers, and the extent to which their caregiving was solo, or under the benign surveillance and direction of the baby's mother. But all of the routine activities of baby care – feeding, bathing, entertaining, changing diapers, soothing to sleep – they all knew how to do, in some cases because they described these activities to me, and in many cases because I saw them in action. Greg's description of his own caregiving – 'basically the only thing I don't do is breastfeed' – could be generalized to all of them.[1]

These men were engaged in different activities from those of the boxers described by Wacquant (1995), or the bouncers described by Monaghan (2002), as noted in Chapter 1. But the point of the exercise I am describing here is to demonstrate that (most) men's bodies are just as capable of caregiving as of boxing (indeed, in many cases they may be better suited to caregiving than boxing), and that caregiving, like boxing, is shaped by embodied resources (and constraints), and requires bodily skills that are learned through practice. So it is necessary to consider the body capital that fathers, like boxers, bring to the job they are doing, and the body techniques they need to learn to make them more competent. I do so here by drawing on the conversations I recorded and the photographs I took during my visits, and the field notes I wrote after each one.

## Body capital

Discussions of body capital build on the work of Bourdieu, as I noted in Chapter 1. Capital constitutes 'the set of actually usable resources and powers' (Bourdieu, 1984: 114) bodies provide; different bodies have different capacities and, therefore, different potentials. When it comes to caregiving of the hands-on, physically engaged kind, mothers are conventionally reckoned to bring more body capital to bear; gestation, childbirth and lactation are biological, capital-generating advantages that are generally considered to trump anything that fathers' bodies can provide. But fathers have resources that constitute capital of a different kind.

### Post-partum fitness

Fathers who are caring for newborns, and other babies in the first month or two of life, bring one invaluable bodily advantage to the work: unlike all but adoptive mothers, they are not recovering from pregnancy and childbirth. This was very clear to Steve, a primary caregiver involved from the start with the care of his first child, and interviewed for the first time when his second was five months old. He joked, 'I had a baby five months ago, but I'm in perfect physical condition!' But there was a serious undercurrent to his comment. He noted the major physical and psychological dimensions of recovery that confront most women after they deliver. 'I don't have to do any of that stuff,' he said. 'I can hammer it!'

Steve's view of the sharing of caregiving labour was that his wife had done the valuable work of gestating and delivering the baby, and then could 'pass the torch.' Not himself needing to recover, he could help his wife recover, by feeding her, letting her sleep, and generally looking after everything at home – including all the baby care apart from breast-feeding. Robert was less explicit about this physical advantage, but had an example which clearly addressed it. His baby had jaundice, requiring multiple medical appointments, and a midnight trip to hospital during her first week of life. In our conversation he seemed clear about the resources he could bring to this situation. 'I mean, she [mother] needed the help, right? She physically wasn't strong enough to carry the seat [baby's carry-seat] probably at that [time], she was so tired. And just to drive and make sure you get there safely. So no, I couldn't imagine not going to those appointments.' Though the issue of their post-partum fitness did not come up in my conversations with other fathers, it is reasonable to assume, on the basis of the caregiving they were clearly doing, that they had made use of it.

## Size and shape

Almost all the fathers in this group of 13 were taller than their partners (in some cases much taller). They had bigger, flatter chests and bigger hands.[2] Those physical characteristics shaped the way in which they carried their babies, and, sometimes, settled them for sleep. A long flat chest made an excellent substitute bed for a baby not ready to be put down in a crib, as Jason could attest. It was his wife who first alerted me to their nine-month-old's changed bedtime routine, built around her preference to fall asleep on her father, and not her mother – in whose arms she wanted to nurse, not sleep. She was also getting too big to lie comfortably on her (fairly short) mother's chest. Jason commented: 'She won't go down for [mother] anymore, so I get the call. I get fuss time!' Babies in cases like this seemed to be able to differentiate between mothers' and fathers' bodies in terms of their capacity for breastfeeding. They 'read' mothers' bodies as (endlessly) available for nursing; they had different expectations from fathers. Fathers' chests provided an alternative comfort. As Paul commented:

> [W]hen he's with [his mother], he does expect to nurse. And if she has just pumped or if she's not able to do it for whatever reason, that frustrates him. But then when he gets handed off to me, he's like, 'Oh, well, okay—I'm not going to be expecting it now, 'cause I'm with Dad.'

Fathers' bigger hands and longer arms affected several activities. A baby may not be any longer than a tall father's forearm. He can carry her comfortably in one arm while doing something else with the other arm. The chest of a small baby being burped can fit comfortably into the palm of a big father's hand – while the other big hand (gently) pats her back. Big hands also have to be trained in the fine motor co-ordination tasks of doing up tiny buttons on very small baby garments, and getting very small arms through very small armholes. Jason, whose size has already been noted, had no time for baby clothes with buttons because it took 'twice as long, three times as long' to change his baby. 'I always go for the ones with the zippers,' he said.

### Strength

The post-partum strength advantage that fathers could offer mothers usually worked on an ongoing basis. Babies need to be carried – at home, when they are distressed or needing to be soothed to sleep, or away from home, when they are being transported from place to place, in car seats, baby slings or backpacks. Some babies whose fathers I visited were carried more than others. In general, whatever the mode of baby transportation, fathers frequently positioned themselves as being better able to do the carrying. In the case of baby slings or backpacks, this involved a close physical connection to the baby. For most of our first two visits, Steve carried his baby in a baby carrier on his chest, and seemed almost unconsciously to rock gently as he talked to me. Steve said he used the baby carrier because it left his hands free to do other things. But he added that it was also 'good exercise.' Martin noted that he did most of the carrying of his five-month-old baby – in a baby carrier – when they were out hiking. His wife could 'do it a bit,' but 'I'm stronger, so I don't notice it as much.' John's carrying strength was demonstrated in another way. He carried his six-month-old baby on his shoulders for quite lengthy periods during our visits – with one hand wrapped behind her back for security. Greg took his baby out frequently, usually in a car seat. He commented: 'I find, I'm, like stronger, so it doesn't bother me to hold it ... But, he's definitely getting up there in weight. You hold the car seat all the time. You know, it's a good little work-out.'

These examples of fathers' strength conform to cultural expectations that men in general will be stronger than women – expectations that fathers themselves are well aware of, especially if they breach them. Douglas, a very tall, fit-looking, 35-year-old father, had suffered damage to his back as a result of years of heavy manual labour. During our visits I saw that he was affectionate and physically engaged with his baby – but he noted that his much smaller wife was the one who carried the baby in a baby carrier when they went for walks. He commented: 'It's kind of funny. I feel odd when we go for these 40-minute walks, and I'm the big whatever, but she's always wearing him!'

### Body techniques

Body techniques, as noted in the previous chapter, are ways of using the body to accomplish certain tasks (Mauss, 1979; Crossley, 2007). Some of the body techniques I observed fathers using might not have been too different from those that mothers would use. Others derived from fathers' distinctive size and/or strength. I have noted already the use of big hands to hold babies, and to 'burp' them, and flat chests to be used as places to soothe babies to sleep. John's method of carrying his baby on his shoulders has already been described. Another distinctively fatherlike hold was demonstrated by Greg (see Photo 1). Still other techniques derived from baby needs that had to be met in father-specific ways.

### Feeding

All of the babies aged less than six months old who were being cared for by this group of fathers were breast-fed; their mothers nursed them when they were at home, and pumped breast milk to be used when they were away from home. So a technique many fathers had to learn

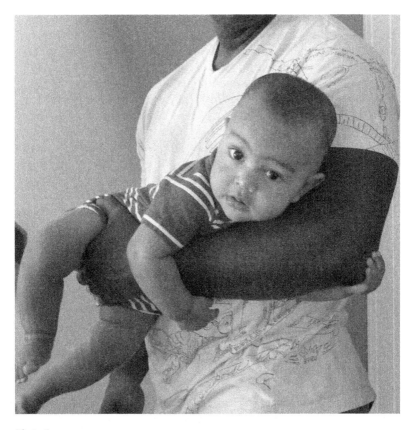

Photo 1

early was to get a baby to drink from a bottle. They had to substitute themselves for the nursing mother – a substitution that in some cases took a little time. Douglas commented: 'He was so fussy with the bottles before. But he's really not now ... He'll eat every time I give him a bottle. And now it's just if he's not hungry, you know it's because he's not hungry, that's why.' Greg commented, 'I'm getting quite good at it.'

Most fathers assumed a posture for bottle-feeding that closely resembled that of a mother breast-feeding, by wrapping the carrying arm around a baby pressed close to the chest. Fathers like Terry continued to hold babies close while bottle-feeding, even when they were well into their second six months of life (see Photo 2). Two others had a different style. Douglas, whose bad back has already been mentioned, braced his baby in an adjustable high chair, and sat beside him to feed him. (On my last visit, when the baby was past 10 months old, he was holding his own bottle – while moving around on the floor.) Martin propped his baby on a big nursing pillow and fed him a bottle with his left hand while leaving his right hand free for other things – like the laptop computer he placed within reach.

Once babies reached the six-month mark (and sometimes, depending on their parents' views, a little earlier) they were started on solid foods. For those who had been exclusively breast fed till that point, the start of solids reduced their dependence on their mothers, and positioned their fathers to care for them for longer periods. Being able to feed their babies, as well as care for them in every other way, was an important stage for many fathers, and they usually embarked on it with enthusiasm. Mothers were clearly not absent from the food planning, and in some cases took care of food preparation ahead of time. But its mealtime delivery, in small spoonful, into small, mobile and not always receptive mouths, was another technique fathers had to learn. I noted some idiosyncrasies in this delivery. By the time his baby was nine months old, Terry had grown impatient with delivering oatmeal by the spoonful, and instead held the bowl itself ('the trough!') up to the baby's mouth. But though casual about delivering it, Terry was scrupulous about what the baby ate. He did all the food preparation, literally by the book (a program for infant feeding he and his wife were following). In Tony's case, both the preparation and the delivery appeared casual. Tony's strategy seemed to be to let his baby explore a wide variety of foods, in very small pieces. At four months, I saw her sucking on a whole banana, held for her by her father. At eight months he sat her on the kitchen counter during my visit and fed her morsels of bread.

Accompanying the actual delivery of food to a baby, however structured or casual its organization, was emotional labour of the kind

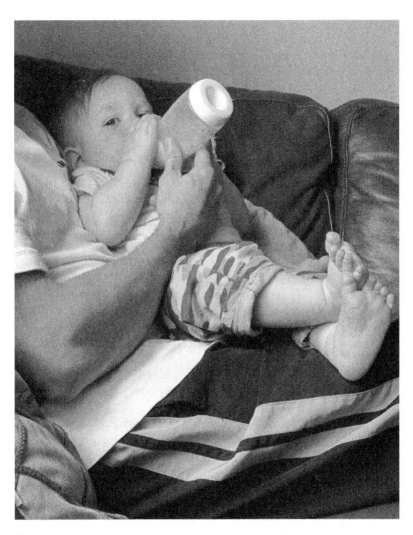

*Photo 2*

described by DeVault (1991) in the context of women's work in 'feeding the family.' For fathers, this labour involved recognizing and accommodating a baby's emerging tastes while also expanding their food horizons and making sure they ate what was needed for healthy growth.

### Doing the 'dirty work'

In Lupton's terms, babies are 'high maintenance bodies' (Lupton, 2012: 39). And some of the maintenance work is not pleasurable. To co-opt

Grosz's (1994) descriptor (from a theoretical discussion of adult bodies), babies' bodies are also indisputably 'leaky.' What's more, to borrow from another study (of incontinence in an adult context) babies' bodies are *unbounded* (Lawton, 1998). In other words, they cannot control their leakiness. Those who care for them must contain and then clean up the urine and feces and, less frequently, the vomit that they produce. This is part of the dirty work associated with any intimate care; by its nature it is work most often associated with women (Bolton, 2005; Isaksen, 2005). So changing diapers – especially after bowel movements – becomes something of a line in the sand, which fathers committed to caregiving must cross. And, of course, they do, because they must.

Changing a diaper is in itself not a difficult technical task. Even taking into account the discrepancies between fathers' big hands, and babies' small bodies noted earlier, diaper changing is greatly simplified for today's fathers by the replacement of the diaper pins of generations past with adhesive tapes and products like Velcro. The point to be made is rather that diaper changing immerses them in a kind of work that most of them have never done before, and that fathers of a generation or two before them, however involved with their children they might have been, would not have done at all.

I saw many examples of diaper changing during my visits to fathers. Invariably it was done quickly and efficiently. In some cases it was accompanied by knowledge-revealing commentaries about creams that had to be applied, or strategies for avoiding diaper rash. In the case of babies eating solid food, there were several matter-of-fact descriptions of the effects of certain foods on babies' bowel movements, and the time that was likely to elapse between them. It was clear, in other words, that this 'dirty work' had become routinized.

## Entertainment and play

I intended, during my visits with fathers, to observe them as they went about their normal activities – many of which, I assumed, would include providing direct, hands-on care to their babies. But while babies would obviously have first claim on their attention, I also wanted to talk to them. So my presence clearly shaped what went on. In some cases, babies were claiming their fathers' attention assertively enough that conversation definitely took a back seat. In other cases, I was able to watch fathers simply *being with* their babies, as companion, playmate and first responder, while they also talked to me. Whether, in my absence, they would have spent the time in this way is a question worth raising. But I got the sense from several of them that the gentle playing and entertaining I was observing did indeed characterize much of the time they were spending with their babies when they were awake. Typically, they sat, or sprawled on the floor, using their bodies as a barrier to block off escape routes for more mobile babies, positioning themselves within easy reach of toys, and allowing their bodies to be used as a climbing frame, plaything and source of comfort. They also brought themselves down to their babies' level, making eye and voice contact more proximate. 'Usually I'm on the floor with her,' said Jason of his then 10-month-old daughter. John, pictured sitting on the floor of his daughters' play room (see Photo 3) commented: 'This is most of our day!'

Fathers' use of play as an embodied way of engaging with their children has been documented by Doucet (2006a, 2006b). I observed it too.

Photo 3

All of the children in the care of the fathers I visited were under two years of age, and most were babies in their first year of life. So there were some constraints on the vigour of the play. Fathers making their own bodies available as climbing frames, as just noted, was one standard 'play' technique. Blowing on a baby's bare belly was another. But to pick up a baby is to pick up a weight – sometimes a fairly substantial weight. Several of the fathers I visited commented humorously on this 'weight training,' and both Terry and Tony demonstrated the way they parlayed playful baby-carrying into exercise routines. 'Breathe in, exhale!' Tony joked as he lifted his baby high over his head. He said he also 'did squats and shoulder stuff' with her. Terry demonstrated some of the exercises he did with his nearly-year-old baby.[3]

Simon, caring for an 18-month-old, was the only father I was able to accompany outside to a playground, where he and his daughter engaged in a game she clearly enjoyed, and that seemed to me quintessentially father-initiated. He lifted her up so that she could hold on to the parallel bars, then took his hands away – and caught her as she let go (see Photo 4). Simon's daughter, at 18 months, was one of only three children in this part of the study who was more than a year old, and for whom this kind of play would have been possible or appropriate. But even so, it was hardly typical of the gentle physical engagement I more often saw between these two – piecing together jigsaw puzzles on the floor and playing imaginary games. 'May I have a cookie?' he would ask her. And she would place an imaginary one in his mouth. He told me they 'dance a lot' during the day. He had also taught her to walk on his feet 'like I did with my dad.' John, perhaps because of his training as a teacher of young children, was especially interesting to watch as he played with his two little ones – a six-month-old baby and a two-year-old. I wrote in my field notes: 'He can turn anything that comes to hand – a couple of blocks, a popsicle container, a puzzle piece – into a game or a task, and the kids are always absorbed.'

### Voice training

Communicating with a baby is not always verbal. Facial expressions and gestures are also involved. Several of the fathers of babies in the 8–12-month age range practised signing[4] with their babies, using common terms ('more,' 'food,' 'milk' and so on) intended to help babies learn to express their needs before they acquired the verbal skills to do so. Drew was possibly the most diligent, having taken a four-week course, along with his baby. 'They say, for what it's worth, that it should help with communication skills,' he said. Drew could see a potential

Photo 4

advantage in his baby being able to sign that he was hungry or uncomfortable. Other fathers admitted to being much less consistent in their signing. But in any case, signing was always accompanied, on the fathers' part, by speech. Talking to babies was another skill they all had to learn.

During my visits to Jamie, Drew and Douglas, I noticed occasionally that their voices moved to a higher pitch when they addressed their little ones. But the shift didn't happen often. Mostly, fathers spoke in normal voice tones. *What* to say was the question. Terry talked to his baby about what he was doing – and since cooking was an important part of his domestic chores, he said he gave the baby a daily cooking lesson: 'I put his little high chair right here, and I show him what I'm chopping, and everything that we're doing.' Greg commented that the baby's mother, when she talked to him, made 'little funny noises.' Greg didn't do that. 'When I talk to him I try to tell him what I'm doing ... I don't know if it's good or bad, but "OK. This is what I'm going to do now."' Greg said it felt odd at first, to think about talking to the baby. 'What are you going to tell them?' he said.

> They're not going to respond back to you. Obviously at that age they don't really understand what you're telling them. But it's good to keep communicating with them. Even when I'm driving and he's awake, I'll talk to him a little bit, here and there. 'Oh, what are you looking at?'

Another dimension of fathers' 'voice training' involved singing. I often asked about singing on the basis of my own experience of its usefulness in soothing a baby, and because I wondered what sort of accommodation singing to a baby might mean for fathers whose voices would not normally be used in this way. From our conversations, it was clear that singing to babies came more easily to some fathers than others. Drew commented that it was his wife, rather than he who sang to their baby, though, he said, 'I have been known to sing.' But other fathers also recognized its effectiveness, and I heard some amusing details about what, exactly, got sung. Martin reported that his baby was very vocal, and seemed to be trying many new sounds. 'We sing different songs to him, depending on the noises he's making,' he said. When the baby was very small Martin sang him the song 'Daisy, Daisy.' 'I don't think I've ever sung that song, ever!' he said. 'But I seemed to remember some of the words to it, and that was the only thing that would make him quiet.' During one visit I heard Jason whistling the French folk song 'Alouette,' which had just been playing on one of his daughter's learning toys.[5] I asked if he sang songs like that to his daughter. 'Not so much,' he said. 'I sing to her when she goes down, but I usually sing country, or ... something I know!' Douglas also found himself 'whistling endlessly' the tunes from his baby's play station. He also sang. 'We'll have CBC Radio on, the kids' station,' he said. 'The songs are ridiculous but I sing along, bopping along ... [The baby] seems to really like it.' John said he also sang, especially when he was doing something like changing a diaper. Most of the time it was 'just random stuff' – commentary on what was happening ('OK, we're eating lunch now'), but sung instead of spoken. Paul said he sang 'all the time.' Because he liked music himself, and played the guitar, he had also started a daily 'music time' by the time the baby was five months old. Sometimes this involved putting music on and walking around singing to him. Sometimes, as on one of my visits, he put the baby on a mat on the floor, and sang to him with a guitar accompaniment.

### 'Perceiving' the baby and learning attentiveness

Body techniques like those just described are, as I have noted, ways of using bodies to accomplish particular tasks. And some of those just described are more likely to be employed by fathers than by mothers. But as Crossley notes, body techniques are also involved in the ways we perceive the world (Crossley, 2007: 90). They involve 'training the gaze' (as well as other senses) in order that our bodies can respond appropriately. This training, I suggest, is not gendered. In caring for babies, fathers, like mothers, must learn to listen for a baby crying, and to distinguish the meaning of a cry. They must learn when a baby is hungry, and how much to feed her; when a baby needs more stimulation, and what kind to provide him. They must learn, in short, to 'read' their babies' signals, and respond accordingly. This learning happens in the course of attending to babies' needs on an ongoing basis. The social practices of caregiving produce a kind of thinking about children's needs which the philosopher Sara Ruddick (1982, 1995) has called 'maternal thinking' – not because only mothers do it (Ruddick is clear that fathers can acquire this form of thinking too) but because it emerges from the kind of practical ongoing daily care that mothers are more likely to do. For Ruddick, it links to a particular capacity of 'attention' very like the training of perception that Crossley has noted. Magaraggia (2013) in her study of Italian fathers of young children, offers the term *paternalità* to capture what can happen for fathers, and for babies, in the 'minute and permanent conditions of everyday life':

> [I]t is in this new daily rhythm that fathers can begin to lay the foundations for *paternalità*, the slow getting to know each other by interpreting gestures and cries of the newborn and so understanding its needs.
>
> (Magaraggia, 2013: 84)

Listening for a baby waking from sleep is one form of perceptual 'training' described by many of the fathers I visited. It began with a recognition of the *need* to listen, and not become so preoccupied with other things that sounds were missed. Listening for a baby is facilitated in many contemporary middle-class households by an electronic baby monitor, which transmits audio (and occasionally also video) signals from a baby's crib to a station within a parent's earshot.[6] Several fathers demonstrated their own monitors, and described how helpful they were. But, interestingly, others preferred, or were able, to trust their own ears. Steve, who used an audio monitor, said he was starting to 'wean himself off it,' because it produced a kind of obsessive dependence he didn't like. 'You spend so much time listening to it terrified they're going to wake up,' he said. 'And really, I can hear him!' Older babies also made enough noise that a monitor was not strictly necessary. Max no longer routinely used one for his 19-month-old – 'he's pretty loud now.'

Beyond becoming aware, with or without technological assistance, *that* a baby was crying, fathers also learned to know what cries or other signs of fussiness actually meant. 'I've gotten the hang of it,' said Tony. 'Once you get to know the different cries. OK, she's hungry. That cry means she's overtired. That cry means, like, "I'm bored." ... That's the most common cry, I find, actually...' Sometimes, he said, 'she just quite simply needs to be held.' Of his baby, Jason said: 'You can see those signs ... I know what's going on now. Sometimes she's just fussy. But most of the time "I'm hungry" or "I'm tired" or "I've got a crappy diaper".' Paul described learning to differentiate cries of distress (which always got a parental response) from cries of anger – the latter kind heard fairly often when he and his wife were training their baby to go to sleep in his crib.[7] I got to hear the difference on my last visit to Paul and his then eight-month-old baby, who was late for his regular morning nap and was visibly – and audibly – cranky. Paul tried several strategies for getting him to sleep as we talked – tucked on his lap, lying beside him on the couch, lying within sight of us in his playpen. When it was clear that these strategies were not going to work, he took the baby upstairs to his crib. The baby roared for about two minutes – as clear an 'angry' cry as could be imagined – and then he went to sleep. Paul said it was now not difficult to decide whether the baby was scared about something in his environment, or just mad that he had been put to bed. 'He's very expressive. Like, there's no ambiguity, I don't think, with him.'

Questions of how, and whether, to respond to a baby's cries link to other aspects of the training of fathers' behaviour – training in which babies themselves soon become active participants, and training that of course involves the other parent as well. In some of the households I visited, there were ongoing debates about whether babies should be left to cry when it was time for them to sleep, or when, during times of wakefulness, they were set down in a baby seat or a mat on the floor. Most of the fathers I talked to found this hard, if not impossible to do. So their response to the cries was to pick up the baby and carry it around – in their arms, like Greg, in a baby carrier, like Steve, on their shoulders, like John. Steve said, 'We bought the books, sleep-training and all – but I can't let them cry it out.'

Babies also present cues that are picked up visually – and they produce in caregiving fathers (and caregiving mothers too) a perpetual watchfulness. If babies' sounds train their parents' ears, so their facial expressions, gestures and body comportment come to 'train the gaze' (Crossley, 2007). On one of my visits to Jason, when his daughter was nine months old, we observed what Jason called her 'pout face' – an expression he had also seen a few days earlier when people came to visit. The expression was 'not crying,' he said, but just more about 'what are all these people doing in my space?' On a visit to Terry and his nearly-year-old baby, Terry jokingly explained the look of rather intense concentration on the baby's face that would shortly result in a dirty diaper. (Needless to say, dirty diapers were part of fathers' olfactory training as well. During my visits I had several opportunities to register fathers' skill at – literally – sniffing them out.) On many occasions I saw fathers looking carefully at their baby's faces and noting early signs of fatigue, or noses that were running, or expressions that signified, to them, a particular state that would soon need attention. Babies' facial expressions were also good indicators of their tastes as different solid foods were introduced. The expression I observed on the face of Jason's baby one lunch time (eating a mixture of pears and greens) was what he called her 'bitter beer' face.

Constant contact, and close observation, meant that fathers also became aware of their babies' cognitive and physical development, and adjusted their own responses accordingly. For example from my conversations with Martin, it was clear that he took a lively interest in his baby's developmental cues, and developed little games with him when he saw what the baby could do. He said he had noticed that he could make the baby giggle by blowing on his belly. But if he made a particular movement in advance of the blowing, the baby would now laugh at the movement. The baby was learning to anticipate, and Martin was learning to encourage it. Martin, whose singing was described earlier, was also very interested in the effects of different styles of music as the baby grew. On my last visit, the baby (then 10 months old) was crying, so Martin played some music by the 1960s pop music group the Bee Gees. He had read that the beat of this music was similar to a human heart beat, and he thought the baby might find it soothing. Martin also demonstrated his new strategy of pulling up some interesting visuals (like shifting kaleidoscopes) on his laptop computer screen, to accompany the music. He had found that this too seemed to soothe the baby and send him to sleep.

Once babies were mobile they produced a watchfulness that was more vigilant. As Terry commented, 'Your eyes are always on them anyway, but it's just you have to be that much more careful.' (On one visit I heard him call 'Danger!' as the baby crawled too close to the gas fireplace in the living room.) But even if the baby was in a safe space and didn't need to be watched in a literal sense, there was a claim on a part of the father's attention that was constant.

## Multi-tasking

Claims on their attention made it difficult for fathers caring for babies in the early months to do anything *but* care for babies. Paul, whose solo caregiving started when his baby was three months old, found the constant demands hard to manage at first – especially since his wife's unusually long working days meant long days of caregiving for him too:

> I thought it would be easy. I thought it would be, 'Oh, well, whatever, we're going for a walk, I'll just put him in the stroller and it's no problem.' But it's not like that, right? Or like, 'Oh, he's hungry, I'll just feed him.' It doesn't work that way, right? Like, there's so many nuances and small details that you just don't think about.

Tony, who was just at the start of a parental leave to care for his four-month-old daughter when I began my visits, commented on more than one occasion that he had trouble doing two things at once. He found it especially challenging to accomplish anything during his day that was not baby-related. He said he didn't like to do any projects of his own with his daughter around, because he needed to 'get into a zone' and focus intensely on them. 'Her time span is a ten-minute window,' he said. 'And I find, especially as a guy, when I get into a project I need more than a ten-minute window.'

According to Simon, at home with an 18-month-old, the best approach – and the way to avoid the frustration he used to feel – was not to *expect* to get too much done. But more experience also helped.

Fathers like Simon who were more seasoned caregivers had learned the cognitive skills that would allow them to attend to other tasks while still being aware of how their charges were doing. They learned, in short, the skill of multi-tasking. Steve, caring for a four-year-old and a baby five months old when our visits started, had the most caregiving experience of all the fathers in the group. Unlike Tony, he had learned that 'you fill up the day five or ten minutes at a time.' Later he put it another way: 'You get time, it's just not time on your terms.' Steve was an exemplary multi-tasker. As I commented in my field notes, 'It's like his antennae are really sharp ... He can attend to the kids' needs while doing other stuff.' Steve himself joked about how, in his 20s, faced with the task of warming a bottle in the microwave, he would have stood and watched it happen. Practice with two babies had taught him that in the time it takes for a bottle to warm 'you can do an amazing amount!' On the basis of his greater experience, he could also deliver a message that would comfort newer fathers like Paul and Tony: 'I think the first six months is all about survival, and you feel like you always have the baby strapped to you. Now he's doing the napping. We're working on nights now.' There was, in short, a little more energy available for other things.

## Effects of caregiving on fathers' bodies

### Wear and tear

Steve, at this six-month turning point, had just bought himself some new running shoes, and was looking forward to using them. Being able to care for his own body would be one of the rewards of survival. (Two months later, he had started running, and had joined a soccer team.) During the early months, even though they didn't also have to recover from pregnancy and childbirth, caregiving affected fathers' bodies as well. The carrying of babies that often fell to fathers could be a source of physical stress, as well as exercise. Drew, like Steve, often carried his nearly-nine-month-old baby in a carrier, in order to be able to get other things done while still having the baby close. But his was a very big baby, and Drew was not a very big man. 'Both my back and my wife's back are a little bit sore because he's a pretty big kid,' he said.

Keeping fit was often a challenge. When I visited him, Max had just started exercising again; he said he wanted to get back into shape and slim down a little. Fathers like Simon and Greg were able to work exercise of some kind into their daytime schedules – Simon, because his daughter was older and able to be left in child care for the length of his daily class, and Greg, a regular gym-goer, because his wife was almost always able to take over at 4 p.m., his regular work-out time. For other fathers, exercising took time they usually didn't have during the day, and for which they didn't always have the energy at night. It sometimes had to be postponed till babies' schedules were more predictable. Terry and his partner were both deeply committed to fitness, but while exercising didn't disappear from Terry's day, it was a scaled-back version. Before he began his caregiving, he worked out at the gym. Now he was trying to fit in a work-out at home – and during the day, because evenings were when his wife worked out. 'I was in much better shape before,' he said. But workouts during the day had to be during the baby's nap time – and Terry, like other fathers I visited, sometimes needed a nap then too. 'When he goes down, depending on whether it's morning or afternoon, and how much I've got done, then ... I'll sit on the couch for half an hour and put my feet up,' Terry said.

Like other fathers who started a parental leave when their partners returned to work, Jason also took on the caregiving 'night shift.' That, he said, was the hardest thing he had to cope with. Getting up in the middle of the night, and then the transition of getting back to sleep after having been up for an hour or so, he described as a 'learned skill' – one he thought, after a month or so of practice, that he was getting better at. Jason was also one of several fathers who answered the question of what they did during a baby's naptime by commenting that it gave them a chance to feed themselves. Jason's naptime chore list read: 'Clean up the kitchen, put a load of laundry in. Eat!' He said he often found himself 'starving' because he hadn't had time to eat earlier. On my first visit to Paul, when his baby was four months old, he told me: 'I haven't eaten lunch or breakfast yet ... just because I can't put him down long enough to boil an egg even, or to, you know, without him screaming.' Max said: 'Sometimes I'll eat, in that [naptime] space. I find I have to eat a lot – because I'm tired a lot too...' Babies' naptime was also the opportunity to take a shower.

Max was the one father of the group who most clearly articulated the observation, implicit in several other fathers' accounts, that personal care had to be subordinated to baby care. 'That, for me, is an adjustment, that I find – being unable to take care of my own needs. He takes precedence.' Paul would have agreed. He noted that he was supposed to have a blood test, which he hadn't been able to schedule, though he'd been trying for a month. 'It's difficult because I have to fast,' he said. 'And, you know, if you're up at 7 a.m. and your appointment's at eleven, I can't – there's no way. So I've just been scheduling them and then having to cancel them over and over again. So I'll get to it eventually.'

Taking on the full-time care of a three-month-old baby was very difficult for Paul, as multiple conversations with him made clear. Of all the fathers in the group, he was the one who seemed most affected by the physical and emotional work of caregiving – perhaps because he took on responsibility for a younger baby than was the case for most fathers, and his wife's long work hours meant his daily caregiving time was extended as well. During our last conversation, when his baby was eight months old, and much easier to care for, Paul looked back on his early months of caregiving. He shared his suspicion, based on some online research, that he might have been experiencing the kind of postpartum depression most often associated with mothers.[8] 'I didn't really notice that I was down until I came out of it,' he said. 'And then, looking back, I was like "wow, that was really bad".' Paul said he had felt 'angry and frustrated' all the time. 'What I found to be the most difficult was that I had nothing to kind of look forward to,' he said. 'When you're looking after a baby, there's no light at the end of the tunnel, basically, right?'

Paul said he experienced physical symptoms as well; every night for about four weeks he felt like he had flu. Gradually, his outlook – and his health – improved, greatly helped by the fact that the baby started to sleep through the night, and to nap regularly during the day. From having 'nothing to look forward to,' Paul said he was able to shift his thinking; the tunnel no longer appeared as dark. But he looked back on those early months as a difficult time in his life.

## The emotion work of caregiving

Feelings of anger, frustration or depression – like those experienced by Paul – were not feelings that fathers would want to communicate to their babies. Paul also spoke of the importance of keeping 'a calm atmosphere' in the house. Terry suggested that some of the fatigue he often felt came from working to maintain 'a positive vibe' for the sake of his baby. He mentioned more than once the importance of being calm. 'You can't get angry, or upset, or feel stressed,' he said. 'Because they feel – you don't have to say anything. If you're tense and upset, they know.' But if this was exhausting, it was also personally beneficial. Terry framed it as a positive effect the baby was having on him, psychologically. 'Probably one of the best things that's ever happened for me, is [the baby], because I'm very calm, a lot calmer, and patient.' Other fathers were not as explicit about the need to manage their own emotions in the interests of their babies' well-being, though they did speak of occasional frustrations, or cited incidents when some reining in of their own feelings would have been called for. 'Patience,' I suggest, is the link to the emotion work that is a critical component of caregiving with young children. DeVault (1999), building on Hochschild (1983) describes this emotion work as 'an intentional management and display of one's own feelings' (p. 53), management which, as other scholars note, is 'expressed through behavior' (Wharton and Erickson, 1993: 458). In the context of caring for very young children, patience might be demonstrated in gesture, or tone of voice, or the repetition of an activity known to bring pleasure. It might also be constituted in the conscious, embodied management of frustration or anger. In all my visits to fathers, I saw no visible signs of *im*patience – but then, I was hardly likely to. My very presence in the interactional mix would have taken care of that. Patience, in the sense I think all the fathers understood it, was something that accrued over the longer term, emerging out of the 'everyday micro-practices of care' (Magaraggia, 2013: 81).

It is through the micro-practices of care that other embodied responses and reactions also occur. Those who care for babies and young children can come to feel an attachment which is not merely emotional, but is also visceral. Mothers are more widely recognized as feeling this visceral attachment (Lupton, 2012), but I found fathers who felt it too. It could be as simple as a sense of absence when the baby was not around. As Greg commented: 'Everywhere I go, he goes, pretty much, during the day ... It almost feels weird now if I go somewhere and he's not with me. I look back, and – "Oh, he's not in the car!"' These feelings move the discussion from a focus on the *practice* of care to how it is experienced – the focus of the next chapter.

# 3
# 'It's a Whole New Level'

In the previous chapter I introduced a group of fathers whom I visited, usually on several occasions, while they were at home caring for their children. I used my observations during those visits, and their descriptions of their activities, to provide a cumulative picture of their caring work as embodied. My main focus, as I noted in concluding that chapter, was on what they were *doing*. The care they were engaged in was routine, and I argue that for that reason, it can be used as a benchmark; *any* father, taking on the engaged, hands-on care of a baby, will be bringing the physical capital of his (male) body to the job, and will learn (with few variations) the body techniques of caring that those fathers described. What remains to be explored is what this embodied care *means* to fathers who perform it. How do they describe the experience of taking time away from their paid employment to embark on this radically different kind of work? What effects do they perceive it to have had, on themselves as fathers, and as men? In this chapter, I move from my earlier focus on the 'doing' of care, to consider how it is experienced.

Steve, one of the fathers I introduced in Chapter 2, clearly made the connection between daily care and its longer-term consequences. He spent a lot of time during my visits with his baby snuggled against his chest in a baby carrier. In fact, he said, the baby did most of his daytime napping in this way. Steve didn't mind. On the contrary, he was relishing this close physical contact, because he knew from experience that it wouldn't last. He had been a full-time, primary caregiver since his first child was six months old. On my last visit, she was nearly four, and the baby was eight months old. He understood the effect that physical contact with his children had – on them, but also on him. It was the reason he had, as he said, 'a lot of trouble being away from them.' He tried to find the words to describe his connection to them:

> It's like a sub-conscious sort of thing. It's a very instinctive, natural process, organic, I guess you could say ... It always just feels like a very natural thing ... It's holistic ... There's a constant feedback, 24/7, right? And we tend to downplay all that stuff, and not embrace it ... That feeling you get with your kids, it's a whole new level.

The 'whole new level' of feeling and attachment described by Steve is an example of the *inner* transformation that ongoing, day-by-day care of a baby can produce in fathers. It is one dimension of the 'interembodiment' described by Lupton (2012). To continue this discussion, and to explore in more detail the experiences of fathers who undertake the kind of benchmark caregiving I have now outlined, I introduce the second set of 21 fathers who had taken parental leave some time in the past, whom I described in the introduction to Part II. These fathers, in all but one case back working at full-time jobs outside the home, were better placed to reflect on the *consequences* of their caregiving, in a variety of family circumstances. Our interviews, with occasional input from the fathers introduced in Chapter 2, are the basis for what follows.

I begin by noting the observation by Brandth and Kvande (2003) that care is relational; it varies with the context in which it is carried out. There were many differences in the context in which all 34 of the fathers I met provided care, but much the most significant was the (daytime) presence or absence of the mother. In 13 cases, fathers took leave when mothers were also at home. In 21 cases, fathers were solo caregivers when mothers had returned to paid employment. Fathers who took leave to be at home with the mothers of their babies usually started the leave at the baby's birth, or a month or two afterwards. In this respect, they were unlike most other fathers in the study in that their caregiving time was directed to very young infants, most of whom were exclusively breastfed. As Doucet (2009a) has pointed out, the early months (Doucet would say the first year) of a baby's life is a time when biological differences clearly differentiate the contributions mothers and fathers can make to caregiving. The embodied work of breastfeeding is usually seen to trump all other work, and to minimize by comparison the embodied dimensions of any other caregiving task. So fathers' role in the care of breastfed infants is often framed as supportive, but clearly secondary to mothers.' Fathers who were solo caregivers usually began their leave when their babies were between four and eight months old – past the early infancy stage, but still often 'breastfed' in the sense that they were fed breast milk delivered (in bottles) by fathers, not mothers. Fathers in this context were hardly secondary caregivers. Clearly, then, the experience – and indeed the activities – of the fathers' caregiving time will be shaped by whether or not the mother is also at home. In what follows, I describe each of the two groups in some detail, before concluding with a discussion of key themes that emerged from the fathers' accounts.

## Fathers' caregiving with mothers at home

In three of the 13 cases in this category of leave takers, it seemed at first sight as if fathers had taken leave for purposes other than to have the experience of caring for their babies. In Vijay's case this alternative purpose was explicit. His wife was not employed at the time their baby was born, so Vijay took four months of parental leave to allow them all to go back to India to visit family.[1] Aidan took a nine-month leave with his second child, in large part to get a break from a less than satisfactory work situation. Alan and his family lived on a farm; he took three months of leave from his paid employment with each of his two children, in both cases timing the leave for the summer months when farm work was most pressing. In the other ten cases where mothers were also at home, fathers' motives for taking leave seemed less ambiguous. They wanted to support their partners, and care for their babies – though the support and the caregiving played out in different ways.

Barry, a 35-year-old physician who took his first leave as a graduate student when his daughter was two months old, was explicit about his place in the caregiving hierarchy. 'I think I was aware that in order for us to have a happy home life, that if I could take time, it would be mostly time to, yeah, spend time with my child, but to support my wife,' he said. 'Most of it was, "Is my wife happy and comfortable?"' So, like many of the fathers in this situation, he spoke of taking care of household work, cooking meals, and running errands, in order to leave his wife free to care for the baby.

But even where mothers' primary role was acknowledged, fathers' support usually extended to active caregiving as well. David, a registered nurse, took a four-month leave when his first child was born. 'The idea was for me to help at home, and because I wanted to be an involved parent,' he said. The baby was breastfed, so David joked that while his wife was responsible for the input, he took charge of the output – everything to do with diapers, from baby changing to laundry. From about two months, however, the baby suffered from serious colic.

Because they also followed the practice of 'co-sleeping' (having the baby sleep in the parents' bed) the baby's unhappy wakefulness affected both parents. David remembered her 'screaming' for an hour and a half at a stretch. So he and his wife took turns walking with her, and, as he said, 'we tried to ... relieve each other when we were getting a little over-whelmed.' His own summing up of this period was simple: 'It was very very hard. It was very hard.'

But he also recalled other dimensions of physical caregiving that were more rewarding:

> I remember, you know, going on long walks with her all the time. We lived close to [major park in urban centre], and I'd be walking with her lots, and going to all the little markets when she was still in the front carrier thing. So she was quite small, and it was nice. You know, spending a lot of time with her at home when she was still quite small ... You don't get that particular experience normally, in life, you know, the first month, you know, first couple of weeks with a really, really tiny infant. That's really special.

David framed his leave time, and the challenging caregiving he and his wife shared, as a partnership which brought them closer together. As he put it, 'You share the love and the responsibility.' His account also suggested the extent to which this early caregiving shaped his ongoing relationship with his daughter:

> Like, my daughter's actually more 'Daddy's girl', and she was even from the early days. She loved mom for, you know, the milk and that, but she often was closer to me, and that was a bit hard for my wife too. She wanted to be with daddy more, even though my wife was literally having the life sucked out of her ... And I don't think that would have happened if I hadn't spent the first four months there every day.

Leave time with a mother at home played out differently when the baby had preschool siblings. This was the case for both Alan and Aidan. During the three months of leave he took when his first child was four months old, Alan said his main job was to be his wife's helper, and, as was the case with Barry, to take over the domestic work to free her for baby care. But his second leave saw him at home with a wife, a newborn baby and a three-year-old. His major responsibility, the second time around, was to take charge of the three-year-old. Aidan had a similar experience, and provided vivid descriptions of how the care of that older child affected him physically:

> I wasn't the baby's primary caregiver, I was the two-and-a-half-year-old's primary caregiver, so um, we were um, like the mobile team and we went, it was great, we did so much outdoor stuff. I got into jogging, um, I just had the time and we had our little routines ... We went to the zoo almost weekly, we had our favorite playgrounds that we would bike to ... The biggest impact was having the time to exercise and get in shape.

Caring for his older daughter had physical benefits for Aidan, but the presence of the baby had a profound effect, even though he was not her primary caregiver. Soon after he returned to his paid employment, he moved to a four-day working week, and cared for both children on the fifth day when his wife returned to work. The multi-tasking, and the cognitive skills required to attend to two children at once, were clear in his account:

> It's just adapting to the different situation ... You have to step up and learn what, what a little kid needs and you know, you got to make a meal for you and a meal for her and then something for the baby and just ... that learning curve of figuring out everyone's schedules and you know, when naps fit in and feeding ... It's just growing and expanding your knowledge and comfort zone.

Among the fathers I visited and interviewed whose partners were also at home during the leave time, there were three situations where fathers' caregiving was especially significant. The first, noted in Chapter 2 in the case of Robert, Greg and Douglas, involved fathers taking over the bulk of childcare from wives who were working full-time from home. Of the three, only Douglas's wife qualified for maternity leave. Robert and Greg both started leaves (of two months and eight months respectively) when their babies were newborn. Douglas started his nine-month leave when his baby was three months old. In all three cases, mothers continued to breastfeed, but during their (home-based) working days, they depended on fathers to do everything else.

The second situation involved fathers who took leave on the arrival of adopted children. In terms of expectations with respect to parent practices, adoption has the potential to level the uneven playing field that biology often establishes. Lacking the attachment advantage often seen to derive from pregnancy, and the caregiving primacy required by breastfeeding, adoptive mothers make the transition to parenting on much the same terms as adoptive fathers. This, of course, has consequences for the fathers, as (in radically different circumstances) both Keith and Tyler discovered.

Keith took a six-week leave on the arrival of his first two children, siblings aged three and two. Some two years later, he took a second leave of six weeks to welcome a seven-month-old baby. Less than a year after her arrival, Keith and his wife were persuaded by the provincial social services authorities to adopt her newborn sibling also. Keith, as primary breadwinner, said he couldn't afford to extend either of his two leaves beyond six weeks, and by the time the baby arrived (so soon after her older sibling), job as well as financial obligations kept him at his workplace, and not at home. But his time at home, though shorter than was the case for other fathers in the study, saw him deeply involved, as a partner, not a helper.

Keith's leave experiences reflected, almost in reverse, the caregiving described earlier by Alan and Aidan, since the older children arrived before the babies. His first leave time involved outings organized around the children's preschool schedule. It was on his second leave that changing diapers and bottle feeding became part of the routine. This too was work he shared; the arrival of babies did not see him taking on primary responsibility for the older children to free his wife for infant care. Partly, this seemed to emerge from the couple's preference to do as much as possible together. Partly, it was because he developed a special role in the care of the babies:

> Obviously she's not nursing so there wasn't any of that time, so I would feed just as much as my wife would feed. In fact, I've established a very good routine that I started with my older baby, and I've carried that into the younger [baby] ... [I'm] always the one that's putting the babies to sleep. And feeding them before they sleep, and then they fall asleep and I carry them into their bed, right? And that's – I've been doing that for two years now ... So that's one thing definitely that I've taken on, strictly.

The training that prospective adoptive parents in Alberta are required to take sensitizes them to issues of attachment, and the work that may be needed to help adopted children feel close to, and secure with, their adopted parents. It was work – just the kind of family emotion work described by DeVault (1999) – that both Keith and his wife were doing on an ongoing basis with their oldest child, adopted at age three with a troubled history. For Keith, it didn't stop when he returned to work. He described occasions when his wife, dealing with a 'meltdown' and having a hard time getting their daughter to settle, would phone him at work so that he could talk to her, distract her, and help her to calm down.

Tyler and his wife also learned about attachment in their pre-adoption training. Their daughter was three months old when they adopted her, and Tyler took three months' leave. From his account, it was clear that attachment issues informed his early caregiving practices. He gave an example:

> I would always look at her and have eye contact. When I talked to her I would [ensure] that I had eye contact with her. When I would be feeding her, and in the early stages it was just a bottle, I would make sure I had eye contact. I wouldn't feed her and watch TV. I wouldn't allow that, and I still don't. Simple. There would be times where I just spent time with her in my arms.

Tyler was a shift worker, accustomed to the routine disruptions of night and day that his job demanded. That experience shaped his early caregiving, too. He described taking on the 'morning shift,' getting up with the baby, feeding her and changing her and 'whatever we needed to do' until his wife took over. During the day, like several of the other fathers already described, he was the 'runner,' doing errands. He took over again for the night shift. 'I think from a physical standpoint, I was more capable of that,' he said. 'Being a shift worker, your body's conditioned to just do what needs to be done regardless of the time of day ... It was just something that was not a problem for me. And I wanted to do it.'

The demands on Tyler's body increased with a vengeance when he returned to work. The four days of 12-hour shifts that were his regular routine were frequently extended into overtime work to accommodate staff shortages. The week he was interviewed was an 84-hour work week. 'There's some days I don't have a lot left in me,' he said. But his account suggested he still did his best to participate in the care of his daughter, who was then a year old. After a day shift, he said, there was usually an hour or so of play time:

> [She] and I hang out, I chase her around the house and she loves that. I crawl underneath the kitchen table and she loves that, we

play. So it's, you know, that's the best I can do. There's an hour of playtime and an hour, hour and a half of doing what we need to do to get her to bed.

When he was working night shifts, he gave up daytime sleep to do more 'hanging out.' He described this as a sacrifice he was willing to make for his daughter's sake.

The third situation in which fathers' caregiving assumed special significance involved three cases where the mother was at home full-time, but was considered by the father to be particularly vulnerable and in need of extra support. In the first case, Laurence took a two-month leave at the birth of his second child, for several reasons: his wife had delivered the baby by Caesarian section, so had to recover from the surgery; she had suffered from post-partum depression after their first child's birth, and he anticipated (accurately as it turned out) that she might do so again; and the older child was only 22 months old when the new baby arrived. Laurence's participation in every aspect of the caregiving was crucial. His experience up to the time of his leave was extensive; he described himself as having been 'very much hands on, right from the get go,' another father who even though at work during the day had taken his share of the night shifts of diaper changing and bottle feeding. (Laurence's wife, listening in on part of our interview, also commented on his care of her. 'He'd also get up in the morning before he went to work and put me out a plate of food because otherwise I wouldn't eat during the day because I was struggling to cope and he'd have all this food chopped up for me,' she said.) Laurence recalled his time on leave as 'very difficult.'

Like Keith, described earlier, Laurence considered he had no choice but to return to paid work, since his wife's extended leave meant his income was needed to support his family. But returning to work (as an accountant for a major energy company) did not relieve him of worry about caring. His account demonstrated the psychic weight of that worry:

> I remember especially the first week, the first two weeks, is that you really don't care, the work seems really trivial compared to what you're dealing with at home and dealing with your kids is so much more important, and supporting your wife is so much more important than whether natural gas flows through a pipeline. It really doesn't matter ... especially our view of it, you know, it wasn't me

sort of maintaining a pipeline so people get their homes heated, right? This was about the [economics of the company].

In Laurence's case, the pull towards home and family eventually won out. After a period in which both he and his wife worked part-time in order to provide full-time parental care for their children, Laurence quit his job, and became the children's primary caregiver, while also doing some paid contract work from home. His wife, the primary breadwinner, worked full-time at a home-based consulting business. Interviewed when the children were seven and five, he positioned himself as the parent doing more of the planning and organizing of family life, along with the worrying, and the reading about parenting. His wife, in what he saw as a subversion of traditional gender expectations, did more of the 'fun stuff.' He said he thought that the children might have been marginally more likely to choose her when they needed comfort, but there was considerable variability, and on many occasions, 'Daddy does just fine.'

Rick and Jeremy took more time on leave than Laurence. Their leaves, unlike his, did not eventually draw them away from their paid employment. But from both men's accounts, the time they spent as infant caregivers provided the foundation for unusually strong connections to their children as they grew. In Rick's case, fatherhood came after 10 years of marriage, when he was 44 and his wife was 40. Rick said they had talked about having children, and he thought he wanted to have them more than his wife did. 'She was just a little unsure about it,' he said. 'We thought we'd let nature take its course.' Even so, the pregnancy when it came was unexpected.

From Rick's account, he was better prepared to care for a baby than his wife was. She had grown up with almost no contact with children, whereas his family circumstances, helping to look after three younger siblings, had given him 'a lot of experience.' So when the baby was born, he took four months of leave, and 'with some trepidation' at the outset, more or less took charge:

> You know, she is the mom, there, you know, there is a bond between the child and the mother. She was a bit of a worrywart, for lack of a better term, she was ... almost to the point of being neurotic, to be quite honest, sometimes. She wanted the best for the child, and ... there's a fair bit of worry. And there wasn't, medically there wasn't anything wrong, but you know, she was unsure so she just wanted to

do the best job as she could. Myself, I was a little more comfortable ... I've changed diapers, I've given bottles, I've done all this stuff.

Rick's active participation from the start was facilitated by the fact that breastfeeding 'just simply didn't work.' So the couple developed what Rick described as a 'tag-team' approach. Initially, his wife did more of the preparation of bottles and formula, and Rick did the actual feeding. He was also the one who bathed the baby, with his wife acting as helper. Then he took on the night shift of care. He spoke warmly about what it meant to him:

> I thought it was fantastic, I mean, it's kind of, it's almost a surreal experience I suppose, you know, when you have something this small that you're basically helping live, you know, you're providing for it ... It was phenomenal, that's the only way I can describe it.

The deep emotional attachment Rick developed to his son resonated through his account. 'I never knew you could love someone as much, when he was born,' he said. So returning to work when his leave was over was extremely painful. Recalling his first days back on the job, he said: 'I was heartbroken. It was very very difficult for me ... I found it hard to leave him.' Rick said the 'real angst' lasted for a month or two, but even beyond that time, he continued to worry, and to check in with his wife during the day:

> I know that she was going through perhaps a bit of a slight case of, you know, [postpartum depression] going on, and you know, she suffered a little bit through that, so I'd be calling to sort of cheer her up and tell her 'we're going to get through this' and 'don't worry,' and so on and so forth ...

Concern for his wife, and his own wish to spend some more time with his son, prompted him to take an additional month of leave when the baby was 11 months old. 'It was kind of important for me for that last month to sort of, you know, help out a little bit more,' he said.

Jeremy was one of the few fathers in the study who had taken two parental leaves, one of six months, the second of five, when each of his children was born. Like Rick, he was (at 41) an older than average first-time father. Unlike Rick, he was in a senior management position for an international company – a fact that significantly shaped his experience of balancing work and family responsibilities. Jeremy's wife did not qualify for parental leave, since she was self-employed. She was at home full-time during both of Jeremy's leaves, and from Jeremy's account tried hard to have him at home too for as long as possible. In one sense, he didn't need persuading; his descriptions of their preparations for the midwife-assisted home birth of their first child, and his view of the birth itself as 'a real high point in our marriage so far,' were clear indications of his willingness to be an involved father. But other factors played in to the decision, apart from his wish to be 'really present for the first weeks and months' of his daughter's life:

> I also wanted to make sure my wife got off to a good start as a mom, and didn't feel isolated and unable to cope and those sorts of things. So you know, two pairs of hands ... If we hadn't done it, there would have been I feel a degree of risk [of] things like post-partum depression ... We both felt it was a high risk period for us and my wife, you know, mentally. She's had a few challenges that way over the years. And uh, we thought it was the best way to proceed. ...We felt it was, on the balance of everything, was something we could do and should do and would give us a great start as parents.

For all the study participants, father-baby relationships were shaped by whether, how often, and for how long, the babies were breastfed. Right after her birth, Jeremy's first child 'didn't want to breast-feed, or couldn't.' He said he spent her first few nights feeding her pumped breast milk from a syringe. Then she learned to drink it from a bottle. Those early days had a profound impact on Jeremy's caregiving, and his subsequent relationship with his daughter:

> [S]he eventually breast-fed just fine, but because she was such a keen bottle-feeder and I wasn't working and I was happy to take the, the late nights and the sleep deprivation, I basically grabbed her as soon as my wife had had enough – 11pm she went to bed. So whatever happened through the night happened, and she came back down for breakfast at nine and the baby's either awake or sleeping or whatever and I got a few hours in. And I've done like lots of feeds and three or four changes and we've ... fallen asleep in front of the TV together. It was very cool.

From Jeremy's account, this early practice had the effect of entrenching him as the baby's main caregiver. 'It just kept going that way,' he said. His willingness to take the long nights, and the baby's willingness to be bottle-fed, along with what he described as his own 'higher toler-ance' for the baby's crying, produced an attachment – on both sides – that was remarkable. At a time in a baby's life when other fathers in the study were reluctant to stray far from home with them, Jeremy and his daughter went on many outings as a twosome, without the baby's mother. 'My wife likes to be quiet, she likes her own space,' Jeremy said.

After six months of leave, Jeremy was persuaded back to work – earlier than his wife had wanted ('she still hasn't completely forgiven me') – in order to move into a new, higher-level job. The persuasion took the form of a generous bonus. He described his return to work as 'the end of a rather beautiful period,' but one that had to end, because the fam-ily needed his income. 'I'm realistic,' he said. 'It was a privilege, [and] a joy, to be off that long.'

It was something of a foregone conclusion that he would take a sec-ond leave, three years later, when his second child was born. 'One of the reasons that I felt I needed to take the second leave was, I'm not will-ing to have one special daughter that we're tightly bound to, and the other sort of spare part that I've barely noticed,' he said. 'I wanted this daughter to be just as special.' A new set of circumstances converged to determine the course of the second leave, however. This time, Jeremy's wife was looking for a different experience:

> My wife [pause] specifically pointed out that, this time around she wants more of the cuddle time, because [with the first baby] she felt like she did a lot of the keeping-the-house-afloat type work and making sure we had clothes to wear and food in the fridge and I was constantly, you know, baby under the arm.

The fact that the new baby, unlike her sister, much preferred breast to bottle, gave Jeremy's wife what she was wanting. He described his sec-ond leave experience as good, but different. In fact it closely resembled the second-baby leaves already described in the case of Alan and Aidan: support for his wife, care of the older child, and 'a lot less cuddle time for dad with this new one, because she always wants her mom.' It was different in another way as well; put simply, the novelty had worn off:

> [E]verything with the first child is new, so you kind of over-think everything, and you're buying gear for the baby and you're trying to make sure you don't trip up on any of the fundamentals. And then the second one is all, 'Well, I've done that before.' It's kind of the same.

For Jeremy and his wife, the decision to take the second leave was based on a desire to be fair to both children. If the leave didn't play out quite as he expected, it did allow him to see the difference that on-going, hands-on care of a baby makes to the bond that can develop between baby and caregiver. Jeremy spoke of the 'really strong bond' he had with his older daughter, and the fact that he hadn't bonded in the same way with the baby, 'mainly [because of ] the way in which she's wanted to feed and be cared for.' But he wasn't concerned; like other fathers of second children, his experience with his first allowed him to take a longer view, because this time, he had a better sense of the changes that were coming.

All 13 fathers described so far were deeply engaged in the embodied work of infant care, even though they were not solo caregivers. Research like that of Doucet (2009a), noted earlier, suggests that in this situation, the biological advantage of the breastfeeding mother tends to position fathers as helpers or secondary caregivers. Fathers like Barry or Aidan, described above, would agree with this assessment. Yet many of the other fathers in this group offered caregiving support that was much more significant than the 'helper' description would suggest. Where babies were not breastfed, or were breastfed but willing to take a bottle,[2] where babies were particularly demanding, where fathers had prior childcare experience that mothers lacked, and where mothers were vulnerable and in need of extra support, fathers' caregiving was not so secondary.

## Fathers as solo caregivers

The 21 fathers who had solo caregiving experience had one critical family characteristic in common: the mothers of their children were all employed professional women. In most cases, these mothers earned as much as, or more than the fathers, in careers to which (from their partners' accounts) they were strongly committed. So fathers, at least partly for rational, economic reasons, were called on to do a larger share of caregiving, and on different terms from the fathers described earlier, whose partners were also at home.

In 16 of the 21 cases, fathers' caregiving was organized as a portion of the year of parental leave available for eligible Canadian parents to share. How much of the leave fathers took on as their share shaped their experience in two main ways. First, and obviously, it dictated the length of time they would be away from their own paid employment. Second, it determined the age of the baby for whose care they would be responsible; the longer the father's leave, the younger the baby at its beginning. Four of these fathers took what one of them described as the 'easier shift' – the final three or four months of the allowable year of leave, when their babies were eight or nine months old. Six of them took five or six months of leave – more or less a half share with their partners – when their babies were six months or so old (John and Charlie had done it with each of their two children). Four of them took on the bigger share of the leave, spending eight or nine months (in Mike's case on two occasions) with babies who were in most cases three or four months old when they took over.[3] One other father's leave took a different form: Jim's wife took the full year of formal parental leave; when she returned to work he took a full year of unpaid leave (rationalized for his employer as 'parental leave') during his child's second year.

For all of these fathers, full-time solo caregiving was an experience set up to last for the duration of the leave. Then they, like their partners, returned to their paying jobs, or (in the case of most of the fathers still on leave when I visited them) were planning to do so. For these fathers, the leave time was an interlude (though usually a highly significant one). For four other fathers, introduced in Chapter 2, transitions between paid work and caregiving played out differently. Steve and Max each took six months of formal parental leave when their firstborn children were six months old. At the end of the leave, both resigned from their paid employment to become full-time, home-based caregivers. Neither Simon nor Paul qualified for formal parental leave, so both stopped their full-time paid employment to become full-time caregivers – Simon when his daughter was a year old, and Paul when his son was three months old. In order to suggest the range of contexts in which these fathers' caregiving was situated, I have chosen five individual cases from among the leave-taking fathers I interviewed as exemplars. These five fathers voiced many of the experiences other fathers in this group described to me.

### Will: taking the easier shift

When I interviewed him, Will was 41, and the father of two sons aged seven and three. He had taken three months of parental leave from his position as a public sector auditor when the older boy was nine months old. He commented that he had not expected to be sharing the leave; the plan was for his wife to take the whole year. But she had had a difficult time being at home alone, with no family support available, and was anxious to return to work. Will commented:

> The way it worked out it was more like, 'Okay, I need a break, and this is my gift to you. I think it would be good for you to spend time.'

And that's the way it worked out ... Had it been just a great, great year, then ... I would have stayed at work and I wouldn't have even thought of saying 'Hey, how about me getting a turn?'

From his account, Will, like most of the other fathers in the study, entered fatherhood with no practical experience of infant caregiving, as our conversation indicated:

Will:   I know before we had Peter, I had never changed a diaper in my life. I had never really held a baby so it was all very new ... But yeah, we did it.
GR:     You learned.
Will:   You do learn and that's kind of the mindset I went into it. You know all fathers have to start somewhere.

By the time his leave started, Will was no stranger to diaper changing and other caregiving practices. Having shared the caregiving when he got home from work in the months leading up to the leave, he had some idea of what would be expected of him. He registered his biggest concern as learning the baby's schedule, and making sure he was eating healthily. There was also some new learning associated with his role as solo caregiver:

I think the biggest thing I had to learn was just going out in public and knowing how long I had ... and the short windows of opportunity to, you know, go and run a quick errand and, you know, something like that before he was hungry or needed to be changed, or something like that, so that was the biggest thing I had to learn. Because within the house I was used to that, from when I'd get home at five, it was basically the same routine but just extended. So I think going out was the bigger learning curve.

In the Canadian context, the weather is a significant factor in parents' experience of infant caregiving. Those responsible for caregiving during the long, severe winter months are much more constrained than they would be at other times of the year. Will was conscious of the fact that by the time he started his leave, spring was on its way and going out was much more of an option:

I remember buying one of those backpack type of deals and any time ... it was nice out it was like okay, let's get out down the river valley ... I was kind of anxious about showing him that sort of thing, because that was something he was too young to do early, back in the fall or whatever and so it was kind of a new thing we could do together, so it was fun.

As well as taking his leave in better weather, Will was also caring for an older, more mobile and more responsive baby. As he concluded: 'I just had the easier shift.'

Asked whether he thought the leave had made a difference to his relationship to his son, Will said:

[I] definitely felt more comfortable ... I'm not sure if he's felt it at all, if he became closer to me, but I think maybe more on a subconscious level, it like, I'm just feeling like I'm contributing more to the family. It made me feel more comfortable just as our group of three at that point. So, more so I guess than just getting to know him, I think it was just personally, internally, feeling better about things.

Another consequence of the leave was his recognition of caregiving as work, knowing 'what it was like to be the single parent for that day,' and what a 'tough job' it could be.

For all its perceived benefits, however, Will did not take a leave with his second child. He gave two main reasons. First, he was working for a different company, with a workplace culture in which parental leave by fathers, though legally an entitlement, was informally discouraged. Second, his wife was not experiencing the difficulties that had challenged her at home alone the first time; this time, she did not need Will to take over. There was also a sense, implicit in Will's account but more explicit in the accounts of some other fathers, that the leave time was not (only) a time to develop a relationship with a specific baby; it was rather (as noted in Chapter 1) a sort of generic apprenticeship that, once served, equipped the father to do what was needed for the children that might follow. As Will said: 'I got what I needed out of the experience.'

### Ben: getting an early start

When I interviewed him, Ben was 35, and the father of a two-year-old daughter. When she was six months old, he took a five-month parental leave from his work as a developer in a small software company, and was her sole caregiver when his wife resumed her professional job. From his account, the opportunity to have, and to care for a baby was long awaited and much anticipated:

I've always wanted to – not necessarily stay at home, but like, I've known I've wanted to have kids. Like, that's really high on, you know, my life list, right? Not really all that career-focused. Um, I'm more family focused. So that's kind of been – I guess an underlying theme ... Up till that point, you know, we had – both my wife and I worked full-time prior to that. Um, and we both kind of had the understanding that we'd both, you know, feed the baby, change diapers, all that.

Ben's hands-on caregiving got off to an early start. The baby's birth was difficult, and its effect on his wife positioned Ben as the parent in charge:

We actually had to bottle-feed pretty much from the get-go. So the first couple – I would say, four days – I was solely feeding the baby, taking care of her ... We had the help of the nurses and all that too, right? But, you know, it was – it was, again, not the typical start that you would think of.

It was a start that he reflected on with obvious warmth, two years later. 'I loved doing it,' he said. 'You know, you, this six- seven-pound baby in your arms, feeding them, albeit every two hours ... '

From this different start, Ben and his wife moved to divide the caregiving work as evenly as they could over the year of parental leave they shared:

We kind of did, uh, call it 'shift work' at night. Um, we basically alternated evenings, where one of us would be the one that would get up, feed, change, all that. Um [pause] and like any new parent, that's tough doing that plus going to work. And, you know, she took on the brunt of that in the second half as well. So, um, but it was really equitable that way.

Ben's descriptions of the leave time at home with his daughter covered both negative and positive experiences. Among the negatives, he cited the boredom of days alone at home, combined with the challenge and work involved in getting a baby ready to go out. There were also days when his patience was thin:

I remember a couple days when I was at home where ... [I] had to fall back on the technique of 'I can't – I can't deal with this.' And, you know, I put Chrissy in the crib, and I would – I would take a break. And, you know, I remember that being really hard, and beating myself up over it and all that. But, end of the day, it's what I had to do to get through it, for sure.

The positives included an array of activities that revealed Ben's engaged, embodied caregiving. He described days of going for walks in the neighbourhood, occasional play dates with friends who had children, 'singing, or eating, interacting with her at home':

I have this one memory about, uh, having her on the change table and – I don't know why – just singing the A-B-C song. And I would always do this. Uh, I have no idea why I picked that song, but, you know, just the constant repetition of it [pause] to both her and me, right? ... I'm sure you remember, like trying to get through the moments where the kid's screaming, and you're trying to get the will to keep going on without losing it, right? [Both laugh] And so that kind of repetition I think really helped, for both of us.

Like Drew (introduced in Chapter 2), Ben was interested in teaching his daughter to sign – initially as a way of getting her to move her arms and hands to help repair a birth injury. 'My wife was interested, but not in the same way I was,' he said. 'It's something that we continue to do today. And, you know, with her being a little over two, she's starting to get dexterity in her fingers. And, um, and starting to really pick up and be being able to articulate and sign. Which I just find amazing.' And, as he added, 'it was good for me, because it kept my mind occupied while I was at home too!'

Ben recalled other interactions with the baby (unfolding from his leave to the present) that were quite different from those of his wife. He specified his willingness to allow his daughter to take more risks, and his inclination not to rush in when she was unhappy. He also did more rough-housing. But play that involved such 'typical father things' was only part of the story:

I look at [pause] I look at how willing Chrissy is to play. Like in terms of, uh, like physical play, as well as her imagination type play. And, like I really feel strongly I've contributed to both of those styles ... Today, yes, she plays with dolls and plays house and all that. And, you know, my plays change with her, like, you know, we blow kisses and things like that, right? Things that you – a guy typically isn't comfortable doing in public, I'll do, right? ...There's a lot of imagination that goes in there too.

When Ben's leave was over, with his wife already back at her job, it was time to put Chrissy in day care. The visceral connection he felt to her was evident in his description of the first day he left her there. Leaving the house was 'heartbreaking'; he remembered 'taking a couple minutes and sitting in the car, trying to centre myself so I could drive.' Looking ahead, he said, 'I really suspect the same thing's going to happen when she goes to school for the first time.'

Interviewed a year after his leave ended, Ben thought he had returned to 'more of a supportive role,' with his wife doing more caregiving and taking more responsibility for Chrissy's wellbeing. He thought that, if they had another baby, she would probably want to take a longer leave; the first time, she had the much more difficult shift in the baby's first challenging months. 'I will take a month off, however it works out,' he said. 'Like, I've had the experience. I loved it.'

### Harjeet: taking an equal share

At the time of our interview, Harjeet was 37 and the father of a two-and-a-half-year-old son. Two years earlier, he had taken a parental leave of five-and-a-half months from his job as an IT account manager, to care for his then six-month-old baby when his wife returned to work. Harjeet's account of the couple's decision to take consecutive but equal shares of the allowable leave time is worth reproducing in full, because it so neatly sums up the stated rationale of many other leave-sharing couples in the study:

[B]oth of us are career people ... my wife is actually a lawyer ... And, you know, she loves her job, she loves what she does, so to her the career is important. So she wasn't going to be one of those moms that, she was going to have a baby and then stay home. So in terms of how we came to a decision as to how this was going to play out ... both her and I wanted to spend time with [the baby]. And obviously the first six months are important for the mother to be home, for breast-feeding and all those reasons. And she was happy to go back after six months. So even though it was important for both of us to stay home, if she had indicated that she wanted to stay the full year, I would never deny a mother of, of that, even though I would [have] loved to have stayed home with him. But she felt that six months was going to be a good time for her to go back to work, so that's sort of the decision where, where we said, 'Okay, it's going to work for both of us.'

Harjeet, like Will, had shared the caregiving in the months leading up to his leave, especially during the first three months, which he thought had been 'super traumatic' for his wife. He remembered taking on one of the night-time bottle feedings, and being counted on to get the baby to sleep in those early weeks. So he was familiar with the daily routines when his leave started. What was new for him was the disorientation of being suddenly at home alone in the daytime with no adult company – being 'stuck in the house' was how he put it. Harjeet resolved this problem by making sure he had daytime social contact through lunches with friends, or even quick outings to run errands. This solution was made possible by the presence of a mother-in-law willing to visit on a daily basis to give him some support.

Harjeet discovered that caregiving was both active and embodied. Asked what he had to learn, during his time at home, his quick response concerned singing. He said he remembered thinking 'I've never had to sing to a kid before,' and didn't know what to sing. So he copied nursery rhymes from the internet, to add to his repertoire. 'He's a child who loves music, so I kind of took that and tried to do whatever I could, trying to make it work for him,' he said. Another experience he recollected with obvious enjoyment was the transition to solid foods that happened during his time at home. 'We had a book that we were actually referring to all the time,' he said. But he remembered being 'a little bit more adventurous' than he thought his wife would have been in introducing the baby to new foods:

> I'd just try and see the market, what there was and make sure I do the research to see what age they can actually take it at. And give him the things they're suggesting at that age and kind of go from there. But yeah, I think we experimented a lot, and that was lots of fun.

Three months after Harjeet's leave ended, when the baby was just over a year old, he moved to a four-day compressed work week that gave him an extra day at home. His wife, by contrast, worked regular hours, and also had to travel away from home for her job. Implicit in his account was an awareness of the connection between caregiving time spent, and relationships within the family:

> So it's a lot of time, uh, that I spend with him, as opposed to my wife, right? So that, that's always kind of held her back, and saying well, 'He loves you more.' [laughs] She knows at the bottom of her heart that that's not the case, but. And I – I don't know how else that's kind of played out, but for sure, there's a little bit of that.

Asked whether he would take a second leave, if the couple were to have another baby, Harjeet said that he would do it again 'in a heartbeat.' Though there would obviously be workplace considerations in advance of an extended time away, he anticipated a similar arrangement the second time. Rather than viewing his first leave as an apprenticeship that didn't need to be repeated, Harjeet, like Jeremy, framed it as time given to a specific child: 'I would think that it would be wrong for me not to do it, just because, you know, whatever you gave to the first, why shouldn't you give to the second?'

### Charlie: doing double duty

Charlie was 35 at the time he was interviewed, with two children aged three and 14 months. He was an engineer, married to another engineer. Before they had children, they had the sort of relationship where household work was shared. ('We've always split it,' Charlie said.) So sharing caregiving when the children arrived was an expectation too – and as part of this sharing, when both children were born Charlie and his wife divided the parental leave so that each spent about six months at home. Though his turn in each case came in the second half of the year of leave, with babies approaching their first birthdays, in effect he spent almost as much time at home on leave as his wife had done.

Charlie gave two reasons for the decision to divide the leaves. The first was for him to 'have time with the kids and have that part of that experience and for the kids too to have, build that relationship.' The second was in order to advance his wife's career goals. He explained:

> The way we kind of structured our family um, or situation, um we're kind of driving down her career path and her career goals, and my career is going to stay somewhat flexible, or kind of a generalist engineer, so I can kind of take a variety of different jobs … Her career is going into upper management, so she needs to do certain steps to make that happen and taking a 12-month leave probably would have [affected] that substantially, so that was a decision that we made.

The first leave Charlie recalled as being more difficult than he had anticipated. More than once, he spoke of the challenge of being home alone with the baby:

> I really wasn't aware of the isolation component of it, of being at home for several days um, not going outside on those cold winter

days, and it's cold here for several days in a row ... There were times where yeah, we didn't get out of the house, or it was too much of an effort to get out of the house. It was harder for whatever reason, it was harder with the first one.

The challenge was highlighted in retrospect, after his return to work. 'I think that's more when I realized it,' he said. 'Not so much that I went into a depression state or anything. When I came back, I thought, oh, I kind of missed this.'

Charlie's second leave, two years later, was a different experience. For one thing, when it came to the physical caregiving routines of diaper-changing, feeding and so on, he was, as he put it, 'a pro.' And this time, as well as a baby to care for, there was a nearly-three-year-old, with an active round of play group and other activities. Charlie's second leave was necessarily more social. It also had the effect of consolidating his already close relationship with his older child, and building a connection with the baby – with interesting family consequences:

There were times where um mostly, not so much when they were babies, but on the second leave where the attachment between my daughter and I was stronger than with my wife, where she only wanted me to put her to bed, where she only wanted me to bath her, and as it is with our son now. I'm not sure if it's a breast-feeding thing, but I'm the only one that can really feed him [solid food]. When [wife] is around, he struggles with it. He wants out of his high chair, he wants to breast feed, or he's just uninterested in food. He's a funny kid, so is it associated with me only feeding him that I established him getting on solids and cutting up his food? ...Perhaps it's a component of it.

Charlie said his wife, as a 'stereotypical mom,' wanted the children to go to her first, and had a 'hard time' with their clear preference for Charlie. He said he tried to help; they started a night time routine with the older child involving a picture chart showing which night would be 'mommy's night' and which would be daddy's. 'It actually kind of went backwards on me, she only wanted mommy to put her to bed,' Charlie said with a laugh.

It was clear from his account that Charlie's caregiving experience had shaped more than his relationships with his children. It had also reinforced the differences between his career and his wife's that had prompted him to take both leaves in the first place. At the time he was interviewed, Charlie had not long returned from the second leave, and already the challenges of organizing family life when both he and his wife were back at work were becoming evident. He said he was considering the long-term possibility of negotiating with his employer to reduce his working hours in order to pick up more of the family work – positioning himself, rather than his wife, as the one better placed to do so.

## Mike: taking the lion's share

At the time of our interview, Mike was 35 and the father of two boys aged seven and two. He was one of the few fathers in the study to have taken long leaves (of about nine months' duration) with both children. He was also one of only two who began his solo caregiving with a baby only one month old. Though he never said so explicitly, the circumstances of that first leave strongly suggested an unplanned pregnancy; the baby was born when his wife was just finishing her medical training and a month before she was due to start her first professional job. It was a job that was going to pay far more than Mike's labouring job did, so it made financial sense for Mike to be the one to take the leave – especially, as he also noted, since they had very little money in the bank at the time.

Like Charlie, Mike found the first leave to be difficult. He too was home with a tiny baby in the winter, so outside activities were limited. In addition, his wife's job had required a move to a new city, so he had no friends or family close by. Thinking back to that time, Mike said:

> Like, for me personally, I got rid of my job, I had to sell my car, and I had to get rid of my house. So, everything that defined me as an individual was gone. And then there's this little life right there that was redefining me as I was trying to redefine myself.

Seven years later, he concluded, 'I was the one who went through the postpartum depression the first time ... it really was for me, personally, it was a depressing time.' But he could also see it as 'a huge growing experience' – one that shaped his relationship with his son, and also with his wife. In the case of his son, the relationship was forged in the context of daily care that saw him move from novice ('here's the kid – have at it!') to expert. And there were elements of the routine that he remembered warmly, years later:

> One of my favourite parts ... is that we'd just nap on the couch twice a day. And that was like, you know, he'd just [lie] on me and I'd [lie]

on the couch and we'd just nap together. And it was just cool bonding time.

In terms of his relationship with his wife, Mike saw his caregiving experience, with both leaves, as helping the couple grow as a team. Like other fathers in the study, he also noted the enormous value, from his experience at home on leave, of understanding what a day caring for small children was like:

> Even if we weren't doing the same thing, or even in the same house for eight hours, we both knew how the day went. And even when she took parental leave with the second one, and I would come home, I knew how the day went. So that was a huge advantage of the first one, is that the second one – I knew what the day was about. So I'd come home after a hard day of work and I would start cooking dinner because I knew what the day had been like.

Mike's own second leave experience started when the baby was three months old, and his older child was five. There were many differences. For one thing he was assuming the care of a slightly older baby; Mike's wife (who had in his terms been 'ripped off the first time') took a larger share of the leave, and unlike the first time, breastfed the baby. By this time, too, the family had moved back to their home town, and there was plenty of support close by. There was also the need to care for two children at home, not just one. As Charlie also found, the needs of the older child made the leave experience much more sociable for Mike:

> It was easier just because – we were running all over the place. ... The oldest had programs and stuff, so we would go out, and I'd take him to a little gym, and he'd have his playtime ... and it was just me and the little one hanging out. And I think that was a really cool experience because I got to be a dad out in public. And that's something I didn't experience the first time. It was being a dad in public.

Mike's regular job involved shift work. So when he returned to it after his second leave, he was still able to spend time with his children during his wife's working day. After-school hours always gave him special time with his older son. When he was interviewed, he was anticipating a four-day compressed work week that would soon give him special time every Friday with his younger son, while the older one was in school.

## Meanings and outcomes of early caregiving

The experiences of these five fathers, chosen as exemplars of the diverse contexts in which solo caregivers were operating, were shared by many of the other fathers in this group, and in some cases linked to the experiences of fathers described earlier, who were not solo caregivers. From this diversity of experience, three key themes invite further elaboration.

### Attachment to children

The first theme relates to the strong attachment fathers felt to the child(ren) who had been the focus of their caregiving. These feelings of attachment resonated through their accounts, and were visible in many of my observations of fathers who were still at home. Among those who had taken leave in the past, there were certainly some who did not credit their leave time alone as establishing the attachment. With the passage of time, and in some cases the shift to caregiving arrangements that continued to position fathers as prominent care providers, it became difficult for some fathers to separate the leave effects from other factors that brought them close to their children. But others were explicit about the effects that an extended focus on an individual child could produce. As noted earlier, Jeremy described the 'really strong bond' he had with his daughter; David noted that his daughter was still 'Daddy's girl.' Other fathers spoke in similar terms. Of the four months of leave he took, Lucas said: 'It's time that I [had] with my son, that I will never have the opportunity probably to take again, and I loved it. I loved seeing him grow, and learning to get to know him.' Derek took an eight-month leave with his first child. He commented:

> I think with any infant or toddler, mom always wins. And so I think because I was home and took care of her so much, it's more equitable than it would be if I hadn't ... [Becky] and I are quite close because of it, and I'm not sure we would be as close [without the leave time].

What was distinctive about these attachments was that they were formed directly between father and child. They were outcomes of the time fathers invested in daily, hands-on care, and they were not mediated by mothers, as is frequently the case in other circumstances (see for example Townsend, 2002). There is a quality of emotionality and intimacy in these relationships that makes them a new phenomenon, at least in scholarly terms. The 'intimate fatherhood' described by Dermott (2008) comes close in some respects, but is only part of the story. Dermott found, among the 25 UK fathers she interviewed, a commitment to develop relationships with their children that were emotionally close; this closeness was 'performed' both in physical displays of affection and in their talk. Dermott's fathers were clear that the development of such relationships took time. But they felt it was time that could be spent in select activities that brought father and child together – activities like reading, playing, talking and listening – rather than in the routine work of hands-on childcare. It was time, in other words, that resembled the 'quality time' that, as Dermott notes, was 'advocated in the 1980s as a possible resolution to the dilemma of the stressed "career woman" who was trying to balance employment and motherhood' (Dermott, 2008: 141).

The fathers I have described in this chapter were spending much more than 'quality time' with their children. In this respect, they were like the Portuguese solo caregiver fathers described by Wall (2014), or the Norwegian solo caregiver fathers in the study by Brandth and Kvande. These fathers, also on parental leave, learned that 'care is about *using a great deal of time* with the children.' As one of these fathers commented, 'I have much more faith in quantity than in quality' (Brandth and Kvande, 2003: 141, emphasis in original). All these fathers – those I describe, as well as the solo caregivers described by Brandth and Kvande – were not outsourcing the hands-on caring work to others, and reserving for themselves the intimate moments. For one thing, they were caring for babies, with whom intimate moments are so bound up in the practicalities of care as to be almost indistinguishable. As Jamieson (1998: 166) points out, 'It is difficult to spend time with young children and not be engaged in practical caring, and knowing and understanding take time.' Those fathers who were also caring for older children – who had reached the talking and listening stage and were more sociable – were in most cases simply building on attachments formed through hands-on care when they too were babies. They had learned that the combination of time spent and care provided leads to a different kind of intimacy and closeness.

Dermott suggests that 'intimate fatherhood' as defined by the fathers in her study – based on 'quality time' rather than more extended practical caregiving – served to position fathers in a separate category from mothers, who typically invested more caregiving time and were recognized as having qualitatively different relationships with their children. Intimate fatherhood did not challenge maternal primacy, but established fathers as offering something gender-specific and different. The fathers I have described in this chapter, like the solo caregiving fathers in the study by Brandth and Kvande (2003), had been doing the work that mothers traditionally do. So the attachments they developed with their children were *not* qualitatively different, and not (in Dermott's sense) gender-specific. This is not to say gender was irrelevant to the care they provided; in an earlier study of mine (Ranson, 2010) I described fathers like these as 'parenting like men.' But in doing 'everything but breastfeeding' (as Greg put it) – and once past their babies' early infancy, literally everything that the mothers did – they could hardly be viewed in a different category.

'Intimate fatherhood' is a better fit for these fathers as a description of the *exclusivity* of their relationships with their children. These relationships were strong, and committed – and, as I noted earlier, not mediated by mothers. Marsiglio and Roy (2012: 122) note that '[m]ost popular, political, and legal assessments of a father's involvement with his child are filtered through the lens of his commitment to a relationship with his wife or partner, the child's mother.' Removing that lens reveals father-child relationships as more individualized – which, in turn, invites consideration of the work of theorists who reflect on changes of just this kind in contemporary family life. For example Beck (1992) sees family change as a reflection of shifts in the social and economic order, which expose people to risks and hazards associated with freedom from old rules and certainties. For Beck and Beck-Gernsheim (1995), children assume a new importance in this changing and uncertain world, where 'traditional bonds play only a minor role, and the love between men and women has likewise proved vulnerable and prone to failure.' The child becomes a 'surrogate' when other (adult) relationships fall apart (pp. 72–73). This is the sense of the claim by Marsiglio and Roy (2012) that in some cases, parents' real 'marriage' is to their children (p. 122).

An alternative interpretation – and certainly what appeared to be the case for all the fathers I have described here – is that close, committed, life-long relationships with children were developing in the context of marital relationships that were also strong. They were not replacements for intimate adult relationships, but neither were they developing in a vacuum; they existed in a complex web of other relationships around which they had to be negotiated. In this context too there were *mother*-child relationships that were at least as engaged and committed. Inevitably, there was the potential for tension, when sharing the caring work led to sharing of children's attachment also. This tension surfaced in some fathers' accounts. As I noted earlier, Jeremy's wife wanted him to be less involved with infant care on his second parental leave than he had been with his first, in order to give her more time with the baby. Harjeet pointed to his wife's concern that their son loved him more than he loved her. Charlie said his wife, as a 'stereotypical mom,' wanted the children to go to her first, and had a 'hard time' with any preference shown to Charlie.

Gatrell (2007) explored this situation in a study of professional UK couples, in which fathers were seeking to become more involved with their children – usually by sharing care-giving activities once mothers' maternity leave ended. Gatrell framed their interest in the language of 'rights' to children, and suggested that, by actively working to be more involved, fathers were seeking to increase their power at the expense of mothers. They did this, Gatrell suggested, both by spending more time on child care, and also (like many of the fathers described by Dermott) by leaving to mothers the bulk of other domestic chores.

Being 'Number One' in a child's eyes is seductive for any parent, and there was no mistaking the pride with which many of the fathers I have described here spoke of their children's attachment to them. But Gatrell's suggestion that their involvement was impelled by a conscious effort to win power would be misleading, for (at least) two reasons. First, as I have already noted, these fathers were not selective about the activities they undertook in the course of their caregiving. Most saw being a solo caregiver at home full-time as incorporating other domestic responsibilities as well. Second, and more importantly, they took parental leave not only with mothers' blessing, but usually also at their request, to facilitate their return to careers that were very important to them. In other words, they took leave not to usurp mothers' power, but to support them professionally. The bonds that they developed with their children as a consequence were a compensation that was often quite unexpected. And *because* they developed in a context in which the hands-on caregiving and other domestic work was also shared, they could draw fathers into parenting as mothers' partners, not as their adversaries. Alan commented:

> I have an idea of what's going on at home ... increased time with the kids has meant a better understanding of what it takes to make them happy, and make mom happy too.

Aidan's wife was also home when he took a nine-month leave when his second child was born. He said that their relationship 'thrived' during the leave time because 'we were always around, and ... extra hands just made everything a lot easier.'

**Caregiving as work**

One outcome of fathers' sharing of the hands-on caregiving work – and this is the second theme to emerge from fathers' accounts – was that this work became visible to them as they learned how to do it. By doing the work, they recognized it *as* work, and so were able to appreciate it when others did it. This recognition was evident in the accounts of many fathers. David said: 'Now I get it! You are working so hard, 24/7, and it is hidden.' Steve said he thought all fathers should spend six months at home: 'I think if you both have your feet in it, it makes it a lot easier to empathize and communicate.' Derek commented:

> I think it's good because it gives you an appreciation for what stay-at-home moms go through … I'll always be the first to kind of give guys heck when they talk about, you know, 'stay-at-home moms, they got it easy.' Oh, no, they don't. The biggest thing that people who haven't done it don't realize is that you never get a break. You can't just say, 'Okay, I'm going to sit down for ten minutes here and have a breather.' Well, no, you can't … It's absolutely non-stop.

But it was, clearly, a new kind of work, conducted in a different space and at a different pace from the work most of them were used to. For almost all the fathers in the study, the time they spent on leave was the first time they had ever been alone at home for an extended period. While some of the fathers enjoyed what they described as the change of pace, and the chance of a break from their regular work, many of them also found the changed spatial and social context the most difficult part of the leave experience. Charlie, as noted earlier, remembered the 'isolation component' during his first leave – and the cold winter days that made outdoors activities difficult. Harjeet commented:

> It was frustrating at times, because, you know, you're left with the child alone and you're having to deal with it, and you've never done it before. So there were times when you'd get frustrated or feel like, you know, 'I wish I had the human contact a little more.' … So that part of it was actually quite challenging, just being stuck in the house for the entire day.

Fathers like Charlie and Mike, who took more than one leave, found their second leave experience to be much more social. The presence and needs of the older child meant playgroups and other activities in the community. As Mike put it, 'I got to be a dad out in public.' But being publicly visible as a caregiving father also had its challenges. Many fathers echoed the sentiments expressed by those in Doucet's (2006b) study; they were acutely conscious of their status as men in the 'estrogen-filled worlds' of infant and pre-school caregiving. Some fathers, like Jason, were emphatic in their refusal to enter this world. 'I have to get out of the house, or I start going squirrelly,' he said. 'But ... I'm not somebody who wants to befriend women and hang out with women. Like I'm a man's man!' Other fathers, like Tony, were willing to 'step up to the plate' by participating in community-organized activities, even though, as he said, he knew he would be joining 'a sea of women.' Jim's description of his participation in a play group neatly summed up these mixed responses:

> I was definitely the only dad there. It was good. It was interesting. I did hear some comments from a couple of moms saying like, 'My husband would never do this.' And it did feel a little goofy, sort of singing songs and clapping hands and stuff. I was a little uncomfortable with that, but ... it was still fun, and it was nice to have a distraction, and something to do.

Temporal as well as spatial issues factored in to fathers' experience of caregiving as work. All the fathers I have described – those who took leave with mothers at home, and those who were solo caregivers – quickly became involved in the practices of daily care. But when mothers were also present, they were less caught up in – and therefore possibly less responsive to – the ongoing rhythms of infant waking, feeding and sleeping that shaped and organized the caregiving work. Fathers who became solo caregivers had to learn these rhythms. And while this learning was not unique to fathers, I would argue that it was a particular challenge to men accustomed to the structure of another kind of working day – one with a schedule of clearly defined tasks, over whose execution they had at least some control. Having their days controlled by a baby – who was far more demanding than most of them imagined would be the case – was a new experience. Adjusting to the baby's rhythm was a critical lesson of the leave. Brandth and Kvande (2003) describe this changed temporal rhythm as 'slow time,' in which the needs of the children determine how the day is spent, and where there is no other agenda beyond responding to those needs:

> This is a perception of time different from the one that applies in the working lives of the fathers and to life in general, where time is more

a matter of division and fragmentation, all inside the framework of the demand for a high tempo.

(Brandth and Kvande, 2003: 66)

Lucas was one father who found this adaptation to the baby routine difficult – at least partly because the baby in question was unusually demanding. Being away from his regular job made him 'a little bit crazy.' His solution was to impose some of the structure missing from his day by painting the inside of his house:

During his naps, I'd give myself an hour, an hour and a half after he went down, I'd focus on a section. I broke each job down into a wall … It added extra stress I didn't need, but at the same time it was cathartic. You know, kind of gave me a break from having to deal with him.

Martin was another father who tried to inject some personal projects into his days of caregiving. At home on an eight-month leave, he always had an online chess game going, on which he dropped in when he could. He had also decided that learning some French would be a useful home-based project, and so had found some computer-based language learning material. But he selected these projects on the basis that they could fit around the work he needed to do to respond to his baby's needs; they took up the time that the baby allowed.

This changed perception of time was behind Will's comment, noted earlier, about the need to learn 'how long he had' before the baby needed attention. It was behind Tony's recognition that he would only ever have a 'ten-minute window' to do anything that was not baby-related. It emerged in other fathers' descriptions of adjusting to the baby's rhythms. As Mike put it, 'It's funny how the baby defined the routine, and you get into that routine, and then the routine changes because he changes, and you just adapt, and you go with it.'

Learning to be a caregiver, and adjusting to the different spatial and social context in which the caregiving took place, made fathers' time on leave distinctive and memorable – especially if the baby they cared for was their first. Most entered the leave with no prior experience of looking after a baby. At the end of the leave all were competent to do so – in most cases having spent extended periods as their baby's primary caregiver. As Robert said: 'I feel comfortable doing all that stuff.' It was in a sense a training period, which turned caregiving fathers from novices to 'pros.' This perspective returns us to the conception, first introduced in Chapter 1, of time at home learning to care for a baby as the serving of an apprenticeship. This analogy is especially apt when fathers antici-pate that workplace or other constraints might prevent them from taking leave with a second or subsequent child.[4] Will was in just this situation and, as noted earlier, commented that he got what he needed out of the one leave he did take. Ben described his first leave as something to be experienced 'once in a lifetime.' He added:

> I know if I have a second one and try and do it again, I know it's not going to be near as [pause], it's going to be enjoyable, but it won't be as fulfilling, because the experience won't be all brand new.

### The effects of caregiving

Ben in other words served his apprenticeship, and had acquired the caregiving skills he could then use with other children. The further point to take out of Ben's comment is that, for him, this learning *was* fulfilling. Ben's reflection introduces the third theme that emerges from the fathers' accounts: how they understood the experience of their caregiving time. For many, the effect of learning how to care was transformative. It affected not only their thinking about their family relationships, but also their relationship to their paid employment. In a context in which breadwinning continues to be a conventional marker of good fatherhood, and a man's job as a key component of his mascu-line identity, these shifts in understanding are significant.

The leave experience was not in every case entirely positive. As noted, many fathers who were solo caregivers found it challenging to be at home alone with a baby; they missed the sociability and structure of their regular jobs, and many were not sorry to get back to them. But in their accounts they were usually anxious not to allow the challenges to detract from their own overall assessment of the leave, which they described in glowing terms: for example, Alan called it 'fantastic'; Mike called it 'an amazing experience'; Mehtab called it 'a blessing.' And for most the leave marked a shift, however minor, in their relationship to paid work.

This was signalled by their willingness to take leave in the first place. In most cases they were absent from their paid employment for a period of many months – and this, I argue, constituted a clear statement about their willingness to accommodate their work responsibilities to the needs of their families. All the fathers who took leave when their partners returned to work were in most cases doing so *to enable* their partners to return to work. The privileging of mothers' jobs was clear in many fathers' accounts, and links to the second theoretical understanding I introduced in Chapter 1, that these fathers are (in Connell's terms) constructing a new kind of masculinity through new configurations of practice.

Taking leave also constituted a challenge to masculinist workplace norms about men as workers. In several cases fathers requested leave with considerable trepidation, aware that though they could not be prevented legally from taking the leave, they might be subject to scrutiny – and viewed differently – because of their open acknowledgement of family responsibilities. But they did so anyway – and most said they would urge other fathers to do the same. Other fathers, like Jeremy and Drew, were high-level employees whose possibly more public and visible leave-taking could be seen as constituting a model, and a precedent, in the companies in which they worked. As a manager, Jeremy recognized that his own experience of caregiving and family life made him more sensitive to the people on his staff:

> You have an objective discussion about, like, projects and work and expectations and deadlines and so on, but behind the scenes, there's all this happening in their lives too, right? ... They all want to do a good job and try hard, but they've got in the background all this stuff, and probably a little bit more financial stress at times too, which also gets in the way.

A further consequence of the leave-taking, and a shift away from conventional understandings of fatherhood and masculinity, was a shift in their attachment to paid work as a result of their attachment to their children. This shift was certainly not a characteristic of the 'intimate fatherhood' described earlier by Dermott (2008). The parental leave, in almost every case, was just the start of a process of bonding that filtered through every other decision. Though financial provision remained important – particularly in cases where the father was the sole or main provider – it was tempered by a recognition that they had a bond with their children that needed more than financial provision to support. So where once workplace responsibilities would have taken priority over family responsibilities, in many cases there was a subtle shift in priorities, so that work became organized around family, rather than the other way around. They became 'working fathers' in the sense usually reserved for 'working mothers' (Ranson, 2012). Jeremy is once again a case in point: he was being invited to apply for a new position, that would involve more responsibility and more travel. Though his wife was encouraging him to consider it, he had decided to turn it down. It was, he said, 'one step beyond what we can handle.' Eleven of the fathers I have described worked for two large employers, both of whom offered compressed work week arrangements. Several of these fathers had taken advantage of such arrangements, and, like Harjeet (described earlier) spent one full weekday caring for children. In more general terms, their identity as fathers meant their priorities would not be the same as they had been. As Lucas said:

> I would say I'm more patient, I think. I won't say [I] care less about my job, that's not the right wording. But if something were to happen and I would lose it, I'd be less impacted than I would have been before. Life is greater than what happens between these walls at the office.

There are two ways to look at this new masculinity. Brandth and Kvande (1998) in an earlier study of Norwegian men taking parental leave (noted in Chapter 1) raise the possibility that it is the domain of men secure in their masculine identity, and that family involvement is seen as an extension of the 'masculine sphere':

> The new man will not win any more victories in the old public arenas ... but rather through his efforts in everyday contact with his closest family. Care and intimacy with children can be seen as new territories to be conquered. ... Being able to master a new challenge, even if it is childcare is ... regarded as an important masculine attribute.
>
> (Brandth and Kvande, 1998: 309)

This perspective might apply to some fathers, for whom competence in child care becomes a new string to their bow, rather than a challenge to the shape of the bow. And there is no doubt that almost all the fathers I have introduced here, with jobs to return to after their leave, were not subject to the same sort of gender challenges as are fathers who are permanent at-home caregivers. But I suggest that this reconstructed masculinity is more progressive; it seems to be associated with more co-operative parenting arrangements, and fathers who are involved not (as noted earlier) as a means to usurp women's power, but – in David's terms – in order to work with their partners to 'share the love and responsibility.'

# Part III
# Reading Fathers

## Introduction

Fathers' accounts of caregiving – what it consists of, and what they make of it – take many forms. Up to now, I have drawn on the material I gathered in my interviews with fathers. In the next two chapters, I turn to other sources of fathers' accounts: in Chapter 4 I examine a selection of memoirs written by fathers about their experiences of caring for young children, and in Chapter 5 I analyze a series of fathers' online blogs. In both formats, fathers are describing what they are doing, and talking about what it means to them. But unlike the interview material, which was solicited by me as a researcher, delivered in conversation and in person, and provided with the assurance of anonymity, memoirs and blogs comprise material volunteered by fathers who, for whatever reason, want to make their experiences public. These accounts are *crafted*, in a way that interview accounts are not. The stories each tells are controlled by a writer with his own agenda. On that basis, then, it might appear that they should be assessed on different terms, or according to different criteria, and there is a growing literature to suggest how this might be done. In what follows, I draw on some of this material to guide my reading of the memoirs and blogs I have chosen for analysis.

With respect to the memoirs, the first challenge was methodological, and involved selection of appropriate material. When I began my search for memoirs that addressed my research interests, I wanted to find in each a father who was seriously engaged in caregiving, and who was thoughtful about his relationship with the child who was receiving the care. I was searching among memoir writers for fathers who were both describing their caregiving, and *reflecting* on it, in roughly the same way that my interviewees had done. Finding these fathers was not always an easy task. Fathers' published accounts are produced for many purposes, some of which seemed not to fit with mine. Memoir writers, like other storytellers, may use the form to 'remember, argue, justify, persuade, engage, entertain and even mislead an audience' (Riessman, 2008: 8). Fathers whose primary goal seemed, for example, to entertain a popular (and largely uncritical) audience, were among those whose work I did not include.[1] Other memoirs (e.g. Berkmann, 2008) clearly drew on personal experience but were not written in the first person. Instead they were constructed as guidance or 'rules' for new fathers, who were addressed directly as 'you.' The authorial 'I' was entirely absent. Yet others (e.g. Viner, 2013) were retrospective reflections on child-rearing (and in Viner's case many other matters) from the perspective of a father of adult children. They were reflections on *fatherhood*, rather than on *fathering*.

I discovered the memoir *Home Game: An Accidental Guide to Fatherhood*, by the American writer Michael Lewis (Lewis, 2009) in the early stages of this research. It confirmed for me that what I was looking for did exist. One comment from the memoir will show why. It is made following a health crisis in the life of Lewis's third child, which drew him into solo caregiving duty at the 11-week-old baby's hospital bed:

> I change his diapers and feed him and suction the mucus from his nose. I notice for the first time that he has my hands and feet. I study the little heart-shaped birthmark on the back of his head. I discover that if I hold him to my chest and hum against the back of his neck, he falls right to sleep. Tabitha [Lewis's wife] comes and offers to take over, but the truth is I don't want to leave: He feels like my juris-diction. After every new child, I learn the same lesson, grudgingly: If you want to feel the way you're meant to feel about the new baby, you need to do the grunt work. It's only in caring for a thing that you become attached to it.
>
> (Lewis, 2009: 162–163)

Lewis's memoir, in which he explicitly connects his hands-on caregiv-ing work to its effects, provided something of a model. To find others like it I conducted searches using WorldCat, the online worldwide library catalogue system, Amazon, the internet-based bookseller, and the websites of major bookstores such as the UK-based Waterstones. These sources provided me with listings of potentially relevant mate-rial; from there, it was a matter of reading a great many, with my Lewis model in mind. Other criteria developed as I read. I wanted each memoir to include discussion of caregiving to babies and very young children (even if that was not its sole focus); this would establish common ground with the fathers I had interviewed in Canada. But I also wanted to extend the discussion beyond its starting focus on those Canadian fathers, all (apparently) heterosexual married men, who were sharing the caregiving with the mothers of their children. This meant introducing some diversity into the sample, both geographically and in terms of the range of circumstances in which fathers were providing care. I also wanted relatively recent publications (2005 or later). Reading with all these criteria in mind, there was of course a subjective element to my selection as well. With Schwartz, I could say 'There was an element of "I can't define it, but I know it when I see it"' to my search (Schwartz, 1994: 4). In effect, I read till I had found what I was looking for. The result is a selection of eight memoirs that are by no means representative of this wide-ranging literary field – nor are they intended to be. They constitute, instead, a coherent sub-set strategically chosen to illuminate this project's main focus.

A search for direction on the analysis of memoirs as a data source was my next challenge. It led first to the broad field of narrative analysis, and the recognition that memoirs, like research interviews, are stories told about a life, or a segment of life, in particular social and historical circumstances. Like interviews they are personal narratives, which 'offer insights into human agency as seen from the inside out; as such they can bridge the analytic gap between outside positionalities and interior worlds, between the social and the individual' (Maynes et al., 2008: 16). Researchers whose work bridges the social sciences and humanities locate memoirs, like autobiography more generally, as a form of *self-life* writing. Smith and Watson (2010) describe memoirs as a particular genre of life writing which take 'a segment of a life, not its entirety, and [focus] on interconnected experiences' (p. 275).

There is extensive debate, across social sciences and humanities disciplines, about what actually constitutes narrative analysis. Disputes about what a narrative is, whether its focus should be on experience or events, and how it should be read, complicate the analytic task (Connidis, 2012; Andrews et al., 2013). There is, as Riessman notes, 'conflict and disagreement among those holding different perspectives' (Riessman, 2008: 11). In light of the diversity of analytic approaches, and the different data sources available for analysis, Maynes et al. (2008: 13) call on researchers to 'explicate as fully as necessary how they are reading their sources in light of them.'

From the perspective of a narrative analyst in the social sciences, memoirs can be read both as resources and as topics. As resources, 'we come to use them to see what insights they may bring to understanding social life'; as topics, 'we come to see them as matters of investigation in their own right: as topics of interest in themselves' (Plummer, 2001: 36). In the language of Holstein and Gubrium (2012) this distinction translates into 'the degree to which empirical and analytic emphasis is placed on the *whats* as opposed to the *hows* of narrative production' (p. 7). A focus on 'what' is said, rather than '"how," "to whom" or "for what purposes"' is the basis of the analytic approach that Riessman (2008) describes as thematic analysis, in which 'content is the exclusive focus,' and where analysts keep stories intact by 'theorizing from the case rather than from component themes across cases' (p. 53).

The fact remains though that, while those offering guidance in the field of narrative analysis seem to consider memoirs a legitimate, and indeed valuable, data source, social scientists in general have tended to pay much more attention to interview-based material than to written forms of narrative (Maynes et al., 2008; Riessman, 2008; Connidis, 2012). And those scholars (more often in humanities disciplines) who do focus on written, auto/biographical material are more likely to view it, in Plummer's terms, as a topic rather than a resource. One of the few models for the approach I am taking is provided by Canadian sociologist Ingrid Connidis (2012), who compared an extensive research interview and a published memoir as a means to explore gay men's family ties.

Like Connidis, I am drawing on memoirs primarily as a resource; I am interested in *what* the writers are saying, rather than in how they say it. The 'what' in this case relates to their experiences of caregiving – what they (say they) do, and what they make of it. In Riessman's terms, I am reading them as cases, and looking for 'patterns but also distinctiveness' in the lives they represent (Merrill and West, 2009: 2). And like Connidis, I am reading them as companion pieces to the interviews I have already conducted.

I approached each memoir, as Taylor (2009) did, with specific questions in mind. Two in particular linked to the interview material, and my focus on the memoirs as resources used, as noted earlier in Plummer's terms, to 'see what insights they [might] bring' to the topic in hand. Of each memoir, I asked:

- How physically engaged with caregiving does the father appear to be? How is this caregiving described?
- What effect on him as a person, and as a father, does this caregiving appear to have? How does he describe his feelings for his child(ren)?

But it was also impossible to ignore the ways in which the memoirs differed from the interviews. For one thing, they sometimes covered topics (like, for example, sexual intimacy with partners) that my interviewees did not introduce voluntarily, and that I might either have had difficulty broaching, or simply not thought to ask. They also represented, to cite again Frank's description, the 'revised reflections of especially articulate individuals' (Frank, 2012a: 41). This led not only to more complete and thought-through responses to the questions I have noted above, but also, incidentally, to a much stronger impression of the writer as a person and a father, and what his life might be like.

The other major difference concerned the circumstances of each memoir's production. Each was written to satisfy a need, or to fulfil an agenda. The motivation to tell the story, as Connidis (2012: 118) points out, might affect the story being told. It soon became clear to me that, in order to do justice to the writers and to the analysis, I also needed to try to discern the motivation. To that extent, I did consider the memoirs as topics, as well as resources. I asked:

- What biographical information is provided, about father and child(ren)? Was it something about a child, or something about the father, that was the main impetus for the memoir being written?
- What was the writer's declared motivation or guiding question?
- How does he present himself as a father?

I read and reread the memoirs with all these questions in mind. I marked relevant text, took notes on each 'story,' looked for common themes, and examined the ways the memoirs contributed to the broader discussion of fathering and masculinity.

As I noted in the introduction to Part I, it was my reading of memoirs by fathers that led me to a study of fathers' online blogs as a further source of information about fathers and caregiving. Over the past two decades, developments in computer-mediated communication have provided new means for parenting issues to be presented and discussed, and among these new developments, blogs are a burgeoning field. Until recently, this field has been populated almost exclusively by mothers; there is a growing literature in North America directed to the 'mamasphere,' and to the 'mommy bloggers'[2] who inhabit it. More recently, however, fathers have also been claiming space as bloggers in the online parenting world.

Many of these fathers are explicit in their intention to reframe conventional understandings of fathers and fathering, and to position themselves as competent caregivers deeply engaged with their families. Because they are relatively new arrivals on the blogging scene, fathers' blogs have attracted almost no scholarly attention.[3] Yet their growing collective presence and output are a potentially rich source of data for researchers interested in the potential of blogs to shape dominant discourses of fathering. Blogs furthermore are a source of naturalistic textual material that is publicly available, easily accessible, and offering archived content to allow researchers to consider change and development over time (Leggatt-Cook and Chamberlain, 2012: 965).

Blogs may take a variety of forms, but the ones I am interested in are in effect online personal journals. Postings are in reverse chronological order, so that the first post accessed is the most recently written. Blogs typically feature instant text and graphic publishing, archives of past posts, and a feedback mechanism which allows readers to comment, and bloggers to respond (Hookway, 2008: 92). The development of software programs such as Blogger or WordPress has enabled 'virtually anyone with an Internet connection' to create a blog, and makes it easy for them to post 'text, audio, pictures, video and links' (Miller, 2010: 1514). Fathers' blogs contain all of these components. What they offer, in a range of styles, are ongoing stories of family life, from the perspective of writers who are committed to identifying as fathers, and sharing details of their fathering with an extended public.

But with blogs, even more than with memoirs, the first and most difficult question is how to choose which ones to study. While there is general agreement that the field is burgeoning, the number of blogs, like the size of the internet, defies accurate calculation. As Rettberg (2014:16) notes, it is 'impossible to estimate how many blogs there are in the world.' The blogging host WordPress estimated in 2012 that it alone hosted more than 50 million blogs, and that some 100,000 were set up each day. But, Rettberg adds, calculation of blog numbers is made more difficult currently because there is no central registry. Furthermore, the two major blog search engines, Technorati and Google Blog Search, both stopped functioning in May 2014, thus making a systematic search for a particular category of blog – in my case, those written by fathers – next to impossible. The sheer undocumented volume of material available is one of its most daunting features. As Hookway found:

> Entering the blogosphere as a blog 'newbie' was like gazing into a dark and tangled labyrinth. The endless criss-crossing hyper tracks and trails of the blogosphere were overwhelming. 'It' seemed unwieldy and unmanageable – words that immediately arouse anxiety in the

social researcher ... Establishing a road-map in what felt like the 'black hole' of the blogosphere represented a serious challenge.

(Hookway, 2008: 98)

Like Hookway and other researchers interested in using blogs as data, I needed to enter the 'dark and tangled labyrinth' in my search for blogs written by fathers. As was the case with my choice of memoirs, however, I had an early sense of what I was looking for – blogs written by fathers who were actively engaged in hands-on caregiving, and who were reflective about their fathering. I wanted to find blogger fathers like the fathers I had interviewed and those whose memoirs I chose, who were experienced caregivers to babies and young children. I also wanted a selection of blogs that covered the geographic range established in my choice of memoir writers. Beyond these criteria, I was also interested in fathers' blogs as a source of potential change in dominant discourses of fatherhood. It made sense, then, to examine blogs considered by the blogging community itself to have some traction and influence, and which may have attracted attention in conventional media as well.

I began with lists of 'top 50 daddy bloggers' published by parenting websites like *Babble.com* (prominent in the US), and *Tots100*, a collective of UK parenting blogs. I consulted lists of 'top 10 dad blogs' on Twitter.[4] I located fathers' group blogs to extend the range I was considering. I also searched for, or followed up, media accounts of father bloggers in Canada, the US, the UK and Australia. All these sources, after considerable cross-referencing, gave me a pool of father bloggers representing all four countries. From this pool, I then applied my personal criteria to weed out those that did not meet my needs. This was not always easy. Some of the highest-ranked blogs did not match my criteria – notably, those whose focus may have been on older children, or as much about fathers' outside interests as about family matters. Considering the strategies for sampling blogs suggested by Li and Walejko (2008), mine was a combination of quota and convenience sampling. I worked with those I could locate that seemed (with occasional compromises) to fit the criteria I had established. This process produced a selection of 20 blogs, from fathers in the four countries just noted. Like the memoirs, they represent a strategic choice, intended to illuminate the key concerns of this research.

As Hayton suggests, blogs are 'a new platform for life writing' (Hayton, 2009: 201). Like memoirs, they are also stories. So it is tempting to consider that they too might lend themselves analytically to the sort of narrative approach I described earlier with respect to the memoirs.

But blogs are different kinds of stories. They are stories told through words, pictures, and occasionally other audiovisual material. They are interactive; blogs receive comments, to which bloggers respond. A blog is, in some ways, a conversation, a story told in short bursts. Rettberg writes:

> When blogs tell stories, they generally do so in an episodic form, with each post being a self-contained unit that contributes to an overall narrative. Each post makes sense in itself, but read together – not necessarily in sequence – the posts tell a larger story. The story is usually partial and incomplete and does not form a narrative whole as well-formed stories in mainstream literature and cinema do. Instead, the overall story as gleaned from reading a blog is likely to be pieced together from fragments, perhaps supplemented by bits of stories from other places.
>
> (Rettberg, 2014: 119)

Though Rettberg also asserts that a blog 'cannot be read simply for its writing' (Rettberg, 2014: 5) in the few examples of social science research using blogs that I could locate, the textual content was the focus of analysis – though some scholars (for example MacKay and Dallaire, 2014; Hunter, 2015) also included an interview component in their research. Forms of textual analysis ranged from quantitative content analyses (for example Saiki and Cloyes, 2014) to conventional qualitative approaches involving the identification of key themes across a series of blogs (for example Leggatt-Cook and Chamberlain, 2012; Takeda, 2013).

My approach is closest to the qualitative, theme-based analysis just described. But, from the foregoing, it will be clear that to focus too narrowly on the *text* of a blog is to skirt important dimensions of the story – and to risk losing sight of the father who is telling it. It was important for me to consider, to the extent I could know it, the context in which the story was being told, and to acknowledge, as I read, the *person* whose story it was. In many ways this was not hard to do. Anyone who is familiar with blogs of this kind will know that the visual material that surrounds the text, the direct approach to readers that characterizes most blog content, and the shifts and changes in family life reported in the blogs over time together make it difficult to separate the text from its author.

For all 20 blogs selected here, I read at least one year's worth of posts (though from the foregoing it will be clear that 'reading' was not all I did). In some cases, my focus was only on 2014, and (depending on how the blog was classified and archived) I read either every post for the year, or every post relating to children and family life. I also read selectively the posts that many of the fathers wrote for prominent sites[5] outside their own blogs. In many cases, depending on how prolific the blogger was, I read back two or more years, usually in order to make sense of recent posts that drew on past history. Because a key focus in this research is on fathers' caregiving to babies, in cases where a baby was born during the life of the blog, I went back in time in order to capture fathers' posts about the baby's birth and first year or so of its life.

My strategy was to read, in Rettberg's terms, in order to 'glean the overall story' (or at any rate as much of it as my reading could discover). I then made summaries of the blog and its writer, and selected key posts – those that seemed most directly concerned with caregiving to children and ideas about fathering – for closer examination. Because fathers as bloggers are a new phenomenon, I also took account of what they had to say about blogging. Several key themes developed from this approach, which I discuss in Chapter 5.

As the following chapters will make clear, fathers who write memoirs, and those who write blogs, have much in common with the Canadian fathers introduced so far. But they also bring a range of different experiences into view, and provide in most cases much more detail about fathering. Their accounts are an important addition to the interview material.

# 4

# 'You Need to Do the Grunt Work'

As I noted in the introduction to Part III, memoirs provide a valuable alternative source of fathers' stories about caregiving. The ones I have chosen to discuss in this chapter are thoughtful retrospective accounts by fathers who have been involved, in a variety of different family contexts, in ongoing, hands-on care of children – care that began when the children were babies.

The eight memoirs included here are organized into sections in terms of the particular circumstances shaping the father's caregiving experience. In the first section, I discuss memoirs by American writers Michael Lewis and Elisha Cooper. Both are well-educated white middle-class men, who are sharing caregiving of healthy children with the mothers of their children. Their circumstances are not unlike those of most of the fathers I interviewed in Canada. The second section contains the memoirs of the Canadian writer Ian Brown, and the American writer George Estreich. These memoirs take the discussion of fathers' caregiving on to new terrain, as both men are caring for 'special needs' children. The third section contains the memoirs of three men who, unlike any other fathers introduced so far, are caring for babies and young children in the absence of a mother. Matthew Logelin, writing in the US, and Ian Newbold, writing in the UK, are young widowers; Dan Bucatinsky is a gay father raising children in the US. Finally, in the fourth section I discuss the memoir by the Australian writer Ben Robertson, who writes as a home-based primary caregiver.

For each memoir, I use the guiding questions (both resource- and topic-related, as noted in the introduction to Part III – not necessarily in order) to focus my discussion. I draw on the writers' descriptions of caregiving, to demonstrate its embodiment, and also on their reflections about the fathering of which it was an important part. I conclude the chapter with a discussion of the overall contribution of the memoirs to the discussion of fathers, masculinity and embodied care.

## Fathering when all is well

Michael Lewis, whose memoir I introduced earlier, is a writer living in Berkeley, California. The memoir is made up of short essay pieces, in three chronological parts, each organized around the births of his three children, Quinn, Dixie and Walker. It reads very much as if it was written in the moment – as it apparently was. In his introduction, Lewis notes:

> I began keeping a journal of my experience of fatherhood seven months after the birth of our first child ... Most of what follows was written in the hazy, sleepless and generally unpleasant first year after the birth of each of my three children. Most of it was also written within a few days after the incident reported. I found pretty quickly that any thoughts or feelings or even dramatic episodes I didn't get down on paper immediately I forgot entirely – which was the first reason I began to write stuff down. (pp. 13–14)

However, his professed 'main reason' for recording his experiences was to address 'this persistent and disturbing gap between what I was meant to feel and what I actually felt' (p. 14). He writes: 'Expected to feel overcome with joy – "It's a boy! You must be so happy!" – I often felt puzzled. (I shouldn't be just as happy if it was a girl?) Expected to feel outraged, I often felt secretly pleased; expected to feel worried, I often felt indifferent. ("It's just a little blood").' All this, for Lewis, suggests an 'extensive cover-up,' by fathers all around him, all 'pretending to do one thing, and feel one way, when they were in fact doing and feeling all sorts of things' (p. 14).

He elaborates on his motivation in writing after the arrival of his second child, Dixie. He wants to address the 'central mystery of fatherhood' as he experienced it:

> How does a man's resentment of this ... *thing* ... that lands in his life and instantly disrupts every aspect of it for the apparent worse turn into love? A month after Quinn was born, I would have felt only an obligatory sadness if she had been rolled over by a truck. Six months or so later, I'd have thrown myself in front of the truck to save her from harm. What happened? What transformed me from a monster

into a father? I do not know. But this time around I'm keeping a closer eye on the process. (pp. 75–76)

The resolution to the 'central mystery,' as he discloses it in the excerpt cited in the introduction to Part III, lies in the transformative effect of 'doing the grunt work.' To repeat the insight evoked by his care for his hospitalized third child, '[i]t's only in caring for a thing that you become attached to it' (p. 163).

Though he claims to have been drawn into it reluctantly, Lewis is directly engaged in the physical care of his children, and, as noted earlier, he is explicit about its effects in making him feel the way he is 'meant' to feel. There are multiple descriptions, throughout the memoir, of literally hands-on caregiving, beginning with the outline of his morning ritual with his eldest child, Quinn, when she is eight months old. The ritual involves singing 'Old MacDonald Had a Farm' as he lifts her from her crib; distracting her as he sets her on the change table (by dancing and waving a trash bag above his head); changing her diaper and 'dancing all the while,' then tucking her under his arm 'like a football,' and taking her to her mother to be nursed (p. 30). Caregiving episodes ranging from infant diaper changing to feeding and dressing toddlers to taking them on outings are framed in humorous terms, but the humour does not detract from the practical knowledge and experience they imply.

Lewis also describes his memoir as 'a snapshot of what I assume will one day be looked back upon as a kind of Dark Age of Fatherhood.' We are, he says, 'in the midst of some long unhappy transition' between models of fatherhood – the past, represented by his own father (the man from whom, he says, he inherited his gift for avoiding unpleasant chores), and 'some ideal model, approved by all, to be practiced with ease by the perfect fathers of the future.' The transition is characterized by a lack of standards for fathers' behaviour; Lewis acknowledges that some might view him as 'a Neanderthal who should do more to help my poor wife with the kids,' and others who view him as a 'Truly Modern Man' for being 'both breadwinner and domestic dervish – doer of approximately 31.5 per cent of all parenting' (pp. 10–11).

Lewis travels in his own mind between these two positions. With his characteristic wry humour, he describes as one example caring for two-and-a-half-year-old Quinn, to allow her mother to concentrate on newborn Dixie. This caring involves the broken night sleeping with her downstairs (Dixie and her mother are upstairs), the struggle to 'dress her in clothes she does not want to wear' and feed her 'a breakfast she does not want to eat,' before getting her to 'school' (presumably daycare or a preschool) (p. 66). At this point, Lewis describes his 'brief feeling of satisfaction'; he is 'coping manfully with a great big mess'; he is 'preventing [his] wife from further suffering'; he is 'the good soldier who has leapt on the hand-grenade, so that others may live'. This feeling lasts until he comes home to find his exhausted wife in tears, and liable to comment that she is 'going through this alone.' Such a comment 'neatly undercuts my belief that I am carrying far more than my share of our burden; indeed, it makes it clear that I am not a hero at all but a slacker, a deadbeat Dad' (p. 67).

Lewis undoubtedly knows, on the evidence he presents throughout the memoir, that he is not a slacker; indeed, the existence of the memoir is itself a sign that he is not. Though, as noted earlier, he may only be doing '31.5 per cent' of the parenting, he appears (like Aidan and Alan, interviewed in Chapter 3) to have played a major role in caring for the older child(ren) on the birth of each new one. And his humour glosses events such as the post-partum panic disorder his wife suffers after Walker's birth, when, '[a]mazingly, the only thing that makes her feel better is me' (p. 140). He is forthright about all the things his wife does for the children that he does not do, and professes his own incompetence on many fronts, from doing his daughters' hair to dealing with spots and a fever. When it comes to babies, he says, the American father 'is really just a second-string mother.' In his own case, he is required in an emergency to 'holler' for his wife, and then 'take my place at her elbow and await further instructions' (p. 43). The baby's mother is very clearly positioned, throughout the memoir, as the parent in charge. Hers are the rules.

He is not the primary parent, but he positions himself as a highly engaged second-string. He suggests, ironically, that family involvement like his is likely to be regarded by women with 'gentle condescension,' while men 'just look away in shame.' (p. 42) But his self-representation as a father, and a man, strikes a different note when the memoir is considered as a whole. Lewis is highly educated, and is a successful professional writer. In Frank's (2012a) terms, noted earlier, he is the model of the 'especially articulate individual.' He is writing for an educated middle-class audience, some of whom may know of him as a father, but many of whom are probably more familiar with his best-selling work as a financial journalist.[1] He is challenging conventional masculinity, but from an elevated position on the masculine ladder, and as one who, in the terms of Brandth and Kvande (1998) introduced in the previous chapter, seems secure in his own masculine identity.

This security shows up in several stories. He writes of taking Quinn to a Gymboree class in Paris (where the family was living for a time); he is the only man among a gathering of nannies and 'actual mothers,' and is treated as 'a charming oddity: the wonderful father who has taken the morning off from work to spend it with his baby daughter.' All the women 'find the notion of a man free in the middle of the day amusingly lovable, which is what, of course, I strive to be' (p. 37). He jokingly refers to 'us mothers' in his description of the class. Another story involves the discovery that Quinn's teachers have been choking back giggles in his presence because she has announced at school that he has a small penis. The third concerns the circumstances, and the details, of his vasectomy. The vasectomy story is effectively the end of the memoir, as it is the end of his procreative life. It is also, characteristically, a funny story.

I would argue that the choice to tell these particular stories is the choice of a man who does indeed feel secure in his own masculinity; he is unlikely to feel it threatened by his involvement as a father. We are invited to conclude that he is the 'Truly Modern Man' rather than the Neanderthal that was his earlier basis of comparison. But his ironic references to himself as the 'good soldier' who 'copes manfully' also leave no doubt that for all his domestic engagement he is very much a man.

The Lewis memoir describes a father's life with three children, and covers a chronological span of several years. The memoir *Crawling: A Father's First Year*, by Elisha Cooper (2006) zeroes in on a much shorter time span, and focuses on only one child – the author's firstborn, Zoë. Over the period described in the memoir, Cooper, like Lewis, was living in Berkeley, California. He too is a professional writer; but while he shares many dimensions of privilege with Lewis as a white, well-educated middle-class man, his world is different. He is also an artist, probably best known for his illustrated children's books, and he works from home. He also becomes, by the end of the memoir, Zoë's full-time caregiver. While professing himself a man who 'had never liked children,' and who, when he was in his 20s, would like most men of that age 'sooner have been handed a bomb than a baby' (p. 10), he knew that some day he would have them, though he 'just didn't know how to get there with any grace' (p. 12). His memoir, in a series of short essays, uses daily doings to trace his experience of becoming a father, and to grapple with its meaning.

As it turns out, the transition for Cooper (unlike for Lewis) is not so much about coming to feel how he was 'meant to feel' about his daughter. That connection seems to have been in place from the start. Of her birth, Cooper writes:

> [Out] it came, a gangly thing covered in blood. The thing was turned to me and it looked into my eyes with the hugest, most startled eyes I have ever seen and our eyes locked. I thought, *I know you.* (p. 6)

He describes the day of her birth, a day filled with calls to family and friends, the drinking of champagne, and his wife Elise learning to breast-feed. For his part, he writes: 'I just stared at Zoë whenever she slept on my chest. She kept both fists in front of her face like a boxer and sometimes started awake and punched me' (p. 9). That description is characteristic of many throughout the memoir; all signal his close attention to the baby as an embodied presence, and his own embodied engagement with her. If he feels he 'knows' her at her birth, he comes to know her much more deeply as the year described in the memoir passes.

More problematic are the changes that he knows will be expected of him as a father, and the implications for his own sense of himself as a man when (as the title of one essay puts it) 'two becomes three.' Like Lewis, Cooper ponders the currently 'awkward and undefined condition of fatherhood' (p. 12), in which fathers are portrayed either as 'bare-chested and holding a naked baby, throwing a ball on a sunny field with the child as they get older,' or as 'potbellied and holding a beer, yelling at the child during a Little League game with beatings and abandonment and years of therapy to follow.' There is, he says, little space between 'too soft' and 'too hard,' between the 'detergent ad' and the 'deadbeat.' The image of fatherhood has not kept up with the current reality of fathers 'increasingly involved' with raising children; those fathers have few if any models to guide them (p. 13).

But, Cooper concedes, this is at least partly because 'we as men want to hold on to our own images.' He notes:

> It's hard to lay a claim to fatherhood when we're so worried about what we think we're giving up. We don't want to lose our idea of ourselves as lone actors. Carefree, caring for nothing. Driving to the mountains, having sex in the afternoon, playing sports whenever we want. How does a baby fit into that? Each new father wonders: will my child still let me be me? (p. 13)

This is one of the central questions Cooper addresses as 'two becomes three.' His domestic circumstances when Zoë arrives are actually not unlike those of the Canadian fathers described in Chapter 3, who took parental leave while the mothers of their children were also home. Cooper works from home, so does not experience his time off work in quite the same way. But his descriptions of his role in the early days of caregiving are similar. Given the many things he says he can*not* do for the baby (soothe her, nurse her, or put her to sleep well) he turns instead to supportive roles he describes as 'sous-chef' (cooking, cleaning, bringing glasses of water) and 'busboy' (bringing the baby to her mother, and putting her back to bed). Gradually, he too takes on more of the practical care, as they wean the baby off constant night time feedings, and Elise, a PhD student completing her dissertation, begins to spend more time in her campus office.

The accommodations he needs to make, when he is caring for the baby by himself, contain another lesson. He is determined not to give up the routines that structure his day and set him up to do his creative work. So Zoë comes with him, for example, on his morning walk to his favourite coffee shop. He carries her first in a sling, then (as she grows) in a more substantial baby carrier. He picks lemons from a tree for her to smell; he talks to her about the people they are passing; sometimes she sleeps, and sometimes she is interactive. Her presence, inevitably, transforms the routine. When she is eventually too big for the carrier, and he takes her in a stroller, he misses having her against his chest and 'being able to see what she saw' (p. 48). New rituals develop. And contrary to all his expectations, they don't detract from his ability to paint – they enhance it. The lesson he is learning is 'acceptance of change,' which is 'at the heart of parenting' (p. 49).

It is a hard lesson. It confronts him again as he describes his worry that Zoë is 'a liability on my ability to pick up and go.' In the face of this worry, he writes, 'I am doubly insistent that we go places' (p. 53). Some early outings – a baseball game, an art exhibition – do not go well. They stay at a friend's beach house, but do not take an anticipated trip to another favourite beach further away because the weather is bad, and Zoë will like neither the wind nor the drive to get there. 'I surrender reluctantly to reason,' he writes (p. 56). But later, holding Zoë on the porch of the beach house, he frames things differently:

She kneads her fingers around mine and furrows her brow. She's so serious. I think I'm falling in love with her, here on this porch. And my love for her is a small wave, one that will expand and flow, a love that I hope will grow to understand that we don't have to be anywhere but where we are. (p. 57)

In the spring of her first year, he starts taking her to playgrounds, and extends his experience of embodied caregiving:

> Playgrounds have become my new habitat. My shoulder bag, which always had a sketchbook, now has a diaper and a hat and a snack. I've learned to find the swing in the shade, to test metal slides and see if they're hot. I've learned how to put sun block on Zoë's nose with one hand while putting her sun hat on with the other. I've learned, without thinking, to lift Zoë's rear to my nose to check her diaper. And I do all this with something approaching naturalness. (p. 117)

As Zoë approaches her first birthday, and the memoir nears its end, the family moves to Chicago, where Elise has a university internship. Elise flies there with Zoë; Cooper drives across country with a friend. He misses them both, but he misses Zoë in the visceral way that Steve, introduced in Chapter 2, has described. He writes: 'I miss her in my arms, pointing out something she might like. The space within my arms feels emptier than ever ...' (p. 136). Much later, he describes being asleep one night in Chicago during a tremendous thunderstorm. When the first lightning struck, he writes, 'I felt my legs getting out of my bed before my mind: *must check on girl*' (p. 156).

In Chicago, he becomes Zoë's full-time caregiver. He has learned the skills of physical caregiving, and has established a very close bond with Zoë in the process. But learning what it means to be a father – not just Zoë's father – is another difficult lesson, to be learned in the public world, not in private. Many of his early encounters are positive. The students he meets as he walks the baby across the Berkeley campus are gratifyingly enthused by what they perceive to be 'the cutest baby in the world.' But the women students also look favourably on him. 'I think I'm a glimpse into their imagined future,' he says. 'I'm the representation of what they want, not now, but sometime later. *The good guy*. The man who loves his wife and carries the baby' (p. 62).

In Chicago, he visits more parks and playgrounds – and here the encounters are more challenging. One playground in particular is populated by *mothers*, and, like the caregiver fathers described by Doucet (2006b), he is trespassing into an estrogen-filled world. 'I just wasn't part of the culture,' he writes. He was unshaven, dressed in shorts, and 'here in the middle of the day, which meant I didn't have a real job.' There was 'an ovary-level nonacceptance' (pp. 149–150). He confides to Elise that 'being a parent would be better if it weren't for mothers' (p. 151). He decides he and Zoë will manage on their own, and for a while avoids the mothers' playground – then after a time realizes that Zoë *likes* the playground and the other children, and so he returns. There is an echo of Lewis's description of 'us mothers,' when he writes: 'The mothers gave me big welcoming smiles and we talked about our favorite kitchen appliance, our hardworking husbands, our impending move to the suburbs. I'd almost missed them' (p. 153). But Cooper's version of 'us mothers' is different from Lewis's. Lewis's usage is a joke – one he can make because he has elsewhere taken care to establish that he is *not* a mother. Lewis is playacting for a morning; Cooper, as Zoë's full-time caregiver, is in the mothers' territory for the foreseeable future.

It's not the only territory he visits; he and a friend, also a father, occasionally take their daughters to daytime baseball games. He feels a 'wishful camaraderie' with the fans around them 'whose concerns don't revolve around diapers and daycare.' But he has experienced the same wishful camaraderie with the mothers in the park – watching them, 'I wished I were a mother' (p. 154).

The memoir closes with his realization that he no longer struggles with 'being the parent to this child in my lap'; any worries about being *her* father 'have dissipated to the point where I don't even remember what they were.' It is, he says, 'as if Zoë has always been with me.' The challenge he takes forward is how he can 'fit in as a father' – how to protect and support her out in the world (p. 154), but also how to fit in a world where models of fathers parenting as he does are still hard to find.

These two memoirs illuminate the connections I am seeking to establish between the hands-on, embodied caregiving that men can and do provide, their feelings for their children, and their sense of themselves as fathers. As professional writers, Lewis and Cooper are indeed 'especially articulate' in making these connections. They are perhaps helped to do so because the context of their caregiving is normative, not to say ideal; though their domestic circumstances are different (a difference I take up later in the chapter) they are both well-educated middle-class men in heterosexual relationships, caring for children who appear to be developing normally. From this 'ideal' context, I move to examine memoirs by fathers dealing with more challenging circumstances.

## Fathering children with special needs

As earlier chapters in this book have established (and as the memoirs just described have illustrated), fathers learn the techniques of hands-on caregiving which, in the learning, become routinized. Like any 'body techniques,' the techniques of embodied caregiving become part of a repertoire that fathers acquire, and that can be performed without conscious thought. I argue that they are also the foundation of the bond that develops with the children on whom – or with whom – the repertoire is practised.

All the fathers introduced in this book so far have been caring for children whose development could be classified as 'normal.' So there has been a certain standardization also in the repertoire of techniques they have acquired, as their children grow from helpless infants to mobile toddlers to sociable, verbal pre-schoolers. The repertoire is not so standardized when it comes to caring for a child with special needs. Perhaps *because* it is not standardized, it is easier to see. Of all the memoirs I considered for this chapter, in none are the techniques of embodied caregiving made more poignantly visible than in Ian Brown's memoir *The Boy in the Moon* (2009). If Lewis and Cooper represent the normative, Brown's experience can perhaps be read as the extreme case.

Brown is a Canadian journalist, author, and television anchor living in Toronto. He is a feature writer for Canada's largest national newspaper *The Globe and Mail*, where parts of the memoir story first appeared. His son Walker was born with an 'impossibly rare' genetic mutation, cardiofaciocutaneous (CFC) syndrome (p. 1). His condition is the source of multiple physical limitations; he is mobile, but cannot speak, or feed himself (or indeed eat solid food by mouth, or swallow easily – he is fed at night through a tube attached to his stomach). His arms are encased in firm tubes to prevent him constantly damaging himself by hitting his head, or scratching his skin. Developmentally, he's 'somewhere between one and three years old' (p. 9) For the first nine years of his life, he lived at home with his parents and older sister. At the time the memoir was published, he had been living for four years in a group home, with three-day visits home every 10 days. He requires 24-hour care, which is shared when he is at home by Brown, his wife, and the family's long-term and beloved nanny, Olga.

The memoir opens with a description of a night – a night, Brown tells us, like every night during Walker's first eight years of life, a night which requires 'the same routine of tiny details, connected in precise order, each mundane, each crucial' (p. 1). The routine is triggered by the sound of Walker awake, and hitting himself in the head. He must be put back to sleep so that he doesn't hurt himself. That means taking him downstairs to make him a bottle. But that in turn requires disconnecting the feeding system – a bag on an IV stand connected by a line to a valve in Walker's belly. It's a complicated process, and Brown names all the tiny steps that must be taken, including, crucially, turning off the pump, before he can lift Walker (all 45 pounds of him at the time of this description) out of his bed.

This night, he also needs a diaper change. So, says Brown, 'we detour from the routine of the feeding tube to the routine of the diaper' – a routine he can also describe in detail. It too is complicated, because Walker, now much bigger than baby size, must be immobilized so he doesn't hurt himself or spread the excrement in the diaper:

> I hold his left hand with my left hand, and tuck his right hand out of commission under my left armpit. I've done it so many times it's like walking. I keep his heels out of the disaster zone by using my right elbow to stop his knees from bending, and do all the actual nasty business with my right hand. (p. 4)

When the diaper is changed, they head downstairs to the kitchen, where the 'bottle ritual' (p. 5) is performed. It involves the (one-handed) mixing of a precise combination of formula and oatmeal ('he aspirates thin fluids; it took us months to find these exact manageable proportions that produced the exact manageable consistency') into a particular kind of bottle ('big enough for his not-so-fine motor skills yet light enough for him to hold'), the search in the dish drainer for the right nipple ('one whose hole I have enlarged into an X, to let the thickened liquid out'), the warming of the bottle, and the trek back upstairs to his bed. The description continues:

> Lay him down on the bed. Oh, fuck me dead, forgot the pump! Build a wall of pillows around him so he doesn't escape or fall off the bed while I nip back into the other room. Remember 4 cc's (or is it 6?) of chloral hydrate, prescribed for sleep and to calm his self-mutilation ... Reprogram the pump, restart the familiar mild repetitive whine, his night pulse. (p. 6)

Then, finally, he lies down with Walker, and describes, again in detail, the bodily practices required to restrain and calm his son, until finally – on a good night – he falls asleep. It doesn't always happen. For a variety of reasons, '[i]t's not unusual to have to perform the entire routine again an hour later' (pp. 6–7).

This is a powerful introduction to a particular kind of fathering, in which intense, ongoing, exhausting physical care is required by a child who cannot respond in any conventional way. Walker is 'the boy in the moon' of the memoir's title, because, for Brown, watching him is like looking at the moon: 'you see the face of the man in the moon, yet you know there's actually no man there.' So Brown is left with the question that guides the memoir: '[I]f Walker is so insubstantial, why does he feel so important? What is he trying to show me?' (p. 3). That question is captured in the memoir's sub-title, *A Father's Search for his Disabled Son*.

The memoir is constructed in 14 essay-like chapters, some of which continue the detailed accounts of caregiving begun in the introduction, some of which range more broadly, as Brown travels to meet the families of other children with CFC syndrome, interviews geneticists and doctors in an attempt to understand the underlying causes of Walker's condition, and later in the memoir, visits L'Arche communities[2] as he tries to envisage a home for Walker as an adult. Throughout the memoir, Brown is seeking to understand who Walker is, and what his place in the world can be.

From the foregoing the extent of his physical engagement – my chief question of all the memoirs – is clear. But its effect on him, as a person and a father, is much more complicated. Any discussion needs to begin with his knowledge of the effects of this relentless physical care on his own body. The fathers introduced in Chapter 2 experienced what I there called 'wear and tear,' but this wear and tear is much more acute in Brown's case. Reflecting on life at home with Walker, from some physical and temporal distance (Walker by this time is in his group home), he writes:

> Christ, I was so tired. I can remember literally lifting my legs with my left hand, one after the other, as if they were logs, hefty stumps, up the stairs [to Walker's room], and pulling on the banister with my right hand for leverage. I can remember thinking: *I can't do much more of this*. I was forty-four years old at the time. (p. 225)

He was 50 before a group home placement was found for Walker, who was then nine. By this time, he writes:

> Carrying Walker upstairs was like hauling a canvas bag of iron pellets, all the weight in the bottom of the sack. Three hours of sleep a night for four nights running was beginning to have an effect: visual migraines became a new feature of my life. How long could we keep it up? Despair seemed to come in cycles, especially when Walker's health was compromised. (p. 82)

So did this care – 'grunt work' of the most extreme and difficult kind – produce in Brown the sort of feelings for Walker that Lewis and Cooper and other fathers have described? Brown is clear that Walker can also give pleasure. He smiles, he laughs, there are glimmers of connection. 'The strange thing was that all this darkness could be relieved by a few pinpoints of light,' Brown writes. 'A reaction alone was notable; a smile or one of his glee sprees charmed my afternoon' (p. 46). When he was very young, giving Walker a bath – something he clearly enjoyed – could lift his father's mood (p. 11). They have a 'private language of tongue clicks' that only the two of them share (p. 34). They also have touch – 'our truest hunger.' He writes about another hospital visit: 'Through it all, you hold your child's body, hold its flesh and heat close to you, like a skin of fire, because you need to hang on to what life there is' (p. 65).

Yet – until an impossible situation is relieved by Walker's group home placement – their relationship is also painfully paradoxical. For one thing, so much of Walker's contribution to it can only be imagined, because of his limited intellectual capacity and lack of speech. No-one can really know what, or even if, he is thinking. Reflecting again from that place of physical and temporal distance about the time before Walker left home, he writes: 'Life with him and life without him: both were unthinkable' (p. 68). Later he writes: 'Walker had given my life shape, possibly even meaning. But Walker had made our lives hell' (p. 135). The hell, along with the pinpoints of pleasure, were shared between Brown and his wife Johanna. The caregiving work they both did during Walker's time at home appears from the memoir account to be scrupulously shared. So it was not allocated along gendered lines. It was the same for both parents; they were in effect shift-workers who were 'functionally interchangeable' (Ranson, 2010).

One of my guiding questions was how the memoir writer presented himself as a father. But in this context, 'fathering' and 'mothering' are beside the point. Their functional interchangeability set up Brown and Johanna as people who were *parenting*, though throughout the memoir there are glimpses of masculinity in Brown's version. But the glimpses are poignant and rare, because of the nature of the child involved. He writes, for example, of buying clothes for Walker – the 'first big-boy shirt,' 'his first jeans, his first khakis, his first sneakers, his first baseball cap,' along with many other items that were all 'the emblems of a normal boyhood':

My longing, not his. One day, I'm going to take him with my father and brother to buy his first tie. I know it's futile: the bib he wears to catch his drool will cover it. But that might be the only male ritual we pass down to him. (p. 42)

He writes of his own strength, both literal and symbolic, which he brings to bear as Walker's protector. On one occasion, it emerges when he holds Walker very firmly to enable a doctor to get a DNA swab from his mouth, in a grip that 'startled most doctors we saw, as much as they appreciated it.' Brown reflects: 'It made me feel useful, and it made me feel closer to my boy; his trusted handler, a strong man who would never hurt him' (p. 170). Elsewhere, he writes of 'leaping' to relieve dinner guests of the responsibility for entertaining Walker, because he didn't want anyone to reject him. He would wrap Walker in his 'constant presence' to 'protect him against everything':

He felt like my boy that way ... We were in it together, he and I, it didn't matter about the others. You could hammer away at me, but you'd never get through to him. Like taking a beating: bury yourself, hunker down, survive until the blows stop raining. It was the least I could do as his father, and at least I did that. (pp. 71–72)

Johanna, he writes, is more willing to let others help. But he points to few other differences between them, either philosophical or in terms of their actual practices of caring. In fact, though she is clearly – and necessarily – present as Walker's co-caregiver, and though there is an older child in the family, the memoir is very much about the relationship between Walker and his father – one that, as Marsiglio and Roy (2012), cited in Chapter 1, have discussed, is not mediated by the mother, but unique to the two of them, born of the intensity of Walker's needs, and Brown's endlessly embodied care. It is revealed – to him and to us – as the outcome of his 'search for his disabled son.' The relationship has changed him: he writes of learning 'an almost geological patience' (p. 63), of Walker having 'deepened and broadened' him, made him 'more tolerant and durable, more ethically dependable,' of giving him 'a longer view' (p. 167). At the end of the memoir, he writes of holding Walker as he recovers from a seizure – and recognizing the depth of their connection:

There was no space between my son and me, no gap or air, no expectation or disappointment, no failure or success – only what he was ... my silent sometimes laughing companion, and my son. I knew I loved him, and I knew he knew it. (p. 288)

Brown's memoir, as I noted earlier, represents the extreme case: embodied caregiving made visible by its intensity, in response to the special and ongoing needs of the child who was its focus. Over the years, Walker's needs did not diminish or change; what changed was the way the care was delivered. The American writer George Estreich offers another version of caring for a 'special needs' child in his memoir *The Shape of the Eye* (2013). In this case, the child in question – Estreich's second daughter, Laura – has Down syndrome. Laura, too, required a special kind of caregiving, particularly in the first year of her life. But Laura is not like Walker Brown; the message of the memoir is the extent to which caring for Laura, *in time*, was *not* significantly different from the caring done by Cooper or Lewis, or that Estreich provided for his older child.

Estreich's memoir is a series of 18 essay-like chapters, with an afterword to the second edition. It begins with Laura's birth, and the surreal two-week period before her Down syndrome diagnosis is confirmed. From that beginning, he sets out to explain his own discovery of Laura, not as a *child first* (as some of his early reading had encouraged him to see her – leaving the implications of Down syndrome as an unspoken but looming *second*) but simply as a *child*, unlike *any* other child, normal or disabled. The memoir, he tells us, was many years in the writing. It was first published when Laura was ten. Like Brown, he sets accounts of caregiving in a broader context. The details of attending to her needs are interspersed with discussion of historic and contemporary understandings – both social and scientific – of Down syndrome. There is also family and personal history, some of it troubled.

Like Lewis, Cooper and Brown writing of their own children, Estreich is well qualified to tell Laura's story. He too is a writer – though until Laura's birth he wrote poetry rather than prose. His world, until her birth, actually resembled Cooper's in other ways as well. He too was married to a university professor, (Theresa), and worked from home, writing around caring for the couple's first child, Ellie, first in North Carolina, and then in Oregon. Laura's arrival, and then her subsequent diagnosis, precipitated an unexpected change of course.

Her first year was especially critical. Like many children with Down syndrome, she was born with a heart defect requiring surgery. At nine weeks, she was hospitalized with a respiratory virus – an added stress on a heart already compromised. She was also not gaining weight. In clinical terms, she was 'failing to thrive' – a problem in itself, of course, but one made even more urgent by the need to have her healthy enough for heart surgery. The solution, urged by medical specialists caring for her at the time, was to supplement breast feeding with a feeding tube through her nose – a strategy with serious implications, as Estreich discovered. Infants who are fed in this way for any length of time lose the ability to associate feelings of hunger with the need to eat – to take in food by mouth. This happened to Laura; one day, shortly after the tube-feeding began, she stopped nursing, and refused for many months thereafter to take any nutrition by mouth.

The nose tube was an introduction to the level and kind of caregiving that lay ahead for Estreich. Feeding Laura in this way required its own repertoire of techniques; Estreich's descriptions of inserting the tube (from nostril through esophagus to stomach), and subsequently of injecting just the right amount of breast milk through it, illuminate the skill required. The nose tube, along with the portable oxygen tank that was another constant companion, also meant that in public, Laura was a 'marked child,' gathering stares like 'iron filings round a magnet': (p. 58):

> I'd feed her in the Starbucks, which entailed mating the nose tube to a veterinary-size syringe, filling the syringe with breast milk, and jamming the plunger [on] top to start the drip. I'd eye the sinking meniscus, watching Laura for signs of gagging; if she got too full, she would throw up. Then I'd refill the syringe. It was performance art ... I felt like putting up a sign: THIS IS EATING. (p. 58)

On good days, he 'almost didn't mind' the scrutiny. 'I was a sensitive, competent stay-at-home dad enjoying a morning out with my special-needs child. I would pack up and leave when I was done like any other customer,' he writes (p. 58). But the extra glances, the public recognition of Laura's difference began to show him 'what Laura meant in the world.'

Laura had the surgery to repair her heart defect when she was almost four months old. Weeks of hospitalization followed, during which her father (and her mother) were constant, vigilant presences, learning the 'clipped med speak of the ICU' (p. 93). Estreich reports playing his guitar and singing to Laura in her hospital bed, partly because Laura's blood pressure was high and he thought it might calm her, but mainly to give himself something to do to make the waiting easier. At the time, he remembers feeling that 'all this would be much worse if it were Ellie in the bed' (p. 88).

Through all the weeks from her birth to this point, Estreich notes, he had been looking after Laura, but he 'did not yet love her.' Perhaps, he speculates, 'those early weeks were only a down payment on a love we might come to feel,' or perhaps 'I did not allow myself to love her, in order to save myself the pain' (p. 100). But by the time he had this insight, after she was home from hospital, he knew it was no longer true. He describes the deeply embodied memory of this realization – a moment in his workshop, holding Laura, searching for something he now can't remember:

> She was braced in the crook of my left arm; I leaned away from her, to keep us both balanced. She twisted this way and that, inspecting the piles of off cuts from the finished projects, the flickering shop lights ... and as I stood by the pull-down ladder, the late morning sunlight turning the dust over in its hands, I saw Laura, and realized what she was to me. I gathered her against me and told her so, in the best words I could find at the time. Then I carried her back into the house. (pp. 100–101)

Laura came home with a repaired heart, and a feeding problem that had only been exacerbated by her time in hospital. While still dependent on the nose tube for feeding, she now not only refused to eat, but actively resisted any approach to her mouth, whether by nipple, food or finger. She was facing the prospect of a permanent, surgically placed gastronomy tube with a port directly to her stomach.

Over several months, involving considerable trial and error and, finally, advice from a new feeding clinic, Estreich learned to get her to eat. Once again the descriptions are detailed – the stimulation of her mouth with a little tool called an Infadent, the spoon-feeding of tiny tastes of a wide variety of foods (including processed cheese spreads, guacamole prepared with mayonnaise, bean dip) chosen for their strong taste and high calorie content, the frequent management of her gagging. Eventually, Estreich tells us, it was ranch salad dressing that had her opening her mouth to ask for more. The combination of that dressing, in powdered form, with formula thickened to the consistency Laura would tolerate, constituted a mixture that was nutritionally adequate. From here, there was no looking back.

The strategies he learned to get her to eat are some of many new techniques he also describes, all aimed at helping Laura to develop to her full potential. Unlike the progress of their first child, Ellie, who developed (like most 'normal' children) according to a more or less standard schedule, and whose development unfolded rather than required active encouragement, Laura's development had to be much more carefully programmed. As her main caregiver, Estreich was positioned to deliver most of the program. The memoir is rich with descriptions of how he did so.

For example, Laura needed to be encouraged to crawl, as the precursor to walking. He describes pushing two couches together to make a Laura-sized alleyway, and getting her to crawl towards him by putting her at one end and a sheet of crumpled typing paper at the other. He writes: 'Typing paper was to walking what ranch dressing was to eating: a "motivator," as the therapists call it' (p. 127). She needed to be encouraged to communicate, and when her speech development seemed to be stalled, signing seemed the best option. After many months of parental signing, there was no response from Laura; Estreich writes that he and Theresa reached the point of signing automatically, without any *expectation* of a response, even to the much-used sign for 'more.' Then, one day, it came. Laura in her high chair wanted more rice, and there was the sign. By her second birthday, she had 40 more.

Laura's development – slow, but undeniably taking place – is tracked through the memoir with many descriptions, which also reveal Estreich's engaged and embodied role. Working at toilet training, he keeps her seated on her potty by hiding in the adjacent bedroom and entertaining her by lobbing stuffed animals past the open bathroom door. He notices she has discovered, on her own, how to hold a pencil, so he works with her to draw a circle, a jagged line. His work, in many ways, has morphed into the work any father in his situation might do in the process of caring for a child. Much of it is routine caregiving; much of it is the kind of emotion work practised by the fathers introduced in Chapter 2. Another kind of emotion work, however, is more specific to a child like Laura. He must advocate for her in a wide variety of situations.

One such situation is described in detail: the playground of the Oregon State University Child Development Center, where Laura, the only child in the class with Down syndrome, is 'learning how to be with other children, and they are learning how to be with her' (p. 246). When he goes to pick up Laura, he unfolds an extended clown routine with the children who sit on the swing with Laura: 'I pretend to get knocked down by the swing, then do somersaults and come up covered with bark chips. I pretend to take naps, until the kids wake me up with their screaming.' All of this, he describes as a 'calculated game of inclusion':

> Since it is about momentum and silliness and screaming, and not, say, numeracy, Laura's deficits become temporarily irrelevant. Besides, I'm

happy to embarrass myself for her sake. If the kids associate Laura with Fun, Laughter, and Incompetent Clown Dad, that's fine by me. It beats the hell out of Weird-Looking Kid Who Can't Talk. (p. 248)

The 'clown dad' appears in several other places in the memoir, and is one of the few ways that Estreich appears in explicitly gendered terms as a 'dad.' Consistently through the memoir, he writes as 'we,' not 'I,' acknowledging Theresa's share in the parenting, even though he does the day-to-day work. He notes differences between them – Theresa is no clown, she is 'steady but not distant,' while he is volatile, a clown who can also be stern and remote. But he claims to find the question of gender differences in nurturing 'uninteresting,' and is unwilling to take gender stereotypes too far. Reflecting on the 'reversed traditionalism' begun with his (more conventional) care of Ellie, he says: 'I was not Papa Bear. I did fine, and mostly enjoyed it' (p. 135). The 'tug of the Inner Guy, the resistant whine of the masculine' did not last. It was replaced by 'an out-of-the-wayness,' a life that was 'difficult to explain' (p. 135), and – like Down syndrome with its many labels – difficult to name. 'Stay-at-home dad' came closest, though '"staying" hardly begins to describe the work of raising children' (p. 136). Yet, in contrast to many of the fathers I have introduced so far in this book, he writes dismissively of caregiver fathers who 'whine about playground snubs and a sense of isolation.' In his words there is also an uncanny echo of Brandth and Kvande's suggestion, cited earlier, that 'care and intimacy with children' may represent new territories to be conquered for men already successful in the public arena (1998: 309). Estreich writes:

> The fact that men now can and do get to watch kids, in addition to running the world and getting paid more than women for equivalent jobs, is an *expansion* of the male domain: this is one more thing we get to do, and those of us who do get to stay home are lucky to do it. (p. 136)

Caring for Laura, certainly at the beginning, would have tested his claim to be lucky. It was hard work, physically and emotionally. The occasional references to lack of sleep, or the 'irritable exhaustion' that comes to primary caregivers in the late afternoon (p. 132) gloss more significant effects, which he mentions only in the afterword (written two years after the memoir was first published). At Theresa's prompting, he acknowledges that he was a poet who gave up poetry and had spent nine years writing prose; and that the depression which, in one passing reference in the memoir he notes 'has accompanied me for as long as I can remember' (p. 118), became acute enough, towards the end of those nine years, that he finally sought help.

The memoir is a testament to his love for Laura, the resolution of his need to explain the way his vision of her had changed. The happiness she had brought the family was 'real, without dilution or asterisk' (p. 238).

## Fathering without mothers

I noted earlier the 'normative' experience of caregiving described by Lewis and Cooper – fathers in heterosexual partnerships, caring for developmentally normal children – as a kind of benchmark. As Brown and Estreich have demonstrated, fathers' experience of caregiving is different when the children are not developmentally normal. But they, too, are sharing caregiving with their children's mothers. Other memoir writers illuminate the different and often challenging experiences of caregiving for fathers for whom, in different ways, the 'heterosexual partnership' descriptor does not fit, and there are no mothers in the picture.

Matthew Logelin and Ian Newbold, in memoirs published respectively in 2011 and 2013, describe their experiences as young fathers suddenly widowed. Logelin's wife Liz died (of a pulmonary embolism) the day after their first child was born. Newbold's wife Samantha died (of complications from a pre-existing heart condition) when their first child was seven months old. Both fathers became full-time caregivers for an extended period, at a time in their children's lives when even the most involved fathers are seldom the primary parents, let alone sole parents.

There is no discernible guiding question in either memoir. Rather, the motivation seems to be to tell a story of tragedy and survival, and to provide a glimpse of a particular kind of fathering that is both rare and intimate. Unlike the memoir writers introduced so far – established writers for whom fathering became a new topic to explore – both Logelin and Newbold appear to have turned to writing as a means to deal with the particular experience of fathering after losing their partners. Both wrote their memoirs having first established blogs that attracted an apparently wide readership, and gave their authors a much appreciated parenting community. For both, writing is now an alternative career route.

Like Cooper's, Logelin's memoir, *Two Kisses for Maddy: A Memoir of Love and Loss*, describes the first year of his daughter Madeline's life, and was published when she was three. Newbold seems to be covering a similar period, but from a greater distance – the memoir (*Parenting With Balls*) was published when his son Max was eight. They're also written in different countries; Logelin at the time was living in Los Angeles, Newbold in a town (undisclosed in the memoir) in the English Midlands.

There are further differences: Logelin took his newborn from hospital to the home he had lived in with his wife. 'I knew that I was going to have to live alone with Madeline, so I figured the best thing to do was to jump right in,' he writes (p. 118). There were no close family members living nearby. Newbold, in contrast, decided he could not return to his own home, and moved in with his parents – though their very large house actually gave him extensive separate living space. He acknowledges the benefits: 'I could pop out for things if I needed to. I was well fed and watered, leaving me able to concentrate on looking after Max' (p. 50). His wife's parents lived in the same town; with an abundance of family members seeking to help with Max, his challenge was (to quote the title of one of his chapters) 'fighting them off.'

There were differences also in the kind of care they initially needed to provide. Newbold was taking over the care of a healthy seven-month-old with whose needs he was already familiar. Logelin was caring, on his own and with no background experience, for a premature newborn. He gives a vivid description of 'body techniques' that were called on during their very first night at home, when he woke to hear Madeline 'choking and gasping for air,' with vomit coming from her nose and mouth. He writes of trying, unsuccessfully, the techniques he learned at hospital in the baby CPR class. There follows, in some detail, his account of his search for the nasal aspirator, still in its package, and his fumbling attempts, finally successful, to get her breathing normally again. He writes of then lying down in the middle of the floor, mentally exhausted and crying, holding Madeline to his chest and rubbing her back (p. 121).

The memoirs also share many similarities. Both writers position themselves as having planned to be closely involved with raising their children in any case, before tragedy struck. (Newbold had some time to practise, starting with nearly a month of leave at Max's birth; he writes of crying the night before he had to go back to work, and feeling distracted, and envious of his wife at home, when he did return.) But both also had envisaged their partners as taking the parenting lead. Logelin writes:

I planned to take an extremely active role in raising our daughter, but I sort of felt that as a man, I didn't have the motherly instinct. I knew

I had a lot to learn, but I was confident that Liz [his wife] would lead the way. (pp. 49–50)

Both write of dealing with the grief of loss, tempered by the imperative to care for the child who remained. In both cases, it is the child who offers the way out of an otherwise unbearably painful time. Logelin calls Madeline 'my reason for living' (p. 78). Newbold calls Max 'my obvious purpose' (p. 81). In both cases, the loss of one parent instilled in the surviving one a resolve to compensate by doing the best job possible. In both cases, 'best' is stated in heroically masculine terms. Newbold writes that Samantha's death inspired him to be '[t]he best damn single parent the world had ever seen' (p. 41). Logelin is more defiant. Implicit suggestions that, as a man, he would not be able to cope alone angered him, and left him with 'the rankling feeling that I had something to prove' – not just to those close to him, but to 'the world':

I knew I would forever be judged as being incapable, if not totally incompetent – unless I was great. I had to be better than great. I was going to be the best fucking father there ever was. (p. 111)

What both memoirs add to the discussion of fathering and embodied caregiving provided so far is their focus on fathering *in the absence of* mothering. The question of what mothers might provide that they cannot looms large as both writers, growing more confident as caregivers as time passes, enter the public world of parenting – Newbold through a play group with which his wife and mother had been involved, and Logelin through an online parenting group. Contact with mothers allows them to ask their own versions of the critical question: whether there is such a thing as a 'mothering instinct' or 'maternal intuition' and, if so, whether its absence from their own brand of caregiving is likely to disadvantage their children. Both decide independently that good caregiving is not a matter of instinct. Mothers, writes Logelin, can be as 'clueless' as men are – 'they're just more willing to ask for and accept help' (p. 147). As their children continue to flourish, their confidence continues to grow. But though they may feel more comfortable in the public world, they are also anomalies. Both write of the constant scrutiny they receive as fathers out on their own with babies. 'Where's the mother?' is a question they say they confront more or less graciously, depending on the circumstances. The underlying assumption is frequently that they won't know what they're doing and will need help.

Both write as undisputed full-time primary caregivers.[3] Since there are no partners to pick up the slack, they are actually doing more caregiving than conventional stay-at-home dads would be doing – partly because they must, and partly (as both acknowledge) to compensate their children for the mothers' absence. But the children also provide compensation; both memoirs movingly describe the relationship each father develops with his child. As Newbold writes:

> There is something very special between my son and I ... with Samantha's death, we've spent more time together, and experienced so much more as a duo, than we were ever set to ... It has been the greatest privilege to have this time with my boy, and to be his dad. (p.168)

Memoir writer Dan Bucatinsky shares with Logelin and Newbold the situation of caring for very young children without a mother in the picture. But unlike them, he is not a solo parent. His two children have two fathers – Bucatinsky and his partner Don Roos. The children, biological siblings aged six and four when the memoir was published in 2012, were adopted at birth as part of an open adoption plan. The memoir's title – *Does This Baby Make Me Look Straight? Confessions of a Gay Dad* – gives some indication of its style and content. Living in Los Angeles at the time he produced the memoir, Bucatinsky is a writer, director and actor in film and television, married to a filmmaker. He is part of a cultural environment on which he draws in his memoir, which clearly shapes his writing style, and suggests his intended audience.[4] He does not explicitly state his motivation for writing the memoir. But though he claims to have 'no real interest' in being an activist, he also notes that, as a gay man, his life is 'political by its very nature' (p. 159). The memoir is both a description of fathering and a quiet political statement.[5]

The memoir's 27 short chapters are written as stories, in which often breezy descriptions of daily life, consciously written to entertain, are interwoven with Bucatinsky's reflections on parenting, his memories of his own family (particularly his father), and (in a more sober vein) his memories of his own often painful childhood, growing up gay. The chapters are frequently set up as moral tales, with a lesson to be learned – usually by Bucatinsky himself. The hands-on, embodied care he is undertaking is seldom described in detail, though his passing references to a wide range of experiences – cleaning up diaper messes, dealing with head lice, comforting children woken by nightmares, buying them clothes that fit, cooking for (and with) them – are clear indicators of his involvement in caregiving.

Bucatinsky adds another dimension to the discussion of gender and caregiving introduced by Logelin and Newbold. Like Logelin and Newbold, he encounters the scrutiny of people who think a man out in public with babies or young children doesn't know what he's doing – '[l]ike when we would be travelling and *every woman on the plane* would offer us important advice' (p. 10). Like Logelin and Newbold, immersed in the kind of care work traditionally done by women, he wonders about the 'maternal instinct.' But unlike Logelin and Newbold, who question its existence, he asks why it is assumed that only women have it; there is a strong sense that it is something he too would like to claim.

Bucatinsky frames his identity, not just his activities, as maternal. He describes this sense of himself as emerging with the arrival of his first child, Eliza. A friend had told him that adopting a child would allow him to discover 'the father within,' and this was what he was expecting:

> But what I never imagined – what I could *never* have predicted – was finding the *mother* within me. There is no doubt that when Eliza got home, I fully took on the role of mother to my cub. (p. 10)

In two stories, later in the memoir, when the children are older, he takes up the mother issue again. The first describes his children watching a Disney film featuring the adventures of a young captive heroine finally restored to her parents – a mother and a father. It prompts Eliza to comment: 'I wish I had a mom and dad.' It was, says Bucatinsky, a comment that went 'straight to the heart' (p. 213). He acknowledges that his children will 'undoubtedly wish they had a mother from time to time,' that they will 'crave that special feeling of being embraced by a mommy':

> But what is that mommyness, exactly? Can a man bring mommyness to a child's life? I feel that I do. But is it still mommyness if it comes from a man? (p. 213)

This is a question asked by Logelin and Newbold too, but Bucatinsky seems to be more challenged by it, perhaps because the absence of a mother in his children's lives is a matter of choice, not accident. It is a choice he worries about. In his heart, he writes, 'I fear that our situation is just a tiny bit not *as* good as if the kids had a "conventional" family' (p. 212). The story's resolution, its moral, is his conclusion that most children at some time or another wish for parents other than the ones they have, that not every family has to be the same – just as, in his joking terms, there's no need for everyone to have an iPad if there is another device that does the same things but only 'looks different, maybe smells a little different, has a penis, and prefers to sleep with men' (p. 214). If his children had had a mother 'they would've been robbed of the experience of having two dads who love them more than life itself' (p. 214).

The second story begins when he briefly loses sight of Jonah, the younger child, at a busy farmers' market. He sees similarities to his mother and grandmother in his immediate, panic reaction – what he calls their 'gasp reflex' – but there is more to be taken from the incident:

> I discovered something all parents must feel deep within themselves: a boundless desire and responsibility to nurture and protect. I imagine it's what people call the 'maternal instinct.' I'm sure countless other men have shared the feeling, which makes me want to lobby to change the name to 'parental instinct.' What's so female about this feeling anyway? If a sense of *mommyness* is connected to having breasts filled with milk and kids latched on to them for mealtimes, then yes, I'm out. But there's more to it. (p. 219)

Bucatinsky locates the bigger picture of 'mommyness' in the context of a same-sex marriage in which both partners are 'freed from the shackles of traditional gender roles and allowed to explore the gamut of emotions and impulses.' Here the challenge is 'finding the balance between the parts of us that are distinctly *dad* and those qualities that are, in a sense, maternal' (p. 219). In his own relationship Bucatinsky notes that the nurturing and disciplinarian roles may alternate between the pair. 'Whether you call it "maternal" or "paternal" care, the kids are getting both,' he writes. Sometimes, who does what needs to be negotiated, and sometimes, there are feelings of competition. (In another chapter, he suggests that, in a relationship between two men, 'the balance of parenting power can be trickier when both are strong, smart, opinionated people who like to feel in control and *right* most of the time' [p. 99]).

But all that said, he concedes that 'Don's got a natural "daddyness" gene.' Of himself, he writes: 'I do tend to gravitate to a kind of mommyness that Don doesn't spark to':

> I like getting the kids dressed, cutting their fingernails, laying out paper and paint, and making puppets out of old socks. But most of all, I love cooking with them. (p. 221)

Cooking is part of the 'uncomplicated and satisfying' pleasure of feeding them – and something that makes him feel like a mother. The chapter concludes with another story, of Bucatinsky making breakfast pancakes with the children, and their discovery, after breakfast, of a bird's nest outside containing two chicks. The children watch as another bird comes to the nest to feed them. They are certain this is the mother, because, in Jonah's words, 'The mama feeds the babies.' Bucatinsky connects the mother bird's feeding to his own; the chapter's concluding lines refer to 'us mama birds' (p. 223).

## Fathering as primary caregiving

Bucatinsky's easy identification with the 'mother role' (albeit in the context of a same-sex parenting partnership) implicitly frames the work of caregiving as 'mothers' work.' His argument, like that made by scholars such as Ruddick (1982) and Risman (1986), introduced in Chapter 1, is that *men can mother*. Other fathers, particularly in contexts where they have taken over from mothers the bulk of the caregiving work, are generally less willing to see their caregiving in this light. They would agree with critics who challenge the tendency to view fathering only through a 'maternal lens' (Doucet, 2006a: 223). As fathers, living with mothers, they are reluctant to call what they do 'mothering' – even though their caregiving practices may look the same. In terms of identity, they are fathers, not mothers.

The tension between these two positions appears in a number of memoirs that focus explicitly on the experiences of fathers who are at-home primary caregivers in families where mothers are primary earners. What also distinguishes these memoirs from those by writers like Cooper, Estreich or Newbold (all of whom were home-based caregivers) is that the *social status* of the stay-at-home father is often a major focus. The memoir by Australian writer and former journalist Ben Robertson, *Hear Me Roar: The Story of a Stay-At-Home Dad* (2012) is a good example.

Robertson's work, the last of the memoirs I consider in this chapter, is useful because of the threads it pulls together. Like Lewis, Cooper, Estreich and Brown, he offers detailed descriptions of his caregiving, making the extent of its embodiment very clear, and connecting it to his relationship to his children. But as for Logelin, Newbold and Bucatinsky, questions of gender (as both identity and practice) are much more prominent. For Robertson, the gender challenge lies not so much in what he *is* doing – caring for his children – as in what he is (therefore) *not* doing – working outside the home at a 'real job.' Like many of the fathers described in the previous chapter, he finds home-based caregiving of very young children (in his case near the Australian city of Brisbane) a spatial, temporal and social challenge. He is alone at home with his children for much of the time, with tasks and routines determined by the children and not by him. He too experiences 'slow time' (Brandth and Kvande, 2003). For him, as for those other fathers, the tasks and routines are both rewarding and, often, quite boring. Unlike most of those other fathers, however, he is in it for the long haul. The lived experience, and the prospect of its extended duration, take a heavy toll.

The memoir begins, however, on an optimistic note, with the birth of Robertson's first child, Fergus. The decision to have him stay at home to care for the baby is (as it was for all the full-time caregiver fathers introduced in earlier chapters) a pragmatic one. Robertson's wife Darlene is a highly placed project director, who earns much more than he does. If one parent is to be the breadwinner, she is the obvious choice. And he is ready to take a break from the unpredictable hours, and the human pain and tragedy he frequently encountered in news reporting. He writes that the challenge of being a full-time caregiver appealed to him:

Role reversal was still uncommon and I would be a rare species, although from what I'd read more and more fathers were taking up the challenge. Sure, I'd have to endure some difficult moments. Maybe take a hit to my ego. But other, braver men had already paved the way and taken some of the hits for me. (p. 56)

So, in a society becoming 'less judgemental, more understanding,' he too is ready to take up the challenge. He also has something to prove – to his own estranged, abusive father: 'I had a burning desire to be a super dad, to prove that I could do a better job than *he* ever could' (p. 56).

He is enthralled with the new baby. 'I never tired of holding him, of stretching out his long arms and legs, of putting my hand on his chest and feeling his heart beat,' he writes. 'I liked taking off my shirt and laying him on my chest, cherishing the skin-to-skin contact, and the wonderful baby smell of him' (pp. 31–32).

From this start, perhaps not surprisingly, his caregiving expertise builds quickly:

Soon I can tell the difference between a tired cry and a hungry cry and a cry of pain, and the amazing thing is that his are different to those of other children. My nostrils can make out the slightest waft of a poo in his nappy, which is also different to other people's children. I'm like one of those penguins that can find their chicks among thousands of others. I am also the rash master ... (p. 96)

'Mastery' – in the gendered sense of the term – is what Robertson is semi-humorously describing. He talks of his 'competitive juices flowing' as he seeks to perfect difficult tasks, including changing a nappy 'with breathtaking speed, sometimes using only one hand' (p. 97). Over months of practice, he has even honed his 'motherly instincts'; when Fergus falls down he is now 'conscious of the need to be nurturing, to make the appropriate coos and give him lots of cuddles.' This, in contrast to his own instinct 'as a man' to dust him off and 'tell him to get on with it' (p. 98). He is, he says, a 'poor substitute' for Darlene, but he's going to try: 'My child is going to be dripping with empathy' (p. 99). He speaks of 'instincts,' but he treats them as practices that even men can learn.

In private, he is doing what mothers do, and is doing it expertly, single-mindedly and confidently. And he is reaping the reward, in a 'blossoming' bond with his son – a bond so strong that, inevitably, he comes to be the favoured parent when comfort is needed (p. 124). But below the surface, all is not well. For one thing, he is very, very tired. Like Paul, introduced in Chapter 2, he is in sole charge at home for the length of his wife's very long work days. And, like many of the fathers introduced in Chapter 3, he comes to understand just how hard a job he has taken on. He is not just a caregiver, but also the homemaker of the family, responsible for 'all the cleaning and cooking and shopping,' and all the kin work of organizing birthday cards and presents for nieces and nephews. 'Nobody told me how hard all that was going to be,' he writes. 'The bottom line is that I'm fucking exhausted, consumed by tiredness that makes my head spin and my bones ache' (p. 111). All this contributes to the epiphany he describes a little later in the memoir. He writes of finally understanding 'what women have been going through all these years,' and what 'all chauvinistic men choose not to understand.' He phones his mother to express his appreciation for all she did for the family. 'I feel like telling every mother I meet, old and young, single or married, "I understand. I *really* understand,"' he writes (p. 119).

Fatigue is not the only problem. In spite of the initial optimism, he struggles mightily with the role reversal that positions his wife as the breadwinner and him as the stay-at-home caregiver. The feeling of self-reproach ('What sort of a man are you?') that he describes as he watches his wife leave home for her first day back at work after her maternity leave is a feeling that 'never really went away' (p. 66). He has great difficulty telling anyone who doesn't know him that he is a stay-at-home father. Because of this diffidence, and because he is indeed one of a rare breed,[6] he lacks the social resources more available to stay-at-home mothers. When Fergus is a toddler, he tries the conventional preschool gym and swimming classes, but like other caregiver fathers, finds these are indeed 'estrogen-filled worlds' (Doucet, 2006b). He too experiences what Cooper, cited earlier, describes as an 'ovary-level nonacceptance' – in his own words, 'the women do not want me there.' He feels as though he doesn't exist, that he is 'the invisible man' (p. 121). So he becomes increasingly isolated.

But he struggles on, because in spite of everything, he has something to prove. He describes Fergus's birth as a new beginning, 'a fresh start to my distorted view of fatherhood,' the possibility of 'redemption even.' He is determined to offer Fergus what his own father could not provide –'patience, stability and unconditional love,' to be able to say, 'You see, Dad, I'm better than you ... My child will love me more than I love you' (p. 128). So the reappearance of his father, who is dying of cancer, and his death shortly afterwards, together provoke a crisis that is only exacerbated by the arrival of a second son, Henry, when Fergus is two. Suffering from panic attacks and depression, he seeks medical help. Drugs and counselling – along with the discovery of an indoor play centre for the children, and a gym with childcare where he can exercise – eventually bring him back to health.

The memoir ends with Fergus about to start school, and Darlene pregnant with a third baby – a girl. They are both delighted. Robertson writes about this turn in family life as a man who has come through a dark tunnel into the light. In an echo of Lewis on the 'grunt work' and its effects, he writes, 'There's a bond with my children that has been forged through the daily grind of the routine.' As Fergus enters a new stage in his life, his father is comforted to know that until that moment 'unlike most dads I can truly say that I've been there every step of the way' (p. 233). He adds:

Some people ... say that I am not a man, but I know that's not true. How could it be? Staying home with the kids has made me a better man and I didn't have to go off to work to prove it. I have provided for my family in ways that are impossible to measure. (p. 238)

Robertson's view of himself as a 'better man' as a result of his caregiving experience is significant. Though he is clear that the work he has done is usually construed as 'mothering,' he views it in Connell's (2009) terms as 'configurations of practice' – configurations that he is able to learn. In learning them, he does not become a mother, but a different kind of man.

## Learning from memoirs

Earlier, I noted Plummer's (2001) distinction between the use of memoirs as *resources* studied for the insights they might bring to dimensions of social life, and as *topics* in their own right, separate from the social ground they covered. My primary interest, as I also noted, was to consider them as resources. The memoirs discussed here were strategically chosen for their capacity to address the key themes of my extended research project – the embodied caregiving that fathers are doing, and what they make of this caregiving. I also intended them as a counterpoint, and a supplement, to the material provided by the fathers I introduced in the previous two chapters.

In Chapter 2, I used my visits to one group of Canadian fathers to paint a picture of fathers' embodied caregiving in some detail. I described the body capital those fathers brought to their caregiving, and the 'body techniques' they learned on the job. Though all were in the unconventional position of caring as men for infants and young children, the care they were providing was in fact routine. In making the embodied dimensions of their caregiving visible, I intended to establish a benchmark for what *any* similarly situated full-time caregiving father would be doing. Having established this benchmark, I was able to move, in Chapter 3, to a consideration of what this caregiving *meant* – for a larger group of fathers, also Canadian, most of whom had been involved caregivers of babies and very young children during a parental leave. I used my interviews with them to capture their reflections on this time – the *lived experience* of embodied caregiving. This was, inevitably, a partial picture. The constraints of in-person interviewing, as noted, impose limits on both the amount and kind of information that is shared.

The memoirs discussed in this chapter extend the findings of the interviews in several ways. For one thing, the cases I chose provided (somewhat)[7] more diversity. These were fathers who (in all but one case) lived outside Canada, and whose caregiving encompassed a wider range of circumstances. Their accounts of their practices provided in some cases a much richer sense of what embodied caregiving might comprise than my benchmark description would suggest. As writers, rather than interviewees, they were also able to provide far more detail on what their caregiving meant to them as lived experience. And as cases, revealed in considerable, book-length depth, they offered new insights on the connections between caregiving, fathering and masculinity.

As I noted in Chapter 1, I see the first stage in the study of fathers' embodied caregiving as documenting its extent and variety. In terms of the descriptions of physical practices of caregiving – the body techniques required, for example, to change a new baby's diaper (while entertaining her on the change table), or setting up a feeding tube through a new baby's nose – the accounts I have selected speak for themselves. I use these descriptions as further evidence of the kind of embodied care fathers are capable of doing, and are choosing to do. In several of my selected cases (Brown's in particular, in his care of his son Walker) they are far surpassing my benchmark.

Not all the memoir writers included here make the connection between their caregiving and their feelings for their children as explicit as do Lewis and Robertson. But the connection is implicit in the work of all the others. These are men intent on communicating their love for their children along with their involvement as fathers. Circumstances certainly shaped the broader experience of caregiving, however. There are echoes of the fathers introduced in the previous chapters, several of whom described fatigue, boredom, and the difficult choice between social isolation at home and social alienation in public spaces occupied mainly by mothers. Robertson's memoir, in particular, illuminates these issues. There is, in general, a much better sense in the memoirs of the *dailyness* of life with children. Cooper's descriptions of his outings with Zoë over the course of a year, and Estreich's descriptions of the increments of Laura's development, are good examples. As time passes, children change and grow; the memoir writers take the time and space to record these changes. This adds to the authenticity of the claims they are making, or the picture they are building. We come to know these men, and their children, in a way that is not possible through interviews, because we see much more of their lives.

Above all, as just noted, the memoirs shed more light on the connections between caregiving, fathering and masculinity. I described at the end of Chapter 3 the reconstructions of dominant masculinity that emerged in my interviews with fathers as they spoke of the hands-on caregiving they had provided, their relationships with their children, their support of their wives and the reordering of their priorities as (in many cases) they became 'working fathers.' This speaks to Doucet's comment (2006a: 225) about the need to consider the way fathers like these are 'reinventing fathering.' But as Doucet also discovered (in her work with stay-at-home fathers, described in Chapter 1) the process is not simple; narratives of the men she interviewed were often contradictory and tentative, as they struggled to understand themselves as both caregivers and men. Because of the detail available in the memoirs, these complexities can be made more clear.

Of all the memoir writers, Lewis seems the least conflicted about who he is and what he is doing. He positions himself as an 'involved second string,' capable of performing most – though not all – caregiving, but clearly deferring to his wife as the primary parent. He takes on a share of the hands-on work – and writes movingly of how it affects him – but it is caregiving as practice, not identity, that he is taking on. He continues to be the family's primary breadwinner. To apply a term I have introduced earlier, he would not see himself as *interchangeable* with his wife. But neither does he enjoy the kind of 'intimate fatherhood' described in Chapter 1, which privileges closeness and intimate moments with children and outsources the 'grunt work.' As we now know, he considers the grunt work crucial to establishing connections with his children.

So how should Lewis's version of fathering be understood? The temptation is to revert to the conception of the 'new father' proposed by Brandth and Kvande (1998) and cited earlier. This father has nothing more to win in the public world (a fair description of Lewis professionally) and so turns to 'care and intimacy with children' as the 'new territories to conquer' (p. 309). Yet this image also does not fit. Lewis suggests that he has entered these territories reluctantly, and that, like the fathers I interviewed in Chapter 3, he has done so in order to support his wife, not to usurp her power or extend his own. He was not anticipating that the process would be, in his own terms, transformative. In taking on the kind of caring work foreign to the 'Neanderthal' fathers of generations back, he has become (along with all the other fathers introduced to date) a different kind of father. Inevitably, then, he has become a different kind of man – though this is a slightly harder case to make. He is, as I noted in my discussion of his memoir, a man who seems secure in his masculine identity, and his position as a man in the public world remains strong. He delivers a progressive message about fathering and caregiving – but he delivers it from a position of ongoing masculine privilege.

As a white, well-educated, middle-class, heterosexual married man, Cooper is also writing from a position of masculine privilege. But in his case the privilege is muted by other characteristics – he is a writer and painter, who works from home to produce illustrated children's books.

Even before he becomes a father, his masculinity is a reconstructed version of the dominant form. But it is a form that offers him considerable freedom. For this reason, he is particularly concerned about what he would have to give up with fatherhood. He doesn't want to change, but discovers in the course of Zoë's first year that he *can* change – he becomes a man entirely comfortable with 'being the parent to this child in my lap.' The challenge comes from his experience as a father out in the world.

In an earlier study (Ranson, 2010), which featured men like Cooper, taking on the kinds of caregiving more commonly associated with mothers, I introduced the proposition that 'parenting,' rather than 'fathering,' was a better description of what they were doing. But, as one of those parenting men commented, he was 'parenting like a man' (Ranson, 2010: 179). This understanding establishes, on the one hand, that the activities of caregiving can be undertaken both by mothers and fathers, and on the other hand, that the *style* of their undertaking might be shaped by the gender of the parent involved. For Cooper, the challenge is rather that he is parenting *as* a man – a distinction that brings issues of public presentation to the fore. In other words, for Cooper – as indeed for most of the fathers introduced so far – the (private) execution of caregiving activities is not the problem. In the private world of diaper changing and feeding and soothing and putting to sleep, he has become competent at giving care, even if he does it *like a man*; and his love for his child grows as his repertoire of caregiving skills and his time on the job increase. This may be a source of gender transformation – indeed, I will argue later that it is – but it is probably not a source of gender challenge. It is when he is in public, parenting *as a man*, that the challenges arise – and when he and fathers like him may feel that their masculinity is most clearly on the line.

This contrast is demonstrated most sharply in Robertson's memoir. In Robertson's telling, it also translates into spatial terms. In the private space of home, he is an exemplary caregiver. He is also alert to the differences that might come from parenting *like* a man, and makes adjustments. (He tells us he is disinclined to coo, but he adopts this practice in the interests of his child.) Parenting *as* a man, he encounters the same response that Cooper did in the mother-populated public spaces into which he ventures. In Bourdieu's terms, caregiving fathers like Robertson are in a game played mainly by women, on fields they dominate. If Bourdieu's 'fields' are largely metaphoric, these fathers could testify to their literal manifestations as well.

But for Robertson there is more on the line than the public image he conveys as a caregiver. To draw again on Bourdieu's framing, I suggest that men's embodied caregiving challenges the embodied dispositions of a conventionally gendered habitus. But there are many such dispositions, some of which may be more amenable to change than others, and some of which – notably in Robertson's case – are contradictory. He wants to demonstrate (to his own father) his caregiving competence, and his children's attachment to him. He also wants, in more conventional terms, to be the family's provider. His challenge – which at the end of the memoir he appears to have faced down – is to reconcile the contradictions. In so doing, he becomes a 'better man.'

While his inner challenges seem to have been more extreme than those described by Lewis or Cooper, what all three have in common is that they share caregiving with the mothers of their children. For each of them, parenting like a man may be less of a concern because their children can be assured of also receiving parenting by a woman. For Logelin, Newbold and Bucatinsky, concern about parenting like a man is more critical, because there is no woman in the picture. This accounts, then, for their questions about maternal instinct, and whether a man can, in Bucatinsky's words, 'bring mommyness to a child's life.' What is on the line for these three is their competence as both fathers *and* mothers. Whether they ultimately set aside the distinction (Logelin and Newbold) or accommodate it (Bucatinsky), their collective willingness to envisage their own performance as adequate conveys an important message about gender and caring for children. They affirm, as my earlier research has suggested, that the practices conventionally associated with mothering and fathering can all be taken up by both men and women. My proposition, noted earlier, that this sharing constitutes *parenting*, is worth repeating.

The memoirs by Brown and Estreich are further evidence of men who are parenting, not fathering, but here the question of whether they are parenting like men, or as men, seems to fade in the light of more pressing questions raised by the nature of the children for whom they are caring. Brown's descriptions attest to the (masculine) body capital he brings to his caring work, and his sense of the bonds of gender that link his son to the men in his family. But, as I noted earlier, Brown and his wife are in effect functionally interchangeable in their caregiving. He does just what she does. Like Lewis, he is also a well-educated, successful middle-class professional, with nothing to prove in the public domain. Yet any gender privilege he enjoys hardly compensates for the difficulties of his family life. He has become, thanks to his life with Walker, more patient, 'more tolerant and durable, more ethically dependable' – he too has become a better man.

From Estreich we get a different picture, because he weaves his full-time care of his older child through his descriptions of caring for Laura, the daughter with Down syndrome. He too writes as one who shares parenting, though as I have noted, he does most of it as a full-time at-home caregiver. He seldom positions himself in conventionally gendered terms as a 'dad,' and yet acknowledges his male privilege in feminist terms. He comes across as the 'new man' of Holter's (2007) definition, ideologically committed to gender equality and so already actively reconstructing his masculinity.

The memoir writers are very clearly men as they tell their stories; there are glimpses of quite conventional masculinity in their accounts. Whether men who are hands-on caregivers are putting their masculinity on the line – the question raised by Doucet (2006a) and noted first in Chapter 1 – is one I have touched on more than once in this summary. The memoir writers, like the fathers I interviewed, lead me to Doucet's conclusion – that they are not. They do not become mothers – a transformation that would certainly compromise their masculinity. They become, instead, different kinds of fathers.

# 5
## 'Making the Case for a New Kind of Manhood'

In earlier chapters I used interviews and a selection of fathers' memoirs to address my key research interests: fathers' accounts of hands-on, embodied caregiving, and their experiences of that care. I was also interested in the connection between their experiences, and their understandings of fathering and masculinity. But behind these interests is the bigger question of how changes in fathering on the part of fathers like these link to broader social understandings of fathering and masculinity. A theoretical perspective that sees gender as socially constructed also sees practice as shaped by, and contributing to, shifting popular discourses and dominant understandings of fathers and masculinity. So the *visibility* of fathers' caregiving practices becomes a significant factor when change in understandings of fathering is at issue.

The accounts of the fathers I interviewed were not public, but were constructed for – and with – a researcher whose own agenda directed their production. Until their accounts appeared, appropriately anonymized, in this book, these fathers had an audience of one. (I am of course speaking here only of the accounts they gave *me*. Outside the research context, their practices and how they talked about them were certainly available to a wider audience.) The memoirs discussed in the previous chapter were written by fathers with their own agenda, and with an eye to a much wider (book-buying) audience. Unlike the interview accounts, they were not produced in one sitting, but were thoughtful and much more extended reviews of caregiving experiences that were sometimes years in the past. Like the interview accounts, however, they were contained, in this case in a single document, whose publication for practical purposes ended the story.

Contrast this with the scope of fathers' blogs both to publicize caregiving practices and to shape public discourse about fathering in the process. One example will serve to make this point. Doyin Richards is an American 'daddy blogger' and father of two children, who appears to have started his blog 'Daddy Doin' Work' in 2012 when his first child was 18 months old. His second child was born in July 2013. During a month of parental leave, in October 2013, he posted on his blog's Facebook and Twitter links a picture of himself, with his baby strapped to his chest in a carrier, doing his older daughter's hair. The picture, to use common internet parlance, 'went viral'.[1] Richards is a Black man, so the extensive comment it attracted had a racist component that was sadly not surprising. More significant, however, was the reaction to Richards as a father, engaged in demonstrably hands-on care. The picture's global reach resulted in media interviews on US television networks, and in print media in the UK and Canada. In all his press coverage, Richards was consistent in his message that what he was pictured as doing should not be considered as exceptional, that it was what any involved father would do, that it represented the kind of work that all fathers *should* do. In a post on the online magazine *Huffington Post* in January 2014, he wrote:

> This story shouldn't be about placing me on the Mount Rushmore of fathers because of a photo. ... What I will welcome from this ... is a healthy dialogue regarding the roles of modern fathers across the world. As a blogger, author, husband, and dad, this is something I will gladly talk about until I'm blue in the face, because it is a discussion that will undoubtedly make a difference in the way men and women view fatherhood. ... If people view me as the guy to help facilitate that discussion, that's great. But here's the thing – I've been *that guy* long before this photo came to light. I just had no damn clue that a seemingly innocuous picture would be the reason why I popped up on the world's radar. But hey – it's pretty cool that a photo depicting what I do everyday for my kids is sparking a worldwide discussion regarding what fathers should do everyday for their kids. (http://www.huffingtonpost.com/doyin-richards/when-the-story-isnt-the-story_b_4610893.html)

Bemused though he appears to be about it, Richards became a media celebrity, an outcome with consequences, as I will describe later in the chapter. The point for now is that any discussion of blogs written by fathers must of necessity take into account both the nature of the medium, and the blogs' potential reach. So while the *content* of the blogs I have selected is an important focus, as a source of fathers' accounts of caregiving, I intend in this final empirical chapter to use it as the start of a broader discussion of their effects on cultural understandings of fathering and masculinity. I begin with a brief introduction to these fathers and their blogs, to outline their family circumstances and demonstrate the variety of formats and styles their blogs represent. I then move to a discussion of the representations of fathering they contain, and how these representations are taken up, both in the online world and outside it. The chapter concludes with some reflections on the contribution of fathers' blogs to social and cultural change.

## Background on fathers and blogs

In this chapter, I consider blogs (all listed in Table 5.1) written by 20 fathers: four from Canada, six from the UK, eight from the US and two from Australia. All but two were currently providing care to preschool children,[2] and all but one had achieved some distinction, either as award-winners of major competitions, as media resources, or as writers on other widely read sites.[3] Eight were home-based full-time primary caregivers; eight were employed full-time and living with partners who were also employed full-time; and four were employed full-time and partnered with home-based mothers. Three had one child, 13 had two children, three had three children and one had four.

All of the blogs they wrote conformed[4] to the general description of blogs as personal journals, containing brief entries, posted in reverse chronological order. All also contained photographs (some many more than others), either to illustrate a post, or to stand in for one. (For example 'Wordless Wednesdays' featuring a picture with a brief caption were quite common.) Several bloggers also included brief video clips. While my emphasis was on what fathers *wrote* (and specifically what they wrote as fathers, and not, for example, as cooks or outdoor enthusiasts or travellers) my review of this range of material, over an extended period of time (at least a year in most cases) offered insights into bloggers' family lives, their practices, and their thinking, that would not be accessible in any other way.

Most of the blogs contained an 'About me' link in which the blogger disclosed some details of himself, his family, and why he chose to blog. Bloggers in general are either writers or aspiring writers, so the blog as a creative outlet was one obvious reason. Others commented that the blog was a way to record their children's development – in the words of Australian blogger Clint Greagen,[5] it was a 'time capsule.' Some bloggers also articulated a more explicit intention to

*Table 5.1* List of bloggers

| | Blog Name | Website link |
|---|---|---|
| **Canada:** | | |
| Buzz Bishop | DadCAMP | www.dad-camp.com |
| Kenny Bodanis | Men Get Pregnant Too | www.mengetpregnanttoo.com |
| Nick Cheeseman | CanaDad | www.canadad.net |
| Michael Cusden | Like A Dad | www.likeadad.net |
| **UK:** | | |
| John Adams | Dadbloguk.com | www.dadbloguk.com |
| Tom Briggs | Diary of the Dad | www.diaryofthedad.co.uk |
| Henry Elliss | Fatherhood2/Henry's Blog | www.henrysblog.co.uk |
| Simon Ragoonanan | Man vs Pink | www.manvspink.com |
| Ben Tipping | Mutterings of a Fool | www.mutteringsofafool.com |
| Alex Walsh | Daddacool | www.daddacool.co.uk |
| **US:** | | |
| Mike Adamick | Mike Adamick | www.mikeadamick.com |
| Chris Bernholdt | Dadncharge | www.dadncharge.com |
| Aaron Gouveia | The Daddy Files | www.daddyfiles.com |
| Andy Hinds | Beta Dad | www.betadadblog.com |
| John Kinnear | Ask your dad | www.askyourdadblog.com |
| Doyin Richards | Daddy Doin' Work | www.daddydoinwork.com |
| Chris Routly | Daddy Doctrines | www.daddydoctrines.com |
| "James" | Luke, I am Your Father | www.liayf.blogspot.ca |
| **Australia:** | | |
| Clint Greagen | Reservoir Dad | www.reservoirdad.com |
| Matt Ross | Dad Down Under | www.daddownunder.com.au |

share experiences of fathering and build a community with other fathers – they wanted, in the words of US blogger Aaron Gouveia, 'to provide some support and a voice for other dads in the same predicament.'[6] They also wanted to paint another picture of fathers – not as the 'bumbling idiots' of many media presentations, but as involved and competent co-parents.

Even in this limited selection of 20 blogs, there was a wide variety of styles and approaches. Some blogs were straightforward records of (almost) daily doings, which it was easy to imagine being shared with family and (actual, not virtual) friends. Good examples of this style, and particularly interesting given the material introduced in Chapters 2 and 3, were two blogs by Canadian fathers which detailed (among other things) their time on parental leave – Michael Cusden's 'Like a Dad,' and Nick Cheeseman's 'CanaDad.' Cusden in fact wrote an almost daily journal describing his experiences as cook, household manager, and sole caregiver to his sons, who were respectively six months and three years old at the start of his leave. Both blogs strove to be humorous; in many ways they exemplify the 'sub-type' of blogger described by US blogger Andy Hinds[7] as presenting 'an idealized digital portrait of their family life.' This intention was shared by James, another US blogger, who said of his blogging plans for 2015, 'I will continue to diligently tell all who will listen how wonderful my wife and kids are, and how amazing it is to be a father.'[8] Many blog posts in this category took the form of advice or 'life lessons.' Examples had titles like 'Top five things every dad has to know' (from Cusden), 'Five skills all new dads need to perfect' (from UK blogger Ben Tipping) or (leaning more to the humorous than the practical) 'Seven ways a puppy prepares you for babies' (from US blogger Chris Bernholdt).

Other bloggers, while still focusing on daily life with children, included posts that described the challenges fathers (and mothers) faced, and were much more confessional in tone. For example, US blogger John Kinnear described having to deal – not easily – with the tantrum his daughter staged outside her daycare, and the difficult evening with her that followed. He concluded the post:

> Sorry. No lessons to be learned here. Just an unvarnished tale of how sometimes shit gets shitty and then it gets a little better. I don't ever want to *just* paint a picture of the good things. Not everything looks better with an Instagram Filter. I try to do my best and sometimes my best isn't good enough. Hell, sometimes it isn't even my best. Anyway, something something.... (June 12, 2014)[9]

Fathers also used blog posts to describe some of the worrying moments of raising children. For example, UK blogger Henry Elliss wrote about his nearly-five-year-old son's admission to hospital for surgery (April 25, 2013). They also addressed broader parenting issues, like child discipline, or playground safety, or the feeding of fussy eaters. Often they closed 'issue' posts with questions to readers, inviting comments and a continuation of the conversation. Some used their blogs as platforms to address broader political issues, like parental leave for fathers. (In view of the policy changes about to take place, this was a topic that four of the six UK bloggers discussed directly.) A topic popular in many US fathers' blogs (and one that will be discussed in more detail later) was the way fathers were represented in advertising and media.

My reading of the blogs I have chosen for discussion was necessarily selective. The textual material that was relevant for my purposes was embedded in a wealth of other content undoubtedly included with other, regular readers in mind. I should also note that my focus was on blog posts exclusively, and not the comments that they attracted. Though it was beyond the scope of this research to explore the interactive element of the blogs, there is no doubt of its importance. Fathers who blog are opening their fathering to scrutiny in a way that has no precedent.

## Representations of fathering

From the diverse styles of blogging just described, it follows that fathering was represented in diverse ways as well. The starting point for this analysis, and the connection to all the fathers introduced in earlier chapters, must be the accounts by blogger fathers of their embodied caregiving, and how they experienced it. Bloggers' accounts, even more than those of interviewees and memoir writers, are rich sources both of fathers' descriptions of their care, and what they see as its consequences.

### Fathering as embodied caregiving

The journal style of many blogs is an invitation to list and describe activities. When babies are the focus, most of the activities involve embodied care. An excerpt from a post by Michael Cusden, who as noted kept a record of his six-month parental leave, is a good example:

Remember yesterday when I said we got Charlie [the six-month-old] down to five bottles again? Well I think he missed it because he woke up in the middle of the night looking for a little something, something to fill his belly. As the home parent now, I was on duty and after getting woken up by my wife (who is always on duty I think), I was off to see what was up. For a brief moment I thought I was going to pull off the magic [trick] of the year and get the baby back to sleep without a bottle. He tricked me and just when I was feeling pretty good, he unleashed his fury. Before it woke up the whole house I was off to get the bottle. I gotta say, making a bottle in the dark with one hand is a skill I may put on my resume one day. So the bottle was down, but not the baby. He was soaked and changing his diaper meant turning on the light. I tried to avoid it but he was like a mop after washing up the floor. So light on, baby did the WTF face and we were back to square one. No crib for this guy. With a dry bum and a new look on life, I took Charlie to the basement where we would hopefully keep the noise down and maybe, just maybe go to sleep. Guess what? My shoulder is becoming a bit of a closer[10] that even the Blue Jays [Canadian baseball team] would value. For the last few days, my shoulder has been lights out for Charlie. It happened again. We got under the blanket, he played out his little dinosaur noises he does and he was out. (April 5, 2013)

The post goes on to note his own uncomfortable and sleepless night, the lazy day that followed, and the dinner that was planned and would be prepared after he and the baby had collected the three-year-old from playschool. Seven months later, in a guest post for the *Good Men Project*[11] in which he reflects on his parental leave, he writes:

Does our son realize that his dad took on the second six months? Probably not. But I do feel this higher connection, a comfort, with our second son. He melts upon being picked up. I seem to have a control over him that I don't remember from the first time around.

Now maybe it is all in my head, or it is the bond formed during all those bottle sessions and strolls around the house rocking him to sleep. Sitting at work each day, I mostly miss those things. The after lunch bottle and nap. The smile on his face after that same nap when I picked him up.

(http://goodmenproject.com/families/dads-parental-leave-wwh/ #sthash.YTL4mlwd.dpuf November 19, 2013)

In earlier chapters I constructed a 'benchmark' for hands-on, embodied caregiving that, I argued, any father caring for a baby or very young child would provide. It is clear from these posts that Cusden was meeting my benchmark. It is also clear that the experience of providing this care, for Cusden as for many of the fathers introduced earlier, was transformative. I use Cusden's accounts to stand in for the many examples of embodied caregiving and its effects that I found in other blogs, and to (re)establish, this time from the bloggers' perspective, that the original argument still stands.

It is important, however, to set this caregiving in the context of other work that blogger fathers describe – work that also contributes to how fathers are represented. Another Canadian father blogger, Kenny Bodanis, describes the 'work/life' schedule of 'tag-teaming' he and his employed wife established to avoid daycare and keep their children at home for the first three years of their life. He writes for the *Good Men Project*:

> My son is almost 8; we're still tag-teaming. This, coupled with the usual life stuff – home repair and personal projects (you're reading one right now) – means there is little time to stare at the ceiling and contemplate my navel. Supper alone with kids last night (after homework, piano practice, snack, snack clean-up, showers, and obliterating 5 of the 12 sausages I forgot on the barbecue) was spent answering questions about the universe while reminding them if they took too long to eat, there wouldn't be time for the extra-long bedtime story they asked for. Bedtime is spent answering questions about what special plans could be made for the weekend [...] They're asleep ... time to make lunches, clean up from supper, clean up from making lunches, have my own shower and try to stay awake in front of the TV long enough to not lose a major chunk of Dexter's storyline.
> (http://goodmenproject.com/families/parents-whats-more-brutal-the-anxiety-or-the-grind/ October 25, 2012)

The blogs I reviewed contained a great many other descriptions of fathers at work with their children, and heartfelt accounts of how they felt about them. Whether idealized, or seemingly matter-of-fact, or confessional, bloggers' posts were framing their writers as deeply engaged fathers. But the seemingly uncomplicated transition from hands-on infant caregiver to competent, still-engaged father to older children, though it was the most common message, was not the only one.

Among the bloggers whose writing I include here were some who had done a much smaller share of the early caregiving than all the other fathers introduced so far. These were the employed fathers whose partners had either taken extended leave from their paid employment, or were primary home-based caregivers, and so were better placed to do most of the hands-on care. In most of these cases, interestingly, the fathers in this category seemed indistinguishable in their approach to infant caregiving and their attachment to their babies from the fathers who were more experienced; their accounts suggested they were committed to participating in caregiving to the extent that they could, and they wrote about it enthusiastically. But other fathers had a harder time of it. Two fathers in this group stood out, and their posts about lapses in – or absence from – early caregiving merit attention for what they add to the discussion of its transformative effects.

For Aaron Gouveia, the challenge involved dealing with his second child's colic as newborn:

> [W]hen I can't calm him and he won't stop crying, I lose my mind. I've banged my head off every surface of my house. I've screamed at the top of my lungs into pillows, cursing my very existence and bargaining with the universe for just a few hours sleep. Poor MJ [his wife] has had to bail me out repeatedly, especially because I need sleep for work ... I want to reiterate, I love my son. We wanted another baby so badly and now he's here and that's great, but it still doesn't change the fact that there's nothing good, fun, or easy about the first few months. So if I sound a little nuts right now, it's because I am. Because I have a newborn. And newborns suck. (September 13, 2013)

Gouveia struggled to take his turn with the caregiving, but he was working two jobs and under some financial stress. He makes no mention of how much time he had off work when the baby was born, but (like most other US fathers) having no access to paid parental leave, the implication is that he had little, if any, time at home. The post just cited was written when the baby was three months old. Six months later, in another confessional post, he acknowledges the difficulty he had bonding with this baby. This confession is possible because, as he recounts it, the difficulty is over. He writes of learning not to resent the baby's wakefulness, but to soothe him in a rocking chair 'without regard to how long I'd be there – in fact, time really ceased to exist.' He relaxes, and so does the baby; all is well. The story ends with a vindication of his persistence; now, he writes, 'MJ is jealous that only Dad can get Sam back to bed without giving him a bottle at night' (March 31, 2014).

Gouveia's distress is at least partly because, as he also reports, he had no problem bonding with his first child. In another early post he writes: 'With Will I was the Baby Whisperer. He loved me and favored me and I could soothe him like no other' (September 23, 2013). It was his attachment to his first child that made him aware of its absence with his second. His experience also addresses the fact that father-baby bonding is not always easy, and especially in cases where the early caregiving is difficult, may take longer to achieve.

The experience of Canadian blogger Buzz Bishop was different again. Where Gouveia was distressed and apologetic about his fathering 'failure,' posts by Bishop, also the father of two children, strike another note. In a thread that runs through his blog over several years, he writes openly – and unapologetically – of his lack of interest in his children as babies. In a recent post recalling a time when he was left alone with his first child as an infant, his description, both of the baby's behaviour and his feelings, are remarkably similar to Gouveia's. His solution, as he describes it, was to phone his wife (who was out with her friends for 'one of her first times being away from our new son') and without saying a word put the receiver close to the screaming baby. 'I knew the sound would be too much for her, and she would come and rescue me,' he writes. 'It was a dirty trick, but it worked' (February 20, 2015).

In a post on the parenting website *Babble.com*, Bishop writes that he didn't feel close to his first child until he was two, when a period of unemployment positioned him as the toddler's primary caregiver: '[T]hat summer of 2009, spending the time and doing the diapers, feeding and activities – that's when I fell in love.'(http://www.babble.com/kid/not-the-dad-camp-on-vh1-the-dadcamp-on-babble/, April 2, 2012). Perhaps not surprisingly, then, Bishop's posts over the period of his second son's birth and early years of life focus almost exclusively on the first child – he even wrote a post publicized around the world in which he confessed to having a 'favourite child' (who was, not surprisingly, the first-born).[12] Family caregiving was shared on a one-child-per-parent basis, with Bishop always in charge of the older child. He writes that his wife, registering this persistent pattern, insisted that he spend some time with the second as well – when he also was two. They went to a show jumping competition, with horses, marching bands and food. 'We had a great time, and I started to fall for him,' he writes (http://www.babble.com/kid/admit-it-you-have-a-favorite-kid-i-do/).

The experiences of Gouveia and Bishop bring to mind the comment by memoir writer Michael Lewis, introduced in the previous chapter, that 'it is only in caring for a thing that you become attached to it' – so '[i]f you want to feel the way you're meant to feel about the new baby, you need to do the grunt work' (Lewis, 2009:163). Sometimes, as Gouveia discovered, the 'grunt work' is hard to do. But failing to do it may prolong the period of paternal detachment and lack of interest Bishop describes. It bears repeating that, at least according to their written accounts, the other bloggers I reviewed took to baby care early and enthusiastically.

## Fathering, caregiving and masculinity

In their descriptions of their caregiving, most of the father bloggers were clear about how they wanted it to be perceived. The post by Doyin Richards at the start of the chapter is characteristic of the views many bloggers report – that engaged, hands-on caregiving should be what fathers provide as a matter of course. But as many also report, these views do not always match public perceptions of fathers and fathering. The image of the 'doofus dad' has by no means disappeared, even though, as home-based US father blogger Chris Routly notes, it is an image that bears little relation to real-life fathers:

> Oh sure, there are definitely plenty of bumbling idiots out there, but the majority of them are either fictional – existing firmly in the worlds of outdated advertising and lowest-common-denominator sitcoms – or aren't determined by gender. Dads have, as a group, never really been the bumbling idiots they have been portrayed to be when it comes to their abilities to care for their children (never mind themselves) – even if some men have decided that playing the buffoon was a good way to get out of what they saw as less-than-pleasant responsibilities. But the rest of us got the message a long time ago that we can do better than that, and we *are* better than that. (May 15, 2014)

In 2012, Routly was at the forefront of a campaign, organized through his blog, to get the manufacturer of a well known brand of diapers to change advertising that clearly framed fathers as incompetent. The campaign succeeded; the company modified the advertisement to meet with father bloggers' approval, and the bloggers in turn became recognized – and recognized themselves – as a force that other major advertisers needed to reckon with (an issue I will take up later in the chapter). Advertising campaigns were not the only target. An issue taken up more recently by father bloggers in Australia, the UK and the US is the absence of baby-changing tables in men's washrooms; fathers note that their absence signals a failure to recognize that fathers, too, change diapers.

In the post just cited, Routly goes on to dismiss several other 'falsehoods, fabrications, and outright lies about fathers that just won't seem to die' – among them, that fathers are 'not naturally nurturing and capable with infants,' that they 'don't care about parenting stuff,' and that 'those who show the slightest competence at childcare are "Super Dads."' Other fathers, while occasionally amused by the kudos they receive in public as caregiving fathers, also regret the fact that the bar for fathers is set so low; like Richards and Routly, they are usually quick to reframe what they are doing as unexceptional, and (in response to another commonly levied description), emphatically not 'babysitting.' Another home-based father, UK blogger John Adams, notes that he does 'pretty much everything society expects a mum to do' to care for a five-year-old and a 22-month-old – including tasks like ferrying children to school and nursery, cooking meals, shampooing hair, organizing play dates and updating the family calendar. He asks:

> Why wouldn't a man be capable of doing this stuff? I have heard it said that women are naturally more compassionate and more caring by nature. It may be true, but it sounds like a convenient notion to spread so that women can be kept behind the kitchen sink, or rather make women believe childcare is their domain. I genuinely wish I lived in a society where I wasn't a curiosity. (September 8, 2014)

Concerns about how fathers are portrayed – notably in media representations and other cultural images – link to concerns about how fathers who challenge the stereotypes are perceived in the real world. Caregiving fathers may be viewed as 'curiosities' for many reasons – indeed, 'curiosities' in some cases may be too kind a term. Awareness of the stereotype of men as dangerous, particularly to children – and personal experience of its application – appeared in several posts.[13] Bloggers also echoed the discomfort expressed by many of the fathers introduced in earlier chapters, whose caregiving drew them on to mothers' terrain. UK blogger Simon Ragoonanan writes of his encounters with what he calls the 'mum hub' – mothers found in 'playgrounds, playgroups and cafes.' They are 'cliques of (usually) at-home mums whose exclusively female daytime community is by design not accident, that prefer their women only social-parenting life. Who find it odd that a man might want to be at home with their children, perhaps even suspicious ...' (January 13, 2014).

Ragoonanan recognizes that not all mothers feel this way – and indeed there are posts from other bloggers that present a different picture. Kenny Bodanis writes of the occasion when he replaced his wife as evening chauffeur for one of his children's activities – and was invited to join the other chauffeurs (all mothers) for a pub drink while they waited for pick-up time. Nick Cheeseman is matter-of-fact about his participation in the 'moms' group' in which his wife had participated, when he started his share of their parental leave. The 'estrogen-filled worlds' referred to in earlier chapters are more challenging for fathers like Ragoonanan, who are home-based primary caregivers, and who (like memoir writer Elisha Cooper, introduced in the previous chapter) are on mothers' terrain for the long haul.

Ragoonanan is not deterred by the 'mum hub.' He recognizes, in the interests of normalizing the kind of fathering he and others were practising, the need for rapprochement. A post eight months after his 'mum hub' description, titled 'Play groups: a survival guide for dads' (October 6, 2014) is clearly written with this need in mind. He advises other fathers to exchange information about children as a conversation opener, offer to help out, remember people's names, join in the singing, and 'be the engaged parent you are.' But he hasn't forgotten the 'mum hub.' Mother cliques do exist, he tells his readers, so 'if you don't like it, move along.' He notes that it took him 'a few groups' before he found the ones he liked. US home-based blogger Chris Bernholdt had a similar story of moving from avoidance to participation. He admits to having been 'intimidated' by the stay-at-home mothers who could 'make everything happen' and be so at ease with one another. Then he became a classroom volunteer and began to join the conversation. 'I even became a part of a group that called themselves the Y Mommies [who] were the moms of the pre-school kids at our local YMCA,' he writes. 'After some time it didn't matter that I was the only dad among these great moms' (March 13, 2014).

For home-based fathers in particular, however, interacting with mothers was only part of the challenge their gender presented. Their engagement with work traditionally done by mothers courted another judgment – that they were somehow lesser men because of their caregiving. Not surprisingly, then, the most explicit reframings of fathering and masculinity came in blog posts from these fathers. They argued that financial provision was not the only way fathers could contribute to their families, that supporting working partners and taking care of children at home took strength and courage of another kind, and that perceptions of caregiving as 'women's work' reflected a view of masculinity and fatherhood that was 'rooted in the primordial ooze' (Bernholdt, November 25, 2014). All were clear that they were redefining masculinity, and what it meant to be a 'real man.' As Chris Routly put it: 'As to the idea that a man is emasculated by virtue of being competent at changing a diaper? I guess it depends on the man. But for most of us, nothing makes us feel like more of a man than when we serve our family' (May 15, 2014).

So in most cases they resoundingly rejected the 'Mr. Mom' label, and chose instead to degender the work they were doing – which they invariably described by its degendered term, *parenting*. To take up the distinction I raised in the previous chapter, they considered themselves to be parenting as men. Some posts raised the possibility that they might also be parenting *like* men – and so, perhaps, doing it differently from women. Chris Bernholdt, for example, notes mothers' tendencies to hover over their children, and occasionally to micro-manage. He worries that children's play is becoming too organized – in another 'viral' post, he calls for the end to children's 'playdates':

> Let's start by banishing the word playdate and focus on just making our kids play in imaginative ways. Let's lose the structure and the formality and remove the dates so they can just focus on playing. (July 9, 2014)

John Adams shares a personal perspective:

> Men and women possibly parent differently. Thinking of my own relationship, I'm more of a risk taker. Play with me is often outside, usually physical and frequently involves getting covered in mud or water. My wife is more likely to do some baking or read books with the kids. I don't think either is wrong, they're simply different approaches and my kids love both. (September 8, 2014)

But there were many other posts about fathers baking and reading books (and taking on other, more stereotypically 'feminine' activities) – enough to blur, once again, the gender boundaries.

I have suggested that the fathers who were blogging as home-based primary caregivers were at the forefront of efforts to reframe fathering and masculinity. But my sense is that among the bloggers I have selected, as in the wider community of father bloggers, they are the flag bearers of change that all these fathers support. This is evident in a wide array of posts – ranging from Tom Briggs' comments about his time on parental leave to John Kinnear's posts as a working father in a dual-earner family – that do not specifically address issues of fathering and masculinity, but that document engaged caregiving by fathers *as if* it were the norm. In this context, some of the 'advice posts' directed to other fathers have a similar effect. For example, Ben Tipping's post, entitled '5 things dads can do during pregnancy,' and directed particularly to fathers who have other children, is clearly based on his own activities as an employed father with two preschoolers and a pregnant wife. Among other things, he calls on fathers to 'be a domestic god' (by tackling the housework), 'make meals easy' (by preparing things the night before and using the freezer) and spend plenty of weekend time as the older children's solo caregiver. (September 2, 2014)

## Fathers, children and gender

The reframing of masculinity evident in fathers' accounts of their caregiving links to many posts featuring children and gender. They provide interesting evidence of fathers confronting – or being confronted by – their own masculinity, as they consider the women and men their children will grow to be. Raising sons, and raising daughters, pose different questions.

For fathers raising sons, boys and sports featured in many posts. Those by Canadian blogger Michael Cusden, whose parental leave posts were noted earlier, are a good example. Cusden's own love of sports is evident in multiple references to sports viewing as part of his evening schedule, and in his invitations to other dad bloggers to predict outcomes in key sporting competitions. He writes with obvious delight of taking his older son to his first hockey game (the occasion for 'a lot of awesome dad feelings')[14] and later to his first basketball game. But in a post titled 'Do you have high expectations for your kids in sports?' he writes of the need to separate fantasy (his sons becoming professional athletes) from reality:

> If sports never materializes, so what? It could be music, cooking, medicine, writing, or any number of other mediums that interests my boys. I will support them however I can and do what I can to help them reach a goal or dream. If they love to play basketball and don't make the All-Star team, so what. If they play tennis and don't make the National team. No big deal to me. (July 16, 2013)

Aaron Gouveia tells a more nuanced story of men, boys and gender. He confesses to having once been highly conventional in his thinking (he was 'that guy' who got 'all bent out of shape' about pink socks for his baby boy) until 'my wife, common sense, and an army of very wise parent bloggers showed me the light' (February 4, 2014). So he is dismayed when another father suggests in his son's presence that a children's film his son has very much enjoyed is 'girls' stuff.' The dismay is increased when he sees his son start to shift his own play and learning preferences away from anything that might be construed as 'mainly for girls.' He wants to keep fostering his son's love for 'art, fashion and cooking in addition to sports.' But the sports dimension is clearly important. He admits to being hurt that his son doesn't share his great passion for baseball – a bond he treasures with his own father. This story, like Cusden's and many similar blog posts, is constructed as a lesson learned, with a satisfactory outcome – he realizes that 'baseball isn't really the bond that holds fathers and sons together,' that '[l]ove, patience and unwavering support is what matters' (April 10, 2014).

Australian blogger Clint Greagen makes personal circumstances – a chat with his eight-year-old son about the mechanics of sex and babies – the start of a broader blog discussion about social stereotypes of men, and their effects on boys growing into sexual awareness. Recalling weeks of news coverage about abusive men, he laments the 'lack of positive stories about men, about the wonderful, caring, inspiring things that men do on a world scale, at the grass roots level of their local communities and within their own families.' His post (one of several on the subject, this time for an online children's fashion and culture magazine, *Studio Bambini*) continues:

> The constant media reports and campaigns on sexual and domestic violence are important and necessary, but some well-intentioned (yet nonetheless sexist) refrains like 'teach men not to rape' have to be countered with a more positive message before today's boys grow into men who have internalised some damaging untruths. Instead, how about we tell our boys that their gender doesn't come with an inherent badness? I want to make sure my boys understand this, and that male sexuality isn't automatically predatory, selfish or cruel. That while a minority of men can be scary and dangerous, most men are not, and male sexuality itself isn't. It doesn't need to be cornered and restricted. It's not something to be ashamed of. It's something to embrace rather than fear.
> (http://studiobambini.com/2014/03/18/how-about-some-positive-messages-for-our-boys/)

Fathers of daughters have similar concerns about gender stereotyping. US blogger Mike Adamick, the father of a now-school-age daughter, writes about issues ranging from the lack of representation of girl characters – and not just the strong heroines – in children's movies, to sexist advertising and the poor coverage of women's sport. Other fathers tell stories that begin with their own daughters and extend to broader social concerns. Simon Ragoonanan's perspective is evident in the title of his blog – 'Man vs. Pink.' In one post, he writes:

> Part of my approach to parenting is to constantly refer back to my memories of growing up, and use that to positively inform my

approach. The fantastical worlds of comic books and Star Wars loom large in my childhood (and adulthood too) ... I want my daughter to have access to all of this too. Luckily, superheroes and Star Wars are still very much in vogue. It's also fair to say that I'm not a fan of Disney Princesses, and pinkification in general. So as well as simply sharing my enthusiasm for Star Wars with my daughter (she has all my old toys), this is also about me offering her an alternative to girly girl culture before she heads into the school system, and peer group pressure becomes a driving force in her development. (October 23, 2014)

In his blog Ragoonanan strenuously opposes gender-stereotyping of toys, and pushes for toymakers to produce more female superheroes. Other fathers raise similar concerns – and give credit when toymakers and stores 'get it right.' For example, UK blogger Henry Elliss writes approvingly of the decision by a major children's toy store to remove its 'Boys' and 'Girls' store signposts. But he wonders why the manufacturer of a well known brand of chocolate treats, having sold them for decades 'without even a hint of gender stereotyping' has moved to produce pink and blue versions. (October 8, 2013).

Other fathers, while philosophically pro-feminist, are less dogmatic – in some cases having learned from experience that children's tastes can't always be easily controlled. Andy Hinds, the father of twin daughters, in a post for the US news and opinion website *The Daily Beast* titled 'Why I finally let my girls be girly,' writes of his determination to undermine gender stereotypes – 'I would make parenting into a sub-versive act by encouraging my girls to be rough-and-tumble, grass-stained, fort-building, frog-chasing, risk-taking, dungaree-wearing, princess-shunning adventurers!' – only to have his feminist intentions undermined over time by little girls with their own ideas. (They wanted pink-and-lavender bicycles and ballet classes.) Hinds concludes that, contrary to his earlier assumptions, girls and boys in general tend to have 'different interests, taste and aptitudes,' and that gender traits may be a result of the interaction of the social and the biological. But, he adds, 'If I hadn't tried and failed to subvert gender stereotypes in my early parenting, my girls would probably still have the same color bikes and go to the same ballet class; but I might not be teaching them to pound nails and build electrical circuits as well' (www.thedailybeast.com/articles/2014/05/17/why-i-finally-let-my-girls-be-girly.html, May 17, 2014). US blogger John Kinnear has come to a similar conclusion, as he notes in the following post:

My girl can love pink and Disney Princesses and Tinker Bell if she damn well wants to. Sure, we tried to go with gender-less toys. We also tried going with toys marketed to both genders. We swore our baby girl wouldn't be covered in pink. We failed. She loves pink. She wants to be a princess. She wants to be a fairy. She wants to have tea parties. Yes, Batman is invited from time to time, but not nearly as often as Anna, Elsa and Rapunzel. (August 18, 2014)

Kinnear's strategy, as he reports it, is 'to find lessons from whatever she's into that empower her.' So, for example, as far as his daughter knows, the famous fairy Tinker Bell is so named because she tinkers – she is in fact an engineer.

Not all the bloggers whose posts I reviewed here addressed gender issues in child-rearing so explicitly. But there were implicit gender messages also in matter-of-fact descriptions of engaged caregiving – messages that may well have been picked up (through the caregiving itself) by children, as well as readers. Fathers modelling engaged caregiving and active participation in family work are also gender models. Chris Routly notes a practical example – his toddler son likes to 'wear' his favourite stuffed monkey, whom he also 'puts down for naps, feeds, and soothes when she is sad or scared' (April 5, 2014). Chris Bernholdt takes a longer view:

If anything, for my son, I have really taught him tools to be the best man he can be. His future spouse is going to thank me for teaching him manners, how to do his own laundry, and how to cook. You can see it in the ways he treats girls his age and his own sisters. It has shown him that staying home is an option if it fits for his family ... Being at home for my daughters, I have taught them how they should be treated with respect and dignity. I have shown them that a man can be just as loving and caring as [a] woman when it comes to raising the children. I have shown them that limitations should never be put on us because of our gender and that we can accomplish anything despite society's labels. (November 25, 2014)

## Fathers, blogging and gender equality?

From all of the foregoing, it is clear that the fathers whose blogs are considered here are putting out a picture of fathering, and masculinity, that is a departure from traditional forms. Engaged fathers are moving into space that mothers have dominated – symbolically as well as literally. How fathers frame the expansion of their role, and its relation to mothering, is another way to assess change in ideas about gender. In the blogging world, it is tricky ground.

The claim made in many blog posts that fathers can provide the same kind of nurturing hands-on care as mothers can be seen as yet another claim to male privilege – reminiscent of the suggestion by Brandth and Kvande (1998) noted in earlier chapters that caring for children is just another challenge to be conquered for men whose public dominance is already assured. In this light, fathers' relentless online opposition to *any* media image that seems to disparage the nature and significance of their fathering can come to be seen (even by other fathers) as self-important and disrespectful of more significant dimensions of inequality – especially those experienced by women. The tension is more acute when father bloggers engage directly with mother bloggers – a not uncommon occurrence. As Andy Hinds comments, 'the omission or derision of dads in the parent (aka "mommy") blogosphere is a perennial pet peeve.'[15] It is a peeve expressed in no uncertain terms by Buzz Bishop, to give one example. In a post for the *Good Men Project* titled 'An open letter to moms who blog about their husbands,' he is sharply critical of a blogger mother who (in a humorous vein) wrote advice and instructions for the husband she was about to leave for several days in charge of their children. Bishop writes:

> I wonder, Moms Who Blog About Their Husbands, who is really to blame for this situation you find yourself in? I mean, you reap what you sow, right? If you have such a tight grip on your family unit that your husband has no idea what time the kids wake up, what they eat, or what his daughter's favorite night-time toy is, what kind of family do you have? Do you just blog to your husband, or do you actually talk to him? ... If you control the hell out of your family, and do everything for everyone, I'm not surprised you have to Blog About The List You Left Your Husband, because why would he ever want to interfere in your Mother of the Year crusade? You'd bark him right the hell off.
> (http://goodmenproject.com/families/tmb-open-letter-moms-blog-husbands/May 1, 2014)

This antagonistic note is not reflected in the posts[16] of the other bloggers I have considered here. More common instead is the view that fathers sharing caregiving liberates mothers from burdensome expectations that limit their opportunities outside the home. From this perspective, representations of fathers as less than competent caregivers are a disservice to mothers too. And while advertisements or television shows or other messages about incompetent fathers might not seem on a case-by-case basis worth the outcry they produce, they are, in Mike Adamick's terms, part of 'a constant, subtle messaging system that is so pervasive, degrading, and normalized that we can't even tell it's bullshit anymore' (October 2, 2014). Australian blogger Clint Greagen writes of the way overt appeals to men to become more involved in their families are subverted by what he calls the *'drip drip drip* subliminal message' that they are not quite capable of doing what's needed. He adds: 'If men are not able to firstly become aware of that constant all pervasive message on a conscious level it will remain incredibly difficult for many men to rise above it and it will continue to limit the choices available to themselves and their partners' (March 24, 2015). In these terms, changing the message is not in the interests of increasing male privilege, but of gender equality. Where a shift happens, as other bloggers note, it needs to be celebrated – as a sign of 'incremental change toward the perception of parenting as an endeavour shared by both sexes' (Andy Hinds, June 14, 2012).

This perspective is taken up in many accounts. For example, Aaron Gouveia writes:

> As an outspoken proponent of involved fatherhood, I'm thrilled to see working dads spending more time at home as well as the skyrocketing number of full-time stay-at-home dads. And I realize that can't happen without more women entering the workforce and being paid enough to support their families. It's why we write articles highlighting the gender wage gap and seek to end it, and want a better world for our sons and daughters in general. Because we realize this isn't an 'Us vs. Them' battle, as the shifting priorities and goals of men and women are intricately tied together. (May 23, 2014)

It also appears in many posts, notably by the home-based primary caregivers, expressing pride in and support for their wives' career achievements. Overall, the message is that fathers *ought* to be engaged, hands-on caregivers, sharing the whole immense body of work known as parenting in ways that support the interests and needs of both fathers and mothers.

## Blogs and their readers

Up to this point, I have considered the blogs as accounts – covering more ground than the interview and memoir accounts discussed earlier, but still the stories of fathers laid out for comparison with the stories of the interviewees and memoir writers. In the analytic sense, I have treated the blogs in the same way as the memoirs – as resources capable of providing information about the topics that were of interest to my research. In that sense, they have served to strengthen the findings of earlier chapters, about the kinds of engaged embodied caregiving fathers were undertaking, the effects they perceived it to have on them, and the reframing of fathering and masculinity that seemed to be taking place in the process. The memoir accounts extended the findings of the interviews in that they were the work of a (somewhat) more diverse collection of fathers, and, more importantly, they were public. The blogs, however, take the discussion on to entirely new terrain. They too are public, but where the memoirs were received on a one-time-only basis by a largely unknown and passive readership, blogs are interactive, and they take place in (more or less) real time. More than accounts, they represent *conversations* with readers. And though my focus is on only one side of the conversation, it is the conversation that is most likely to affect the practice and experience of fathering over the long term. For that reason, it merits special attention.

## Community building on- and off-line

An early question, in considering the influence of the bloggers' main message about fathering, relates to their readership. On the basis of the blogs considered in this research, it is very clear that a key group of people who read blogs written by fathers are other father bloggers.[17] Working through the 'endless criss-crossing hyper tracks and trails' noted in the introduction to Part III (Hookway, 2008), this cross-readership is readily apparent. Individual bloggers link to posts by others, to guest posts they have written on other blogs, and to their contributions to the growing numbers of group blogs run by several fathers.[18]

Others write explicitly about the community they sought, and found, through blogging – sometimes (though certainly not invariably) in contrast to the *lack* of community they found as fathers in their offline lives. Many posts echoed the sentiments expressed here by Andy Hinds:

> I started reading dad blogs (and mom blogs) as soon as I became a father, so I don't know what it's like to be a dad and not have access to a community of parents who are fascinated enough by the enterprise of child rearing that they would share their stories, theories, joys, and frustrations with one another. When I started my stint as a stay-at-home dad to twins almost three years ago, I was aware of the possibility that I would feel isolated and maybe even

trapped, especially during those first months when interactions with other adults were rare and punctuated by feedings, screaming, and diaper changes. But during naptime, I could always get on the Internet and learn, laugh, or just vent in the interactive world of the dadosphere. ... I suppose I could have gotten along just fine by calling parent-friends, reading books, or maybe meditating during these days alone with my uncommunicative bundles of need. But it was a great salve for me to read stories of other parents – both those in the throes of new-parent anxiety themselves, and seasoned veterans I could look to for advice – and to interact with the people who congregate around their blogs. (May 24, 2012)

In this virtual community they are often joined by 'mommy bloggers,' whom they frequently perceive as sharing common ground – partly through the practice of blogging, but also by virtue of the kind of parenting they are doing. Some of their 'guest' posts are on blogs by mothers, and 'mommy bloggers' are frequently among those who comment on their posts. Aaron Gouveia in his 'about me' comments explicitly notes that 'moms make up the majority of the readership.' And though this cross-tracking is not without its tensions (as noted earlier), there are more similarities than differences.[19] Ben Tipping writes: 'Becoming a blogger is potentially the best thing any parent or parent to be can do because you will never experience such support and kind words anywhere else' (April 25, 2014).

However, the fact that messages about fathers' participation in engaged caregiving are widely circulated in this virtual community is still only part of the story. There are two other aspects of the community that must be noted. The first is the opportunity provided by the virtual community for fathers to meet and form face-to-face relationships as well. Fathers' blogging networks have facilitated the formation of dads' groups in several communities, as US blogger Chris Bernholdt and Australian blogger Clint Greagen have reported. Bloggers' conferences are another site where the virtual is transposed. In the UK, for example, blogger Tom Briggs wrote about his participation in the conference organized by *BritMums*, described on their website (www. britmums.com) as 'Britain's biggest collective of lifestyle bloggers and social influencers' – most of whom are women. He participated in a panel discussion with other father bloggers to represent what session organizers labelled a 'fast-growing trend.'

Father bloggers in the US have also been participants in conferences for women who blog – notably the widely known annual BlogHer conference, which by 2012 had achieved sufficient eminence to warrant an opening address by President Barack Obama. But 2012 also marked the start of the Dad 2.0 Summit, an annual gathering of 'daddy bloggers.' The summit, according to its website, is 'an open conversation about the commercial power of dads online, and an opportunity to learn the tools and tactics used by influential bloggers to create high-quality content, build personal brands, and develop business ideas' (www.dad2summit.com). Of the eight US fathers whose blogs are considered here, all but one had been conference speakers at least once. The business dimension of the summit is significant, and will be addressed in more detail shortly. But what seemed to be at least as important to the fathers who participated was the strengthening of the sense of solidarity and community many had experienced online. Chris Routly reflects the sentiments of other US father attendees in his comments about the 2014 Dad 2.0 Summit in New Orleans:

> It's hard to put into words a weekend like this, where the community built and nourished and strengthened during the evening hours, in the streets and cafes of New Orleans, were as important as the sessions, workshops, panel discussions, and opportunities to meet with representatives from brands who want to work with dads. ... I walked into [the summit] feeling like I was going to the best reunion ever. I was greeted with hugs and handshakes and inside jokes ... by guys who I had never met in person before but feel like I know well, through their honest writing about just trying to be a good dad. (February 4, 2014)

One reason Routly gave for his sense of the summit as a reunion was the fact that most, if not all, of the participants were part of an online Facebook group exclusively for 'dad bloggers' started in 2012 by US blogger Oren Miller. This group, estimated in early posts by several bloggers to number in the hundreds, by March 2015 had an estimated membership of more than 1,000 father bloggers from countries around the world. Miller's death in February 2015 produced emotional responses from many of them. They spoke not only of their appreciation for his tireless work maintaining and supporting the group, but also of its value. From the UK, John Adams (in a *BritMums* post) described the Facebook page as 'not only somewhere to showcase blog posts but a place where dads open up and talk frankly in a way you rarely see elsewhere.' (http://www.britmums.com/2015/03/dad-blogger-round-sad-forward-looking/). From Canada, Buzz Bishop wrote of attending a Dad 2.0 summit session so he could meet Miller and thank him for gathering the group together and allowing deep friendships to form. He added: 'There are dick jokes, political debates, and support. Exactly the sort of things friends would talk about. These are my people' (June 13, 2014).

## Father bloggers as 'social influencers'

The Facebook connection links to the second aspect of the father blogging community that must be noted – the growing significance of its online reach. The rapid – and continuing – development and use of social media like Facebook and Twitter[20] can vastly expand the networks of individual blogs, and hence their potential readers. This has two important consequences. The first concerns blogger fathers' ability to mobilize. The second is the extent to which blogs are being commercialized.

Bloggers' use of their networks to mobilize support for causes of interest to them has already been noted. The successful 2012 campaign against an advertisement about diapers that disparaged fathers' caregiving competence was the first to establish fathers engaged with their families as a group with a collective voice that should be heeded. Now, with increased network connections, this becomes easier to do. A campaign (re)launched in March 2015 is an excellent example. The focus of the campaign was the online marketer Amazon, which among other things offers 'a membership program aimed at helping parents and caregivers in the prenatal through toddler years.' The program, according to its website, 'is open to anyone, whether you're a mom, dad, grandparent, or caretaker' (www.amazon.com). In countries like Canada, the UK and Australia, this program is called 'Amazon Family.' In the US it is called 'Amazon Mom' – exactly the kind of distinction likely to draw the attention of blogger fathers. In 2013 Oren Miller wrote a post encouraging fathers to sign a petition (on the online platform Change.org) in favour of the name change, which at the time had received little support. After his death, members of the Dad Bloggers Facebook group decided to revive this cause in Miller's honour. Supporters were asked to sign the petition, and to send tweets to a specified hash tag. By the end of March 2015, the petition had gathered 11,000 signatures, and there had been some 6 million Twitter posts.

Another effect of the social media activity, in this case as with many of the other causes father bloggers have embraced, was to draw the attention of conventional (print and television) media as well.[21] In this way issues of importance to father bloggers could also be communicated to a new, non-digital audience. Coverage of the 2015 Dad 2.0 Summit also speaks to father bloggers' influence. An article on the website of *Time* magazine was headed 'The Dad 2.0 summit: making the case for a new kind of manhood.' The author commented that '[t]his summit, nearly double the size it was in 2012, has been at the forefront of an ongoing revolution in how America perceives fatherhood' (Steinmetz, 2015).

Policy issues are also a focus of father bloggers, particularly in the UK, where parental leave has been a popular subject. Four of the six UK bloggers introduced here have produced thoughtful posts, both about the changes in fathers' potential share of parental leave that took effect in April 2015, and about alternative proposals put forward by both the opposition Labour Party, and the Liberal Democratic Party, in advance of the 2015 spring election. John Adams has been particularly engaged with this debate. It is an indication of his status as a blogging 'social influencer' that he has met with key politicians, and (on March 27, 2015) published a guest post on parental leave by the then Women and Equalities Minister, Jo Swinson – with posts from other political parties promised to follow.

However, the digital reach of individual blogs has had another effect. Marketers of a wide variety of products and services are recognizing fathers, represented by those who blog, as an influential market. In the US, where this trend seems most advanced, advertising campaigns directed to men are coming to be shaped with the blogger fathers' message about involved fatherhood in mind. A recent example was the television advertisement produced by a brand of personal care toiletries for men that was shown during the televising of the 2015 US Super bowl – the championship game of the National Football League that conventionally attracts record-setting audiences. The advertisement – apparently made using actual fathers and their children – showed a series of fathers responding to children's needs in recognizably real-life situations.

But if blogger fathers are being recognized for what they might buy, they are now increasingly sought out for their potential as advertisers also. Marketers are coming to see blogs as a means to spread their message – and bloggers are increasingly coming to see their blogs as a way to make money. The commercial dimension of the Dad 2.0 summit is understandable in this context; in the 2015 summit, for example, sessions on respecting family members' privacy and sessions highlighting the work of individual bloggers were interspersed with sessions on how to make money online – and frequent opportunities to meet marketing representatives. The commercialization shows up on blogs in a variety of ways, starting with the way they are now set up – more commonly as independent websites than as blogs run by hosts like Blogspot or WordPress. Commercial content may range from product reviews and give-aways to sponsored posts and permanent advertisements. Many blogs now announce themselves to be 'PR-friendly,' and have 'media packages' available for review.

The blogs I consider here illustrate this range. For example seven have little discernable commercial content at all. Most of these are written by fathers who set them up a little ahead of the social media revolution that has transformed the field. Some commercial content is evident in all the others (though it must be noted that at least two other bloggers in this group – Canadians Kenny Bodanis and Buzz Bishop – appear to donate all the money earned through their blogging to non-profit causes.) Several intersperse product-related posts with other, more general ones. Australian blogger Matt Ross is more direct about the business model he is adopting; in December 2013, he posted details of a pre-Christmas social event he attended with 'the agency I'm fortunate enough to be with.' (The agency, known as *The Remarkables*, is described on its website as 'a talent agency for bloggers; creating remarkable blogger-brand relationships' [http://www.theremarkablesgroup.com.au/].) Different again is the blog by Doyin Richards, whose celebrity status I mentioned at the start of the chapter. This is one of the newest blogs I have included; it was started in June 2012. Shortly after the January 2014 media storm, Richards announced in a post that changes were coming. Now the blog seems to be less a blog than a business, mainly to promote Richards as a public speaker. He notes on his website that he has 'spoken at preschools and universities, keynoted a conference for a Fortune 500 company, and will serve as the commencement speaker for a June 2015 graduation ceremony.' He refers all 'interview and PR requests,' as well as organizations wishing to book him for speaking engagements, to his agent. The website also has a store, where t-shirts, children's onesies and mugs (all stamped with the blog's 'Daddy Doin' Work' logo) are available for purchase.[22]

## Professionalizing blogs, professionalizing fathers

Most of the bloggers I have introduced here, as already noted, have promoted products or services, and written sponsored posts, at some time or another. Frequently, these came with disclaimers to the effect that though the goods/services were provided free to the blogger, the opinions were his own. But beyond that, the commercial element was seldom addressed. The fact is, though, that commercial success is dependent on blog readership; the more widely read the blog, the more brands and sponsors it is likely to attract. As Clint Greagen put it:

> The brands 'love' the way you write and 'love' your blog and think you're a 'perfect fit' for their products and they promise not to compromise your writing or your 'authentic voice' and they use words like *collaboration* and *team* but what brought them to you were *numbers*, and the numbers are real people; people who rewarded you beyond cash and prestige by reading your stories and coming back to read your blog again and again and it's those people – and the real exchange you've had with them – that the brands want access to. (October 10, 2014)

So the ability to attract readers is critical – and thoughtful, interesting blog content is only one way this can be done. Provocative posts and headlines (known in internet jargon as 'link bait' and 'click bait') may be written with publicity alone in mind.

Becoming a 'pro' blogger (again to use common internet parlance) is a means for home-based fathers in particular to generate some income, with work that can be fitted around their family responsibilities. As in the case of a blogger like John Adams, it can also be the logical next step for a blog that has become very popular on its own account. As he explains in a guest post for the website *inside MAN*, (provocatively titled 'How I became one of the UK's top dad bloggers') he started his blog with the sole intention of documenting his experiences as a home-based father, and to counter the 'casual sexism' he faced in this role. Then he started to write on a wider range of issues – though still retaining his family focus. And along the way, he 'learned more about blogging and the skills required to make my small corner of the Internet popular with search engines.' This was the background to his decision to 'take the blog professional' (http://www.inside-man.co.uk/2014/07/25/how-i-became-one-of-the-uks-top-dad-bloggers/).

The growth of 'professional' blogs is perhaps evidence of the general acceptance of their commercial element, and the need for bloggers to be somewhat instrumental in cultivating their readership.[23] This attitude is well reflected by UK blogger Alex Walsh. In a post titled 'Am I a pro blogger?', he jokes about the 'PR friendly' label on many blogs (and wonders about the alternative), before explaining his own position:

I don't doubt that some of the people I know who blog make an awful lot of money from it ... That's fine, I'm not criticising it at all. As long as I can read your blog and still find out things that I used to of course. You know, like stuff about you or your family. Important stuff and sort of the whole point of a blog. ... Personally I think the biggest indicator on whether someone is, for the want of a better word, 'pro,' is their motivation behind what they do. Do they have 12,000 twitter followers because they have found 12,000 like-minded people or because they can charge more for a sponsored tweet with 12,000 followers? Are any of their social media interactions, you know, *social*, or are they all just advertising for either stuff they've written or brands they promote? (January 23, 2015)

Even apart from commercial considerations, the growing focus on reader numbers – the page views, links, likes and followers that social media both facilitate and encourage – can change the blogging experience for bloggers. The 20 interested and faithful followers – in Andy Hinds' words, cited earlier, the 'people who congregate' around popular blogs – are a different community from the '12,000 Twitter followers' to which Alex Walsh refers. The difference, according to Rettberg (2014) represents the difference between strong and weak ties – the distinction with respect to networks and their effectiveness first described by Granovetter (1973). Granovetter's interest was in how ideas spread between communities; though he was writing decades before the advent of social media, his analysis exactly captures the function of thousands of Twitter followers in supporting campaigns and lobbying for change. But some bloggers miss the 'strong ties' that faithful followers represent. In a post reflecting on the four years he had been blogging, and the changes in the blogosphere since he started, UK blogger Ben Tipping writes:

I do miss the community feel that I experienced in the first couple of years of blogging, reading back old posts I remembered all the great bloggers I used to 'talk' to via blog comments every week, some who I realised I haven't even tweeted with for a long time ... I know people read what I write (the stats and subscriber list show that) but would love to know what they/you think also. (September 23, 2014)

Tipping is validating Chia's conclusion that 'more than hits, links or votes, bloggers appear to value a virtual pat on the back, a reassuring remark, a sincere conversation' (Chia, 2012 421).

The central dilemma is the balance between the commercial – requiring 'hits, links and votes' – and the personal. While commercial content of some kind is available now to almost any blogger, some worry about what might be lost by its inclusion. Two of the father bloggers I introduce here address this issue explicitly. At the end of three long, thoughtful posts during October, 2014 titled 'Blogging for the soul' Clint Greagen concludes:

> Despite the hours I've put in to justifying my decision to write for brands and despite the many varied motives I've settled upon from time to time ... I just haven't been able to shake the feeling, that every time I agree to a sponsored post, I'm dipping myself into a stinky brown swamp ... After all this time, I just can't see any way to feel comfortable about it. (October 7, 2014)

In a message reflecting on his blog plans for 2014, Tom Briggs writes:

> In the last year ... I think this blog lost its way a little. I've flirted with the idea of trying to become a 'name' with it and have done the product placement thing a little more than I originally intended to as well, but I'm well and truly over that. My blogging and social media time is scarce as it is, so it has to be a pleasure rather than a chore. So I guess my new year's resolution – well, my one for Diary of the Dad anyway – is for it to be a true reflection of me rather than based on how much I can make out of it. (January 4, 2014)

Fathers' blogs, like any other accounts, are unlikely to be 'true reflections,' as Briggs himself came to acknowledge. In a post 10 months later, he comments:

> The Tom I project on here [his blog] is definitely still me, albeit an edited one. He's a lot more confident and capable at the whole parenting lark than I am and is a bit wittier given the extra time he gets to ponder his thoughts before blurting them out. In truth, I keep a lot to myself for fear of presenting any shrinks who land on my blog with a field day. Sure, I openly admit to winging it and sometimes even write about my feelings, but you should see the stuff that goes through my head and doesn't make the cut! Think about the bit of the swan you don't see as it seems to effortlessly glide across water and you get the idea. (November 12, 2014)

Briggs' comment is a salutary reminder about how all blogs should be read. The fathering practices and experiences that are my focus here are particular representations, shaped by the demands of the medium. But as the blogs I have considered here demonstrate, they are the work of fathers who are *thinking about* the kind of fathering they are doing, and the model of fathering to which they aspire – regardless of how they are organized or funded. Andy Hinds writes:

> [B]logging has, in a weird way, kept me accountable as a parent. Not like I don't omit a lot of stories about my worst moments, or embellish the ones about my best. However, having this compulsion to report on my own progress does keep me, if not honest, at least self-vigilant. (March 1, 2012)

In other words, blogging about fathering produces a *consciousness* about fathering that is unrelated to whether or not a blog is 'professionalized.' And this too has consequences. By claiming public identities as fathers, by communicating their ideas about fathering to a more or less extensive audience, and by their ready online accessibility, father bloggers are increasingly being positioned as parenting experts, on call to comment whenever a father's voice is needed. They are becoming professionalized *as fathers*. Father bloggers are increasingly making appearances in the mainstream media, as well as in the blogosphere – in some cases as regular contributors. For example, Canadian father blogger Kenny Bodanis is a frequent guest on his city's breakfast television show, where he is billed variously as a 'parenting author' or a 'parenting blogger.' Doyin Richards is on the online 'parenting team' of the US network NBC's Today Show. (In the introduction to his blog he describes himself as 'your daddy consultant,' and, as noted earlier, he is actively promoting himself as a speaker.) Of the 20 bloggers considered here, four (Bodanis, Adams, Richards and Greagan) have written books about fathering, one (Briggs) has produced an edited collection of fathers' blog posts, and Adamick and Routly have produced books for children.

The 'professional father' designation was actually specified in Canada's largest national newspaper, the *Globe and Mail*, in an online article related to Fathers' Day in 2013. The article was headed 'Need a hand, dad? Top parenting advice from 5 daddy bloggers.' The introduction continued: 'Becoming a new dad? Unsure of what to do once the baby comes? Check out what these professional fathers have to say about the wonderful world of daddyhood.' The article went on to a slide show featuring each of the bloggers, with their captioned advice – beginning with the blogger father whose advice was: 'Lean in. It is stereotypical for dads to not know how to do diapers, or care for kids … Let's be the generation that breaks the stereotype by being active, engaged fathers who aren't afraid to bottle feed, grocery shop, or put on a tea party' (Hernandez-Rassavong, 2013) A similar article in 2014 was headed 'From five dads to another: Top parenting tips from these daddy bloggers' (Hernandez-Rassavong, 2014).

The fact that it was father bloggers who were positioned as the 'professional fathers' able to give 'top parenting advice' must have come partly from their accessibility online, and from the recognition that these would (therefore) be fathers who would not be shy about expressing their opinions in another public forum. But it must also have been due to their self-positioning as experienced and committed fathers. So it is worth revisiting the images of fathering their blogs display, and the broader message about fathering and masculinity that fathers' blogs may be communicating.

## Fathers' blogs, masculinity and social change

With respect to the image of fathering collectively reflected in the blogs discussed here, I suggest that there were many signs of change. From the daily detail of hands-on caregiving to the juggling of paid work and family responsibilities that were reported, traditional 'fathering' was not much in view. Instead, as I have noted, these fathers explicitly positioned themselves as engaged, hands-on caregivers – either through matter-of-fact descriptions of their practices, advice to other fathers, or thoughtful position statements. The message that this fathering represented a new kind of masculinity was also clear.

There is also no doubt that this message is now being disseminated widely. Setting aside for now the fact that both bloggers and their readers are on the privileged side of the digital divide – and bearing in mind also the impossibility of accurately quantifying their reach – the number of fathers' blogs is certainly increasing, along with an exponential growth in their readership. The attentiveness of this readership is also impossible to estimate. As noted earlier a blog's '12,000 Twitter followers' may not be the best estimate of its influence. But bloggers' successful lobbying on a variety of father-related issues, and their growing presence as 'professional fathers' – giving media interviews, speaking at conferences, and writing books – suggest they have made a significant contribution to a cultural shift in ideas about fathering. If fathers' involved, embodied caregiving is becoming entrenched as normative, father bloggers can take some credit.

Blogging about fathering also provides social support for father bloggers. Online, however many followers they interact with, they have each other. And as I noted earlier, the online community leads to real-world gatherings that they find extremely helpful. In fact, the social spin-offs of blogging may be among its most innovative outcomes, for fathers seeking affirmation for their fathering involvement.

As a format, as I have noted earlier, blogs are unique in their capacity to communicate experience. I often felt, at the end of my reading of a year or more of posts, that I had come to 'know' the writer. I needed to remind myself that what I was reading, seeing (and sometimes hearing) collectively contributed to a particular *representation* of fathering that might not necessarily have told the whole story. But the story in the blog was often unusually compelling.

Though entries are always retrospective in that, like memoirs, they too describe past events, the 'past' is very recent. What is distinctive about many blogs is their sheer 'dailyness.' with ups and downs reported in close to 'real' time, and in ways that may speak directly to the experiences of other readers.

What linked those I describe here was a common interest in involved fathering, but they were also interesting for what they did not share. These bloggers represented a variety of domestic circumstances. Though it was seldom spelled out, there were also obvious differences in educational background and, not surprisingly, literary skill. Personality differences were also quite apparent, as were individual tastes and talents – some fathers were keen cooks, others were lovers of the outdoors, others were devotees of music genres or sporting teams. All these differences shaped what was on offer in each blog. Across the range, though, there was material that would engage any interested reader – from matter-of-fact accounts (like those of Michael Cusden) on putting a baby to sleep, to reflections on fathers' representation in advertising (like those of Chris Routly) to beautifully written pieces expressing fathers' love for their children (and often, their partners) like those of Clint Greagen.

To write about blogging, however, is to write about a phenomenon that is far from stable. One of the changes that blogs are undergoing, described earlier, is their increasing commercialization. The attention being paid to fathers by many major brands has been construed as positive in that it is producing more positive images of fathers. But a less benign interpretation is that fathers, as well as mothers, are now being constructed as consumers – a message that is of course also being communicated by individual father bloggers who promote products themselves. The question is whether the commercial message diminishes the blogs as 'social influencers' in the more progressive sense. Certainly among the bloggers I have introduced here, there seems to be enough commitment to the positive 'social influencer' role that it will not disappear. But many of these bloggers will retire from the field as their children get older. Younger fathers will enter a different blogging world.

This links to another change – the growing use of social media like Facebook and Twitter, which are becoming alternative, 'micro-blogging' formats. It could be that blogs as we have known them will be casualties – a passing phenomenon in a rapidly changing technological environment. If that is the case, then the work of the bloggers I have introduced here is all the more significant, for the image of fathering they have helped to promote.

# Part IV
# Joining the Threads

## Introduction

In this final section I pull together the threads of a research undertaking that, like most such undertakings, has gone in some unanticipated directions. It was, in short, a project that grew, in ways that have pushed me to address new questions about fathering, caregiving and masculinity.

In the early pages of this book, I announced my intention to explore a phenomenon that had received little scholarly attention: fathers providing hands-on, embodied care to babies and young children. I noted many reasons why this had not been a focus – most of them linking to entrenched ideas about fathers and masculinity that diverted attention from men as caregivers. I also noted my reasons for pursuing the topic, based on previous research that not only showed me how competent fathers could be as caregivers, but also what some of the consequences of this caregiving could be. The men in my earlier study were confident engaged fathers who seemed to enjoy close relationships with their children and equitable relationships with their partners. And most had started their hands-on caregiving right from the birth of their children. I was persuaded that some close attention to fathers as caregivers – and in particular to those caring for babies and young children – was a worthy focus, particularly since changes in parental leave policies made this option much more of a possibility in Canada.

My interest in fathers' caregiving, and the sense that the earlier in a child's life it began the better, launched me on a study of fathers taking parental leave that became the first phase of the research described in this book. With Doucet (2013) I could say that I did not begin with the goal of studying embodiment; as I noted in the introduction to

Part I, my plan was to visit fathers during the course of their leave, ask them in general terms about the experience of the leave, the challenges of engaging with this new kind of work, and whether it shaped their thinking about their paid employment. It was only in *watching* them as they cared for their babies that I was struck by the extent to which this work was embodied. Its embodiment, furthermore, seemed to matter. Fathers' hands-on caregiving was also, as I then discovered, a dimension of masculine embodiment, and of fathering, which was almost entirely missing from scholarly research.

In hoping to address this gap, my goals were straightforward: I wanted to explore the phenomenon of fathers' embodied caregiving as *practice* – in other words, I wanted to look closely at what they were doing – and as *experience* – I wanted to know what it was like for them to be a baby's caregiver. I started close to home, with Canadian fathers. I watched a group of fathers as they went about their caregiving tasks, at home on parental leave, and I talked to more of them who reflected on the leave time they too had taken, some time in the past, to care for babies. Then, broadening my focus both methodologically and geographically, I added accounts of another kind – memoirs written by fathers. Finally, tapping into a lively contemporary resource, I added a series of fathers' blogs.

This turned out to be an interesting scholarly journey, during which I encountered 62 caregiving fathers. I interacted with them in different ways: by sitting in their kitchens watching them at work, by talking to them in coffee shops, at their workplaces, or over the phone, and by reading about their experiences in book or blog form. All were different kinds of 'knowing,' based on different kinds of accounts. In the introductions to Parts II and III, I have described how I went about analyzing these different sources of material.

My conclusion, at the end of the journey, was that these accounts differed more in level of detail and style of delivery than in form. Connidis, reflecting on her own use of interview and memoir material, reminds us that interviews, like memoirs, are also constructions (even if the circumstances of that construction differ). Blogs are constructions too. Connidis' view is that using narratives from various sources 'may prove helpful in deepening our understanding ... ' (Connidis, 2012: 107). As I will demonstrate in more detail in the next chapter, the three narrative forms I draw on had just this effect.

Another outcome of my work on all three sources was my sense of all of these men – interviewees, writers and bloggers – as fathers with a lot in common. The common ground emerged across all types of accounts, and linked to my focus on the practices of embodied care, and how it was experienced. In short, they were doing the same kind of work, and experiencing it in similar ways. Memoir writer Elisha Cooper's description of a day at home with Zoë would have resonated with most of the caregiving fathers I interviewed. Memoir writer Ben Robertson would have understood very well what blogger Simon Ragoonanan meant by the 'mum hub.' Ben, one of the Canadian fathers who talked about days when his patience wore thin, would have understood blogger John Kinnear's description of a bad evening with his daughter. There were employed fathers struggling with work-family balance, and home-based caregivers challenging stereotypes about fathers and masculinity in each of the three groups.

Of course, they had many other things in common. One of the reasons why I have up to now unproblematically combined accounts of fathers from Canada, the UK, the US and Australia is that, demographically, they share many characteristics. Most are white, well-educated, middle-class heterosexual men. They are living in Western countries with globalized post-industrial economies, in which cultural understandings about fathering, and indeed most of the circumstances of work and family life, are shared.[1] This was, in short, a privileged group of fathers – but their status homogeneity was the price I was willing to pay for their expertise. Men on parental leave were an obvious source of information about fathers' embodied caregiving of babies – even though parental leave is available only to a select group of men (those who are eligible by virtue of their ongoing employment, and those who can afford to sacrifice a sizeable proportion of their income for the period of the leave). Memoir writers require a level of education and literacy not universally shared. Bloggers require digital access and social media skills, along with writing skills. All the fathers I have introduced here had advantages that many other groups of fathers did not. But they were the fathers best positioned to help me address my research questions. As I show in Chapter 6, their accounts served this purpose, and addressed some new issues as well.

# 6
# Fathers, Caregiving and Social Change

The scholarly journey I outlined in the introduction to this section had three stages – visits and interviews with fathers, research on fathers' memoirs, and research on fathers' blogs. The stages were more or less sequential, and each one produced new understandings and new questions.

As I also noted earlier, I wanted to explore the phenomenon of fathers' embodied caregiving as *practice* – in other words, I wanted to look closely at what fathers were doing – and as *experience*. In focusing on this seldom studied phenomenon, I saw the important first step as actually documenting it. I thought, as I noted in Chapter 1, that it needed to be described before it could be deconstructed. So in my visits to the fathers currently on leave, I first set out to establish a benchmark for what, in most circumstances, fathers' embodied caregiving to babies would look like – the 'practice' part of my research undertaking. To explore fathers' *experience* of this caregiving, I turned to my interviews with another group of fathers – those who had taken parental leave some time in the past to care for babies.

Fathers' accounts of this time with their babies, described in Part II of the book, collectively suggested three major outcomes. The first was that they developed strong attachments to the child(ren) who had been the focus of their caregiving. These were attachments that were formed directly between father and child, and were the result of the time the fathers had invested in daily, hands-on care. These fathers were not outsourcing the labour of caregiving, and reserving for themselves only the intimate moments; they were doing the work. In the doing – the second outcome I identified – caregiving became visible to them as work, and made them appreciative of others who also did it. In most cases, it was different from any work they had done before, and it was not always easy. Alone at home, or venturing into a public world not often well set up for fathers and babies, their days were ruled by babies' schedules, and they learned to do what was needed to meet their babies' needs. In this sense, especially if the baby in their care was a firstborn, the leave time constituted an apprenticeship, and gave them a repertoire of skills they could use on an ongoing basis. The third outcome, a logical consequence of the first two, was that learning how to care changed their thinking, not only about family relationships, but also about paid work. Their accounts suggested the leave time was memorable for allowing them the experience of coming to know their babies, and to support their partners in the process. Taking the leave also constituted a challenge to masculinist workplace norms about men as workers. All these outcomes, taken together, suggested the sort of re-visioning of care, fathering and masculinity that earlier research had predicted.

The accounts of the fathers I interviewed also allowed me to address the issue raised by Doucet (2009a: 113), about the nature and significance of fathers' caregiving in a baby's first year – a time when biological and social differences between women and men might tend to sideline fathers. There were many who, as one of them put it, were doing 'everything but breastfeeding' as they cared for babies in the early months. In some cases, where mothers needed extra help, fathers' caregiving was not so secondary.

I turned to the memoirs as a further, and more diverse, source of fathers' accounts of embodied caregiving. Memoir writers Michael Lewis and Elisha Cooper described caring for babies and young children in circumstances similar to those of the Canadian fathers I had interviewed. Ian Brown and George Estreich described caring for children with special needs. Matthew Logelin, Ian Newbold and Dan Bucatinsky described caregiving without the presence of mothers. Ben Robertson wrote as a home-based primary caregiver. These accounts, with their rich descriptions of embodied care, conformed to my benchmark and in some cases surpassed it. They also confirmed, implicitly or explicitly, the connection the interviewees had made between the kind of embodied caregiving they were doing, and the bonds they developed with the children in their care. The memoir writers were also able to provide more considered reflection about how they situated themselves as fathers, and as men, in terms of what they understood to be dominant understandings of fatherhood. In most cases they too saw themselves as reframing conventional understandings of fathering and masculinity by the sort of caregiving they were undertaking.

In Chapter 1 I noted the two theoretical understandings that guided this research. The first was that embodied caregiving involves techniques that are *learned*. Fathers bring particular physical capital to their caregiving, learn the 'body techniques' needed for the work, and become competent with practice. The second understanding was that when fathers do become competent caregivers to very young children, they become different kinds of fathers. In Chapter 1 I described a variety of ways this difference could be described: they would be 'doing gender' differently (West and Zimmerman, 1987) through the construction of new configurations of practice (Connell, 2005). Or their caregiving could be seen as a disruption of the gendered habitus that would otherwise predispose them to more conventional gendered behaviour (Bourdieu, 2000).

On the basis of the accounts in the interviews and memoirs, it seemed clear that these two understandings were resoundingly affirmed. But in their depth and detail, the memoirs allowed me to see more clearly another dimension of fathers' caregiving that also appeared in some of the interview accounts: the effects of fathers' embodied caregiving as both *personal* and *social*. In the memoirs, the distinction came through in Elisha Cooper's growing bond with his daughter Zoë, his realization that 'it is as if Zoë has always been with me,' and at the same time, his awareness that his style of fathering is not the model he sees much of in the real world. It came through in Ben Robertson's stark differentiation between his work at home, where he relishes his growing expertise as his baby's primary caregiver, and his painful struggles with the role reversal that positions his wife as the family breadwinner. In the introduction to Part I, I noted Lupton's (2012) description of *interembodiment* – the relational dimension of embodiment, and the intimate relationships between infants and their caregivers that result. I also noted Connell's (2005) discussion of men's *re-embodiment* as it might happen in the course of infant caregiving. It seemed clear that all these fathers were experiencing the interembodiment produced through their caregiving, and they were becoming re-embodied in the process. At the level of father and baby, the transformative effect of embodied caregiving on fathers was unequivocal. The real question was how it played out in public.

As it turned out, the accounts of the father bloggers were an excellent resource to address this question. As Chapter 5 makes clear, fathers' blog posts, like the memoir and interview accounts, added to the rich detail already assembled on fathers' practices of embodied caregiving, and the bonds with children that ensued. In that sense, they confirmed what was becoming the main message of the research so far: fathers' competence in the embodied work of caring for children, the value of the work for relationships with children (and partners), and the reframing both of fathering and masculinity that followed. Here too were 're-embodied' fathers, deeply engaged in their caregiving work. But these were also, for the most part, fathers with a mission – not only to practise this new form of fathering and masculinity, but to proclaim it publicly. Blogs as a medium are public in a way that even published memoirs are not. So the potential for father bloggers to be 'social influencers' was an important part of the discussion in Chapter 5. There I noted their wide – and growing – readership, and their potential to mobilize around issues of importance to fathers, often through challenges to stereotypical public representations. The take-up of their messages about engaged fathering, by major advertisers, and also conventional media, are powerful and ongoing signs of social change.

My reading of the blogs confirmed my sense of fathers' embodied caregiving as having both personal and social dimensions. The personal encompassed not only the father-child connection, but extended to relationships with partners as well. It was the dimension that, from their accounts, was largely unproblematic. They cared for their children, developed strong bonds with them, and (in most cases) seemed to have mutually supportive relationships with their partners. In the family context, they viewed themselves unambiguously as fathers, and as men. And they considered their caregiving work to be *parenting*. As I noted in Chapter 5, sometimes they did it *like* men, but always they did it *as* men. *As* men – especially men who were primary caregivers – it was the public, social, dimension of their work that was more likely to be a challenge.

Like the fathers I am citing, and as I have noted in earlier chapters, I too consider that family work, when it is shared without attention to the gender of the person undertaking it, should be called 'parenting.' But it is a label that needs to be used with care. In earlier research, I made the point that 'parenting' was conventionally used as 'an ostensibly gender-neutral label for childcare practices that are generally assumed to be carried out by mothers' (Ranson, 2010: 173). Now, however, I think enough fathers have appropriated it that the term is losing this connotation. At the same time, as Ruddick (1997) warns, it is important to ensure that 'parenting' in its degendered sense doesn't lose sight of the gendered contributions that fathers, as well as mothers, bring to the job. Parenting 'like a man' is one way to get around this problem. It suggests differences of style, but not necessarily of substance, in the practice of parenting. But parenting 'as a man' shifts the discussion to more controversial gender turf. It risks raising, once again, the comparisons between fathers' caregiving and mothers' caregiving that I addressed in the previous chapter, in my analysis of fathers' blogs.

The father bloggers were generally agreed that the importance of establishing fathers' competence as caregivers was not because men wanted to acquire yet more privilege, but because men's sharing of caregiving work was necessary to the achievement of gender equality. With the exception of memoir writers Logelin and Newbold, who were widowed, all the other fathers I have introduced in earlier chapters were sharing the caregiving work with partners, in ways that worked for both. A high proportion had taken on solo caregiving (as parental leave, or as home-based primary caregiving) explicitly to support their wives' careers. Each had become, in the process, a new kind of father, and so, inevitably, a different kind of man. In Messerschmidt's terms, these fathers might collectively be producing 'equality masculinities' (defined as legitimating 'an egalitarian relationship between women and men, between masculinity and femininity, and among men' (Messerschmidt, 2012: 73).

There are both personal and social dimensions to this reframing of masculinity also. At the personal level, Bourdieu's description, cited earlier, of gendered habitus disrupted, is one way to account for the change in fathers as individuals. In social terms, to draw on both Connell (2005) and West and Zimmerman (1987) a reframing of masculinity is evident in changing configurations of practice as individual fathers 'do gender' differently. I have suggested that the personal transformations resulting from fathers' embodied caregiving are generally unambiguous, and unequivocal. The social changes that might be anticipated are, inevitably, slower to emerge.

But this is not to say that change of the kind to which caregiving fathers are contributing is not happening. I repeat a conclusion from my earlier research (Ranson, 2010) that, in Sullivan's terms, it is 'a slow dripping of change' that may be 'unnoticeable from year to year' but that 'in the end is persistent enough to lead to the slow dissolution of previously existing structures' (Sullivan, 2006: 15–16). It is evident in the shifts in popular discourse that father bloggers and others have been working to produce. It is also evident in policies intended to increase the opportunities for fathers to participate in caring for babies. The Canadian fathers introduced here, almost all of whom were taking or had taken several months of parental leave, are an important model for the changes in fathering that such early involvement in caregiving can produce. Policy changes effective from April 2015 promise to give eligible UK fathers similar opportunities.[1]

The accounts of all the fathers introduced in earlier chapters have resoundingly demonstrated that fathers can be competent providers of hands-on, embodied care to babies and young children. In the process of learning what to do, they become 're-embodied' as men, and engaged, committed fathers, likely to remain involved for the long haul.

I view this as a desirable outcome. Like the fathers I have cited, I too view fathers' sharing of caregiving as essential for gender equity – not through the imposition of a particular division of labour on parents, but to provide more choice and opportunity, for fathers and for mothers too.

# Appendix: Details of Interviewees

## Introduced in Chapter 2

*Robert*[1] was a 34-year-old software engineer. He took two months of parental leave right after his baby's birth, to supplement the care provided by his wife, who was self-employed and therefore did not qualify for maternity leave. She worked from home on a part-time basis during the time Robert was on leave.

*Greg* was a 36-year-old warehouse supervisor who took a full eight months of parental leave, starting when his baby was born. His wife was also self-employed and did not qualify for maternity leave. She too worked from home, on a close to full-time basis, while Greg was on leave.

*Terry* was a 47-year-old graphic designer, who also took a full eight months of leave from his job, starting after his wife returned to her full-time job when their baby was four months old. Terry planned to quit his job at the end of his parental leave, and become a full-time caregiver to the baby.

*Drew* was a 38-year-old engineering manager. He started a six-month leave after his wife returned to her full-time job when their baby was six months old.

*Douglas* was a 35-year-old construction worker. He took a nine-month leave that started when his baby was three months old. His wife, who had taken the first three months of leave, was employed full-time, but did most of her work from home. Douglas also had a teenage daughter from an earlier relationship, in whose care he had participated.

*Jason* was a 35-year-old research technologist. He took a four-month leave after his wife returned to work when their baby was eight months old.

*Steve* was a 34-year-old former high school math teacher. He took a six-month parental leave after his wife returned to work when their first baby was six months old. When his leave ended, Steve resigned from his job, and became a stay-at-home primary caregiver – a role which he was continuing with the birth of their second baby nearly four years later.

When we met, he was about to resume sole day-time charge of both children on his wife's return to work after a two-month leave.

*Tony* was a 37-year-old high school English teacher. He started an eight-month parental leave on his wife's return to full-time work when their baby was four months old.

*Simon* was a 35-year-old art director. Having been self-employed, he didn't qualify for parental leave, so left his full-time job when their baby was six months old in order to share caregiving with his wife during the remaining six months of her parental leave. When their baby was a year old, his wife returned to her full-time job and Simon continued as primary home-based caregiver – a role he had carried out for nearly six months when we met.

*John* was a 34-year-old elementary school teacher, and the father of two children. He had taken a two-month parental leave with his first child. When we met he had just started a six-month leave after his wife returned to work, when their second child was six months old, and the first child was two.

*Paul* was a 32-year-old freelance journalist. Ineligible for parental leave, he had greatly reduced his working time to become a full-time home-based caregiver. He assumed this role after his wife's leave ended and she resumed her full-time job when their baby was three months old.

*Max* was a 36-year-old former IT project manager, who had taken a six-month parental leave when his wife returned to full-time employment seven months after their baby was born. When his leave ended, Max resigned from his job to become a full-time home-based caregiver, a role he had been filling for about a year when we met.

*Martin* was a 35-year-old senior environmental health official. He started an eight-month parental leave after his wife returned to full-time employment when their baby was four months old.

## Introduced in Chapter 3

*Will* was a 41-year-old public sector auditor, who took a three-month parental leave to be the solo caregiver to his first child, aged three months when the leave started. When interviewed, his two children were aged seven and three.

*Laurence* was a 40-year-old accountant, who took a two-month leave, while his wife was also home, when his second child was a newborn.

He later became a full-time home-based caregiver, while also doing some part-time consulting work. When we met, his children were seven and five.

*Aidan* was a 37-year-old salesman, and the father of three children.[2] He took a nine-month leave, with his wife also at home, when his second child was born.

*Jim*[3] was the father of two children, aged nearly four and 18 months when he was interviewed. He took a year of unpaid leave to care for his first child when his wife returned to her full-time job. She had taken the full year of parental leave.

*Lucas* was a 32-year-old bank manager who took four months of parental leave as a solo caregiver on his wife's return to her full-time employment when his first child was eight months old. At the time of the interview, the child was nearly two, and was an only child.

*Rick* was a 49-year-old instrumentation technologist, interviewed when his only child was five. He took a total of five months of parental leave – the first four months when his child was a newborn, and the fifth month when his child was 11 months old. His wife was also at home.

*Alan* was a 35-year-old maintenance technician who took three months of parental leave when his first child was four months old, and four months when his second child was a newborn. In both cases his wife was also at home. At the time he was interviewed, the children were aged five and two.

*Charlie* was a 35-year-old engineer and the father of two children, aged three and 14 months at the time he was interviewed. Charlie had taken six months of leave when his first child was six months old, and five months of leave when his second child was seven months old. In both cases, his wife had returned to her full-time employment and he was a solo caregiver.

*Brian* was a 42-year-old research technologist, and the father of one child, aged five at the time of the interview. He took a three-month parental leave after his wife returned to full-time employment when his child was nine months old, and then extended his time away for another four months of unpaid leave.

*Tyler* was a 48-year-old plant operator, and the father of one child, one year old at the time of the interview. He took a three-month leave, with his wife also at home, when they adopted their child as a three-month-old.

*Ben* was a 35-year-old software developer, and the father of one child, aged two at the time of the interview. He took a five-month leave as a solo caregiver after his wife returned to her paid employment when the child was six months old.

*Mike* was a 33-year-old construction worker, and the father of two children aged seven and two at the time of the interview. For both children, he took nine months of leave to be a solo caregiver on his wife's return to her paid employment. The first child was one month old, and the second was three months old, at the time of each leave.

*Jeremy* was a 44-year-old senior manager, with two children, aged three and one at the time of the interview. He took six months of leave with his first child, and five months with his second, in each case when the baby was born. His wife was at home during both leaves.

*Harjeet* was a 37-year-old systems analyst, and the father of one child aged two-and-a-half at the time of the interview. He took a parental leave of five-and-a-half months to be a solo caregiver on his wife's return to her full-time employment when the child was six-and-a-half months old.

*Ross* was a 35-year-old engineer, and the father of two children, aged three-and-a-half and one at the time of the interview. His wife returned to her full-time employment when the second child was four months old. Ross took four-and-a-half months of parental leave as a solo caregiver.

*Vijay* was a 33-year-old transit employee, and the father of a child who was 20 months old at the time of the interview. He took a four-month leave, with his wife, who was not in paid employment when the child was nine months old. Vijay and his wife used his leave time to visit family in India.

*Keith* was a 35-year-old senior programmer, and the father of four adopted children aged eight, six, four and 14 months. He took six weeks of parental leave, with his wife also at home, on the arrival of the first two children (siblings aged three and two), and another six weeks when the third child, aged seven months, joined the family.

*David* was a 42-year-old nurse. At the time of the interview, his two children were aged eight and 10 months. He had taken a four-month parental leave when his first child was a newborn, and one month when his second child was born. For both leaves, his wife was also at home.

*Mehtab* was a 41-year-old IT manager, and the father of two children aged five and two months at the time of the interview. He had taken 11 months of leave when his first child was one month old. His wife returned to her full-time employment when the baby was three months old, leaving Mehtab as the solo caregiver.

*Derek* was a 29-year-old operations foreman, the father of one child who was two at the time of the interview. He took eight months of leave after his wife's return to her paid employment when the baby was three months old. He was a solo caregiver during his leave.

*Barry* was a 35-year-old physician, and the father of three children aged four, two and one month at the time of the interview. He took six months of parental leave when his first child was two months old, and four months of leave when the second was three months old. On both occasions, his wife was also home.

# Notes

## Part I   Setting the Scene

1. To make his case, Hamington draws on the work of Merleau-Ponty, cited in more detail in the next chapter, and also on Carol Gilligan's understanding of 'care ethics' (Gilligan, 1982). He argues, in short, that men who learn to care also develop an ethic of care.
2. The two were *The Boy in the Moon* by Ian Brown (2009), and *Home Game, by* Michael Lewis (2009), both of which are discussed in detail in Chapter 4.
3. I discuss these challenges in more detail in later chapters.
4. 'Similarly situated' is a critical qualifier. I am of course aware of the somewhat privileged homogeneity of my sample, and address the issue more directly later in the book.

## 1   Research Context

1. Miller (2011b) describes her own use of the term 'caring' to refer to 'men's description of meeting the needs of a new and growing baby through hands-on practices, activities and emotional thinking, commitment and responsibilities' (Miller, 2011b: 5). She notes alternative descriptors such as 'nurturing' or 'involvement.'
2. While just over 90 per cent of women with pre-school children reported doing primary child care both in 1986 and in 2005, men's involvement jumped from 57 per cent to 73 per cent. There was a corresponding increase in the amount of time they spent caring for children (Marshall, 2006).
3. Since its original articulation by Connell, the concept of hegemonic masculinity has been widely taken up in gender research, and has also been the subject of considerable critique and refinement. Connell and Messerschmidt, in the article significantly titled 'Hegemonic masculinity: Rethinking the concept,' suggest their own reformulation in the light of others' (re)theorizing. They also note, 'The importance of masculine embodiment for identity and behavior emerges in many contexts' (p. 851).
4. Messerschmidt (2012) in a further elaboration, introduces two forms of masculinity which involve power relations among men: dominant masculinities, which involve 'the most celebrated, common or current forms of masculinity in a specific social setting' (p. 72), and dominating masculinities (which involve the exercise of power and control.) These masculinities are only *hegemonic* if they also legitimate hierarchical relations between women and men – an essential part of the Connell and Messerschmidt reformulation of hegemonic masculinity. Demonstrating hegemony is, as Messerschmidt also points out, a complicated exercise, and not necessary for my purposes. Unless I am quoting another source directly, I prefer to speak of 'dominant' masculinities.

5. As Gavanas (2004) found in her study of conservative fatherhood politics in the US fatherhood responsibility movement, an essentialist view of a caring father poses a dilemma for such groups, since it requires both the 'masculinizing of domesticity' and the 'domesticating of masculinity.'

6. Solomon's US study in fact suggested none of the ambiguity and nuance about caregiving experience that Doucet's study of home-based caregivers indicated. It is important to note that Solomon's study was much smaller, involving only 26 US fathers, who were all 'middle and upper-class straight white males' (p. 56). Doucet's Canadian research involved more than 200 fathers, who were much more diverse in terms of class, race/ethnicity, sexual orientation and domestic circumstances.

7. Research on men who do perform caregiving as a component of their paid employment mainly focuses on men in nursing. Here too, men are found to distance themselves from the feminine, by reframing their caring work in more masculine terms – for example strength in lifting, or in subduing violent patients, or an affinity for the high-tech elements of specialties like emergency care (Williams, 1989; Dahle, 2005) – or achieving distance in a more literal sense by taking the 'glass escalator' to management positions removed from direct care (Williams, 1992).

8. Gabb (2012) notes that these perceptions of men's bodies as dangerous shape everyday practices of father-child intimacy also. She writes, 'Paradoxically, while physical and emotional closeness is being encouraged at the social level, as part of healthy fatherhood, the *innocence* of publicly displayed relationships between men and children (fathers and offspring) remains a source of cultural apprehension' (p. 646, emphasis in original).

9. Twigg's reference to the absence of research on embodiment in specific occupations highlights another lack of convergence – between sociological studies of the body, and of paid employment. Wolkowitz (2006) notes the scant research within the sociology of work on embodied approaches that are 'concerned with how it feels to be embodied.' She finds even less attention paid to employment in sociological studies of the body (p. 16). Monaghan (2002) and Hockey (2009) are exemplary in combining the two fields.

10. The sub-title of *Body and Soul,* Wacquant's ethnography of boxing, is *Notebooks of an apprentice boxer* (Wacquant, 2004). See also Mauss (1973), Silva (2005).

11. I am grateful to Liza McCoy for pointing out this connection and its implications.

## Part II   Seeing and Hearing Fathers

1. Living and working in Canada, they had access to shared parental leave provisions which are, considered in a global context, relatively generous. Since December 2000 the federal Employment Insurance Act has offered a year of paid parental leave to eligible parents; fathers can share up to 35 weeks at 55 per cent of average earnings up to a ceiling of $49,500. Fathers' uptake of the leave has been slow; the proportion has hovered around 10 per cent of eligible fathers over recent years – though in 2013 an estimated 12.2 per cent had

claimed or were planning to claim leave. The province of Quebec opted out of the federal plan in 2006, and introduced its own Parental Insurance Plan. This plan offers more generous benefits than the federal plan, and includes three to five weeks of non-transferable paternity leave – the 'daddy weeks' also available in some Scandinavian countries, notably Norway. Not surprisingly, there has been a much greater uptake of leave by Quebec fathers – some 83 per cent of eligible fathers took leave in 2013. All the fathers described in Part II were living outside Quebec, and therefore were subject to the federal act.

2. One exception was a father who had taken six weeks of leave, on two separate occasions, to accommodate the adoption of two sets of infant and preschool-age siblings. The second was a father whose wife took the full year of paid parental leave with their first child. He took a full year of unpaid leave when she returned to work. An exception of a different kind was the father who took two months of parental leave, returned to work, and then resigned from his job to work part-time from home while acting as his children's primary caregiver. I felt the circumstances in all cases were sufficiently illuminating to warrant their inclusion in the study.

3. One father was doing part-time contract work at home, and was acting as the primary caregiver for two school-aged children.

## 2 'Everything but Breastfeeding'

1. More information on all the fathers introduced in this chapter and the next is provided in the Appendix.

2. Of course this is not the case for all fathers. But it is the case for many fathers, especially in comparison to the mothers of their children, as exemplified by the participants in this study.

3. These practices are clearly widespread. An online search using 'father-baby exercising' as a search term produced more than 70 million references.

4. The phenomenon of 'baby signing,' which uses modified gestures from American Sign Language, has made its way into many contemporary Canadian childrearing programs.

5. Many of the contemporary toys designed to entertain children as they sat, or practised standing, or lay on a mat on the floor, came equipped with push-button music (along with lights and other sounds).

6. The widespread use of baby monitors links to Lupton's observation that the infant body is 'culturally primed for intense and constant surveillance on the part of its anxious parents' (Lupton, 2012: 45)

7. 'Sleep training' by allowing babies to cry while adjusting to being put down to sleep in their own beds is a contentious parenting issue currently. Paul and his partner opted for sleep training, but other parents were more inclined to the philosophy of 'attachment parenting,' which opposes the practice of leaving children to cry.

8. A study published in the *Journal of the American Medical Association* (Paulson and Bazemore, 2010) estimates that about 10 per cent of fathers may experience some prenatal or postpartum depression, and that the incidence is higher in the 3–6-month postpartum period.

## 3 'It's a Whole New Level'

1. Vijay joked that during the visit, he had to compete for the chance even to hold the baby. But after their return to Canada, Vijay's wife started a job. They began to work alternating shifts so that their baby, by then a year old, could have exclusively parental care. Vijay's arrears of caregiving were very soon made up.
2. I have made multiple references to fathers bottle-feeding breast milk to babies. These passing references have not acknowledged the time-consuming and often painful work of pumping breast milk that mothers undertake to make it possible.
3. Mehtab actually started his leave when his baby was a month old. For the next two months, his partner was also at home. Then she returned to work, leaving him in sole charge, when the baby was three months old.
4. For some fathers, the parental leave was not merely an apprenticeship in caregiving, but the opportunity to develop a relationship with a specific child. These fathers, like Jeremy, introduced earlier, saw taking one leave per child as an issue of fairness to each child.

## Part III Reading Fathers

1. A US magazine reviewer of one such memoir spoke of the 'sit-commy cliché' to which the writer on occasion resorted, and commented: 'You want him to go deeper than he does' (Bry, 2013). A UK newspaper reviewer, assessing a number of books on fatherhood, commented on the 'dilemma about how to approach the subject,' and concluded that the choice 'boil[ed] down to two choices: jokey or mawkish' (Lezard, 2005).
2. See for example Friedman and Calixte (2009), Lopez (2009), Friedman (2013).
3. The study by Asenhed et al. (2013) of first-time Swedish fathers' blogs is the only example I was able to find.
4. Lists like these are put out by the tracking software company Cision. Cision's list of top ten UK father bloggers for 2014 was published, with blog descriptions, in the *Daily Express* newspaper online.
5. Details of these sites are provided in Chapter 5.

## 4 'You Need to Do the Grunt Work'

1. Lewis has noted that much of the memoir first appeared as part of 'a peripatetic series in the web magazine *Slate*' (p. 189). His financial writing includes, most recently, the book *Flash Boys: A Wall Street Revolt* (Lewis, 2014).
2. L'Arche is a worldwide network of communities, founded by the Canadian humanitarian Jean Vanier, made up (according to L'Arche Calgary's website), of 'people with and without developmental disabilities, sharing life in communities belonging to an International Federation.'
3. Logelin returns to work when Madeline is six months old; Newbold has an unspecified but more extended time away from paid employment.
4. Testimonials on the memoir's back cover are provided by actors Rosie O'Donnell and Gwyneth Paltrow, among others.

5. Shonkwiler (2008) discusses in detail the political motivations of gay fathers.
6. The Australian Bureau of Statistics (2006) reports that, in 2003, families in which the father was the full-time home-based caregiver accounted for 3.4 per cent of all families with children aged 0–14.
7. The diversity is mostly limited to geographical location and domestic circumstances. The memoir writers, like the fathers I interviewed, are a privileged group – a point to which I return in later discussion.

## 5 'Making the Case for a New Kind of Manhood'

1. The expression is used with respect to internet content that is spread rapidly through a population by means of email and other social media.
2. In two cases, the children in 2014 were school-age. But information supplied on the blogs made it clear that both fathers had been active caregivers when their children were infants.
3. The one exception was a US father, employed full-time, who took parental leave to care for a second baby. I considered this background – rare in the US – was important to include.
4. All the bloggers included here appeared to be active online at the time of writing (early April, 2015), but as I note later in the chapter, the blogosphere is in a constant state of flux. I use the past tense to signal that my analysis refers only to blog material available at the time of writing.
5. My decision to use Greagen's name – and the names of all but one of the other bloggers I am introducing here – was made after careful consideration, and links to an ongoing debate about the need to respect the privacy of those (bloggers and others) who post material on the internet. The issue is that, though this material may be publicly accessible, as is the case here, its take-up by researchers may violate bloggers' own understanding of what 'public' means. When I began doing research on blogs in 2012, I agreed with scholars (for example Kozinets, 2010; Eastham, 2011; Wilkinson and Thelwall, 2011) who felt that researchers should conceal bloggers' identities. In the intervening years, however, the rapid expansion of social media as tools to promote blog material has expanded the definition of 'public' to the point where researcher scruples about confidentiality are almost irrelevant. In this research, all but one of the bloggers either provided their full name on their blogs, linked to material in which it was used, or wrote under their full name for popular sites which linked back to their blogs. The full name of only one blogger was not available through any of these methods, and (though it was in fact not hard to discover it) I have not used it. Three other considerations shaped my decision to name the bloggers. First, it was a requirement of the publisher that the blogs themselves be cited. Second, as the material to follow in the chapter will show, most of these men are, as blogger fathers, already public figures to some extent, and others aspire to be. Third, the material I draw on is not highly sensitive; further, I am using it to discuss issues they care deeply about, in a way that I am confident would meet with their approval.

6. http://www.daddyfiles.com/about/.
7. http://goodmenproject.com/featured-content/why-parent-blogging-is-exactly-like-punk-rock/ September 7, 2012.
8. James blogs only by his first name, in a blog called 'Luke, I am Your Father.' This post was found at www.liayf.blogspot.ca (January 24, 2015).
9. My practice in this chapter is to supply only the date for a post that comes from the blogger's own blog – for which the link is provided in Table 5.1. Full link details will be provided in the text for guest posts to other outlets.
10. A 'closer' in baseball is the relief pitcher who can get the last hitters out.
11. The Good Men Project is an online media company and magazine described on its website as 'a diverse community of 21st century thought leaders who are actively participating in a conversation about the way men's roles are changing in modern life—and the way those changes affect everyone.' (www.goodmenproject.com/about)
12. In a recent post (April 2, 2015) Bishop reframed his definition of 'favourite' – relating it not to the child, but to the *age* of the child. Using this criterion, his second child, now five, has become the favourite!
13. See for example the incidents reported by Australian blogger Matt Ross (www.daddownunder.com, January 13, 2014) and UK blogger Simon Ragoonanan (www.manvspink.com, July 29, 2014).
14. www.likeadad.net, February 25, 2013.
15. http://www.thedailybeast.com/articles/2014/06/17/move-over-ladies-dove-does-dads.html, June 17, 2014.
16. In this research I am considering only *posts*; fathers' *comments* on the posts of others may well be less conciliatory.
17. Similarly, Tucker (2009) comments that the core audience for mother-bloggers is other mother-bloggers.
18. Fathers' group blogs include Life of Dad (www.lifeofdad.com) in the US, dadzclub (www.dadzclub.com) in the UK, and Aussie Daddy Bloggers (www.daddybloggers.com.au) in Australia.
19. Another father blogger, not otherwise included in this analysis, commented: 'We support broads who blog, birds who tweet, fillies with followers, etc. and so on. We are one in the blogosphere. We just pee differently.' (Kevin McKeever, http://blogonkevin.blogspot.ca/, July 24, 2012).
20. Other social media, like the micro-blogging platform Tumblr, and the photo-sharing website Pinterest, are also widely used.
21. The media network CNN, and the *Washington Post* newspaper, were among many media sources reporting on the issue.
22. A note on Richards' website indicates that $5 of every $20 t-shirt purchase will be donated to Operation Homefront, a non-profit organization assisting military families.
23. Rettberg (2014) also notes the increasing acceptance of commercial blogs and social media. She cites Dean (2010) who 'uses the term "communicative capitalism" to describe the somewhat uneasy symbiosis between our love of communicating in social media and the firm hold that commercial companies have on our social media platforms … ' (Rettberg, 2014: 153).

## Part IV   Joining the Threads

1. Pleck (2013) notes the globalization of American and European cultural practices – including father involvement. Schachtner notes the effect of digital media on cultural flows – including 'values, social rules, world views and patterns of behavior' across national boundaries (Schachtner, 2015: 228).

## 6   Fathers, Caregiving and Social Change

1. Along with two weeks of paid paternity leave, and subject to various eligibility criteria, UK fathers are now able to share up to 50 weeks of leave (37 of them paid) with partners during a baby's first year of life.

## Appendix: Details of Interviewees

1. All names, and occasionally other details, have been changed to preserve the anonymity of the interviewees.
2. The ages of Aidan's children were not collected.
3. Jim's age was not collected.

# References

Andrews, Molly, Corinne Squire and Maria Tamboukou (eds). 2013. 'Introduction: What is narrative research?' In *Doing Narrative Research (2nd edition)*, edited by Molly Andrews, Corinne Squire and Maria Tamboukou. London: Sage.

Ariss, Robert, Gary W. Dowsett and Tim Carrigan. 1995. 'Health strategies of HIV-infected homosexually active men in Sydney, Australia.' *Journal of Gay and Lesbian Social Services* 3(3):49–70.

Asenhed, Liselotte, Jennie Kilstam, Siw Alehagen and Christina Baggens. 2013. 'Becoming a father is an emotional roller coaster – an analysis of first-time fathers' blogs.' *Journal of Clinical Nursing* 23:1309–17.

Ashbourne, Lynda M., Kerry J. Daly and Jaime L. Brown. 2011. 'Responsiveness in father-child relationships: The experience of fathers.' *Fathering* 9(1): 69–86.

Atkinson, Michael. 2008. 'Explaining male femininity in the "crisis": Men and cosmetic surgery.' *Body & Society* 14(1):67–87.

Australian Bureau of Statistics. 2006. 'Fathers' work and family balance.' Retrieved from http://www.abs.gov.au/AUSSTATS/abs@.nsf/7d12b0f6763c78 caca257061001cc588/acf29854f8c8509eca2571b00010329b!OpenDocument/ April 9, 2015.

Backett, Kathryn. 1987. 'The negotiation of fatherhood.' In *Reassessing Fatherhood: New Observations on Fathers and the Modern Family*, edited by Charlie Lewis and Margaret O'Brien. London: Sage.

Ball, Jessica and Kerry Daly. 2012a. 'Father involvement in Canada: A transformative approach.' In *Father Involvement in Canada: Diversity, Renewal and Transformation*, edited by Jessica Ball and Kerry Daly. Vancouver: UBC Press.

———. 2012b. 'Looking forward: Father involvement and changing forms of masculine care.' In *Father Involvement in Canada: Diversity, Renewal and Transformation*, edited by Jessica Ball and Kerry Daly. Vancouver: UBC Press.

Beck, Ulrich. 1992. *Risk Society: Towards a New Modernity*. London: Sage.

Beck, Ulrich and Elisabeth Beck-Gernsheim. 1995. *The Normal Chaos of Love*. Cambridge: Polity Press.

Beissel, Adam S., Michael Giardina and Joshua I. Newman. 2014. 'Men of steel: Social class, masculinity and cultural citizenship in post-industrial Pittsburgh.' *Sport in Society* 17(7):953–76.

Berkmann, Marcus. 2008. *Fatherhood: The Truth*. London: Vermilion.

Bianchi, Suzanne M., John P. Robinson and Melissa A. Milkie. 2006. *Changing Rhythms of American Family Life*. New York: Russell Sage Foundation.

Björk, Sofia. 2013. 'Doing morally intelligible fatherhood: Swedish fathers' accounts of their parental part-time work choices.' *Fathering* 11(2):221–37.

Bolton, Sharon C. 2005. 'Women's work, dirty work: The gynaecology nurse as "other." ' *Gender, Work and Organization* 12(2):169–86.

Bourdieu, Pierre. 1977. *Outline of a Theory of Practice*. Cambridge: Cambridge University Press.

———. 1984. *Distinction: A Social Critique of the Judgment of Taste*. London: Routledge.

———. 1990. *The Logic of Practice*. Stanford: Stanford University Press.

———. 2000. *Pascalian Meditations*. Cambridge: Polity Press.

Brandth, Berit and Elin Kvande. 1998. 'Masculinity and child care: The reconstruction of fathering.' *The Sociological Review* 46(2):293–313.

———. 2001. 'Flexible work and flexible fathers.' *Work, Employment and Society* 15(2):251–67.

———. 2002. 'Reflexive fathers: Negotiating parental leave and working life.' *Gender, Work and Organization* 9(2):186–203.

———. 2003. 'Father presence in childcare.' In *Children and the Changing Family*, edited by A.-M. Jensen and L. McKee. London: Routledge-Falmer.

———. 2009. 'Gendered or gender-neutral care politics for fathers?' *Annals of the American Academy of Political and Social Science* 624:177–89.

Brannen, Julia and Ann Nilsen. 2006. 'From fatherhood to fathering: Transmission and change among British fathers in four-generation families.' *Sociology* 40(2):335–52.

Braun, Annette, Carol Vincent and Stephen J. Ball. 2011. 'Working-class fathers and childcare: The economic and family contexts of fathering in the UK.' *Community, Work & Family* 14(1):19–37.

Brown, Ian. 2009. *The Boy in the Moon: A Father's Search for his Disabled Son*. Toronto: Random House Canada.

Bry, Dave. 2013. 'Fatherhood memoirs multiply: Bring on the daddy wars.' *New Republic*, May 13. Retrieved from www.newrepublic.com/article/113149/two-fatherhood-memoirs-reviewed-dave-bry, July 11, 2015.

Bucatinsky, Dan. 2012. *Does This Baby Make Me Look Straight? Confessions of a Gay Dad*. New York: Touchstone.

Burnett, Simon B., Caroline J. Gatrell, Cary L. Cooper and Paul Sparrow. 2013. 'Fathers at work: A ghost in the organizational machine.' *Gender, Work and Organization* 20(6):632–46.

Chabon, Michael. 2009. *Manhood For Amateurs*. New York: HarperCollins.

Chapple, Alison and Sue Ziebland. 2002. 'Prostate cancer: Embodied experience and perceptions of masculinity.' *Sociology of Health and Illness* 24(6):820–41.

Chesley, Noelle. 2011. 'Stay-at-home fathers and breadwinning mothers: Gender, couple dynamics and social change.' *Gender & Society* 25(5):642–64.

Chia, Aleena. 2012. 'Welcome to Me-Mart: The politics of user-generated content in personal blogs'. *American Behavioral Scientist* 56(4): 421–38.

Coltart, Carrie and Karen Henwood. 2012. 'On paternal subjectivity: A qualitative longitudinal and psychosocial case analysis of men's classed positions and transitions to first-time fatherhood.' *Qualitative Research* 12(1):35–52.

Connell, R.W. 1987. *Gender and Power: Society, the Person and Sexual Politics*. Cambridge: Polity Press.

———. 2005. *Masculinities (2nd edition)*. Berkeley: University of California Press.

Connell, R.W., M.D. Davis and G.W. Dowsett. 1993. 'A bastard of a life: Homosexual desire and practice among men in working-class milieux.' *Australian and New Zealand Journal of Sociology* 29(1):112–35.

Connell, R.W. and James W. Messerschmidt. 2005. 'Hegemonic masculinity: Rethinking the concept.' *Gender & Society* 19(6):829–59.

Connell, Raewyn. 2009. *Gender (2nd edition)*. Cambridge: Polity Press.

Connidis, Ingrid Arnet. 2012. 'Interview and memoir: Complementary narratives on the family ties of gay adults.' *Journal of Family Theory & Review* 4:105–21.

Cooper, Elisha. 2006. *Crawling: A Father's First Year*. New York: Anchor Books.

Craig, Lyn and Killian Mullan. 2011. 'How mothers and fathers share childcare: A cross-national time use comparison.' *American Sociological Review* 76(6):834–61.

———. 2012. 'Australian fathers' work and family time in comparative and temporal perspective.' *Journal of Family Studies* 18(2-3):165–174.

Crossley, Nick. 1995a. 'Merleau-Ponty, the elusive body and carnal sociology.' *Body & Society* 1(1):43–63.

———. 1995b. 'Body techniques, agency and intercorporeality: On Goffman's relations in public.' *Sociology* 29(1):133–49.

———. 1996. 'Body-subject/body-power: Agency, inscription and control in Foucault and Merleau-Ponty.' *Body & Society* 2(2):99–116.

———. 2001. 'The phenomenological habitus and its construction.' *Theory and Society* 30:81–120.

———. 2007. 'Researching embodiment by way of 'body techniques.' *The Sociological Review* 50(1):80–94.

Dahle, Rannveig. 2005. 'Men, bodies and nursing.' In *Gender, Bodies and Work*, edited by Berit Brandth, Elin Kvande and David Morgan. Aldershot: Ashgate.

Daly, Kerry, Lynda J. Ashbourne and Jaime Lee Brown. 2009. 'Fathers' perception of children's influence: Implications for involvement.' *Annals of the American Academy of Political and Social Science* 624:61–77.

———. 2012. 'A reorientation of worldview: Children's influence on fathers.' *Journal of Family Issues* 34(10):1401–24.

Day, Randal D. and Michael E. Lamb (eds). 2004. *Conceptualizing and Measuring Father Involvement*. Mahwah, NJ: Lawrence Erlbaum Associates.

Dean, Jodi. 2010. *Blog Theory: Feedback and Capture in the Circuits of Drive*. Cambridge: Polity Press.

Dermott, Esther. 2008. *Intimate Fatherhood: A Sociological Analysis*. Abingdon: Routledge.

DeVault, Marjorie. 1991. *Feeding the Family: The Social Organization of Caring as Gendered Work*. Chicago: University of Chicago Press.

———. 1999. 'Comfort and struggle: Emotion work in family life.' *Annals of the American Academy of Political and Social Science* 561:52–63.

Dolan, Alan. 2014. '"I've learnt what a dad should do": The interaction of masculine and fathering identities among men who attended a "dads-only" parenting program.' *Sociology* 48(4):812–28.

Doucet, Andrea. 2004a. 'Fathers and the responsibility for children: A puzzle and a tension.' *Atlantis* 28:103–14.

———. 2004b. '"It's almost like I have a job, but I don't get paid": Fathers at home reconfiguring work, care and masculinity.' *Fathering* 2:277–303.

———. 2006a. *Do Men Mother? Fathering, Care and Domestic Responsibility*. Toronto: University of Toronto Press.

———. 2006b. '"Estrogen-filled worlds": Fathers as primary caregivers and embodiment.' *The Sociological Review* 54(4):696–716.

———. 2008. '"From her side of the gossamer wall(s)": Reflexivity and relational knowing.' *Qualitative Sociology*, 31: 73–87.

———. 2009a. 'Dad and baby in the first year: Gendered responsibilities and embodiment.' *Annals of the American Academy of Political and Social Science* 624:78–98.

———. 2009b. 'Gender equality and gender differences: Parenting, habitus, and embodiment.' *Canadian Review of Sociology* 46(2):103–21.

———. 2013. 'A "choreography of becoming": Fathering, embodied care, and new materialisms.' *Canadian Review of Sociology* 50(3):284–305.

Doucet, Andrea and Natasha S. Mauthner. 2008. 'What can be known and how?: Narrated subjects and the Listening Guide.' *Qualitative Research* 8(3): 399–409.

Dowd, Nancy E. 2000. *Redefining Fatherhood*. New York: New York University Press.

Eastham, Linda A. 2011. 'Research using blogs for data: Public documents or private musings?' *Research in Nursing and Health* 34:353–61.

Eerola, Petteri and Johanna Mykkanen. 2013. 'Paternal masculinities in early fatherhood: Dominant and counter narratives by Finnish first-time fathers.' *Journal of Family Issues*. Published online before print. Oct. 10. doi: 10.1177/0192513X13505566.

Eggebeen, David S., Chris Knoester and Brandon McDaniel. 2013. 'The implications of fatherhood for men.' In *Handbook of Father Involvement: Multidisciplinary Perspectives (2nd Edition)*, edited by Natasha Cabrera and Catherine Tamis-LeMonda. New York: Routledge.

Ehrensaft, Diane. 1987. *Parenting Together*. New York: The Free Press.

Estreich, George. 2013. *The Shape of the Eye: A Memoir*. New York: Tarcher/Penguin.

Fagan, Jay, Randal Day, Michael E. Lamb and Natasha J. Cabrera. 2014. 'Should researchers conceptualize differently the dimensions of parenting for fathers and mothers?' *Journal of Family Theory and Review* 6:390–405.

Featherstone, Mike and Bryan S. Turner. 1995. 'Body & Society: An introduction.' *Body & Society* 1(1):1–12.

Finn, Mark and Karen Henwood. 2009. 'Exploring masculinities within men's identificatory imaginings of first-time fatherhood.' *British Journal of Social Psychology* 48:547–62.

Fisher, Kimberly, Muriel Egerton, Jonathan I. Gershuny and John P. Robinson. 2007. 'Gender convergence in the American Heritage Time Use Study (AHTUS).' *Social Indicators Research* 82:1–33.

Foucault, Michel. 1977. *Discipline and Punish: The Birth of the Prison*. New York: Vintage Books.

———. 1978. *The History of Sexuality*. New York: Pantheon.

Fox, Bonnie. 2009. *When Couples Become Parents: The Creation of Gender in the Transition to Parenthood*. Toronto: University of Toronto Press.

Fox, Elizabeth, Gillian Pascall and Tracey Warren. 2009. 'Work-family policies, participation, and practices: Fathers and childcare in Europe.' *Community, Work & Family* 12(3):313–26.

Frank, Arthur W. 1991. 'For a sociology of the body: An analytical review.' In *The Body: Social Process and Cultural Theory*, edited by M. Hepworth, B. Turner and M. Featherstone. London: Sage.

———. 2012a. 'Practicing dialogical narrative analysis.' In *Varieties of Narrative Analysis*, edited by James A. Holstein and Jaber F. Gubrium. Thousand Oaks: Sage.

———. 2012b. 'Conclusion: The varieties of my body: Pain, ethics and *illusio*.' In *Routledge Handbook of Body Studies*, edited by Bryan S. Turner. Abingdon: Routledge.

Friedman, May. 2013. *Mommyblogs and the Changing Face of Motherhood*. Toronto: University of Toronto Press.

Friedman, May and Shana L. Calixte (eds). 2009. *Mothering and Blogging: The Radical Act of the Mommyblog*. Toronto: Demeter Press.

Gabb, Jacqui. 2012. 'Embodying risk: Managing father-child intimacy and the display of nudity in families.' *Sociology* 47(4):639–54.

Gatrell, Caroline. 2005. *Hard Labour: The Sociology of Parenthood*. Maidenhead: Open University Press.

———. 2007. '"Whose child is it anyway?": The negotiation of paternal entitlements within marriage.' *Sociological Review* 55(2):352–72.

Gavanas, Anna. 2004. 'Domesticating masculinity and masculizing domesticity in contemporary U.S. fatherhood politics.' *Social Politics* 11(1):247–66.

Giddens, Anthony. 1991. *Modernity and Self-Identity*. Cambridge: Polity Press.

Giesler, Mark A. 2012. 'Gay fathers' negotiation of gender role strain: A qualitative inquiry.' *Fathering* 10(2):119–39.

Gillies, Val. 2009. 'Understandings and experiences of involved fathering in the United Kingdom: Exploring classed dimensions.' *Annals of the American Academy of Political and Social Science* 624:49–60.

Gilligan, Carol. 1982. *In a Different Voice: Psychological Theory and Women's Development*. Cambridge, MA: Harvard University Press.

Goffman, Erving. 1963. *Behavior in Public Places: Notes on the Social Organization of Gatherings*. New York: Free Press of Glencoe.

———. 1972. *Relations in Public: Microstudies of the Public Order*. New York: Harper Colophon.

Gottzen, Lucas and Tamar Kremer-Sadlik. 2012. 'Fatherhood and youth sports: A balancing act between care and expectations.' *Gender & Society* 26(4):639–64.

Granovetter, Mark S. 1973. 'The strength of weak ties.' *American Journal of Sociology* 78(6): 1360–1380.

Gregory, Abigail and Susan Milner. 2008. 'Fatherhood regimes and father involvement in France and the UK.' *Community, Work and Family* 11(1):61–84.

———. 2011. 'Fathers and work-life balance in France and the UK: Policy and practice.' *International Journal of Sociology and Social Policy* 31(1/2):34–52.

Grosz, Elizabeth. 1994. *Volatile Bodies: Toward a Corporeal Feminism*. Bloomington: Indiana University Press.

Halrynjo, Sigtona. 2009. 'Men's work-life conflict: Career, care and self-realization: Patterns of privileges and dilemmas.' *Gender, Work and Organization* 16(1):98–125.

Hamington, Maurice. 2001. 'A father's touch: Caring embodiment and a moral revolution.' In *Revealing Male Bodies*, edited by Nancy Tuana. Bloomington: Indiana University Press.

Hanlon, Niall. 2012. *Masculinities, Care and Equality: Identity and Nurture in Men's Lives*. London: Palgrave Macmillan.

Hawkins, Alan J., Shawn L. Christiansen, Kathryn Pond Sargent, and E. Jeffrey Hill. 1993. 'Rethinking fathers' involvement in child care: A developmental perspective.' *Journal of Family Issues* 14(4):531–49.

Hawkins, Alan J. and David C. Dollahite. 1997. 'Beyond the role-inadequacy perspective of fathering.' In *Generative Fathering: Beyond Deficit Perspectives*, edited by Alan J. Hawkins and David C. Dollahite. Thousand Oaks: Sage.

Hayton, Kavita. 2009. 'New expressions of the self: Autobiographical opportunities on the internet.' *Journal of Media Practice* 10(23):199–213.

Henwood, Karen and Joanne Procter. 2003. 'The "good father": Reading men's accounts of paternal involvement during the transition to first-time fatherhood.' *British Journal of Social Psychology* 42:337–55.

Hernandez-Rassavong, S. 2013. 'Need a hand, dad? Top parenting advice from 5 daddy bloggers'. *The Globe and Mail*, May, 21. Retrieved from http://www.theglobeandmail.com/life/parenting/fathers-day/5-daddy-bloggers-share-insight/article19146343/), April 9, 2015.

———. 2014. 'From five dads to another: Top parenting tips from these five daddy bloggers'. *The Globe and Mail*, June 13. Retrieved from http://www.theglobeandmail.com/life/parenting/fathers-day/5-daddy-bloggers-share-insight/article19146343/), April 9, 2015.

Himmelweit, Susan. 1999. 'Caring labor.' *Annals of the American Academy of Political and Social Science* 561:27–38.

Hochschild, Arlie. 1983. *The Managed Heart.* Berkeley: University of California Press.

Hockey, John. 2009. '"Switch on": Sensory work in the infantry.' *Work, Employment and Society* 23(3):477–93.

Holstein, James A. and Jaber Gubrium. 1994. 'Phenomenology, ethnomethodology, and interpretive practice.' In *Handbook of Qualitative Research*, edited by N.K. Denzin and Y.S. Lincoln. Thousand Oaks: Sage.

———. 1997. 'Active interviewing.' In *Qualitative Research: Theory, Method and Practice*, edited by D. Silverman. Thousand Oaks: Sage.

———. 2008. 'Constructionist approaches in ethnographic fieldwork.' In *Handbook of Constructionist Research*, edited by James A. Holstein and Jaber F. Gubrium. New York: Guilford Press.

———. 2012. 'Introduction: Establishing a balance.' In *Varieties of Narrative Analysis*, edited by James A. Holstein and Jaber F. Gubrium (eds) Thousand Oaks: Sage.

Holter, Øystein Gullvag. 2007. 'Men's work and family reconciliation in Europe.' *Men and Masculinities* 9(4):425–56.

———. 2012. 'Towards a new fatherhood: Fathering practices and gender equalities in recent Nordic research.' In *Fatherhood in Late Modernity*, edited by Mechtild Oechsle, Ursula Müller and Sabine Hess. Berlin: Barbara Budrich.

Hook, Jennifer L. and Christina M. Wolfe. 2012. 'New fathers? Residential fathers' time with children in four countries.' *Journal of Family Issues* 33(4):415–50.

Hookway, Nicholas. 2008. '"Entering the blogosphere": Some strategies for using blogs in social research.' *Qualitative Research* 8(1):91–113.

Hunter, Andrea. 2015. 'Lesbian mommy blogging in Canada: Documenting subtle homophobia in Canadian society and building community online.' *Journal of Lesbian Studies* 19(2):212–29.

Isaksen, Lise Widding. 2002. 'Masculine dignity and the dirty body.' *NORA (Nordic Institute of Feminist and Gender Research)* 10(3):137–46.

———. 2005. 'Gender and care: The role of cultural ideas of dirt and disgust.' In *Gender, Bodies and Work*, edited by Berit Brandth, Elin Kvande and David Morgan. Aldershot: Ashgate.

Jamieson, Lynn. 1998. *Intimacy: Personal Relationships in Modern Societies*. Cambridge: Polity Press.

Johansson, Thomas. 2011. 'The construction of the new father: How middle-class men become present fathers.' *International Review of Modern Sociology* 37(1):111–26.

Johansson, Thomas and Roger Klinth. 2008. 'Caring fathers: The ideology of gender equality and masculine positions.' *Men and Masculinities* 11(1):42–62.

Kaufman, Gayle. 2013. *Superdads: How Fathers Balance Work and Family in the 21st Century*. New York: New York University Press.

Kilkey, Majella and Harriet Clarke. 2010. 'Disabled men and fathering: Opportunities and constraints.' *Community, Work and Family* 13(2):127–46.

Kimmel, Michael S. 2012. *Manhood in America: A Cultural History*. New York: Oxford University Press.

Kozinets, Robert V. 2010. *Netnography: Doing Ethnographic Research Online*. Los Angeles: Sage.

Kvande, Elin. 2005. 'Embodying male workers as fathers in a flexible working life.' In *Gender, Bodies and Work*, edited by Berit Brandth, Elin Kvande and David Morgan. Aldershot: Ashgate.

Lamb, Michael E., Joseph H. Pleck, E.L. Charnov and J.A. Levine. 1985. 'Paternal behavior in humans.' *American Zoologist* 25:883–94.

Lammi-Taskula, Johanna. 2006. 'Nordic men on parental leave: Can the welfare state change gender relations?' In *Politicising Parenthood in Scandinavia*, edited by A.L. Ellingsaeter and A. Leira. Bristol: Policy Press.

Lawton, Julia. 1998. 'Contemporary hospice care: The sequestration of the unbounded body and "dirty dying".' *Sociology of Health and Illness* 20(2):121–43.

Leggatt-Cook, Chez and Kerry Chamberlain. 2012. 'Blogging for weight loss: Personal accountability, writing selves, and the weight-loss blogosphere.' *Sociology of Health and Illness* 34(7):963–77.

Lewis, Michael. 2009. *Home Game: An Accidental Guide to Fatherhood*. New York: W.W. Norton & Company.

———. 2014. *Flash Boys*. New York: W.W. Norton and Co.

Lezard, Nicholas. 2005. 'Invasion of the pregnant dads.' *The Guardian*, January 26. Retrieved from http://www.theguardian.com/society/2005/jan/26/childrensservices.healthmindandbodyreviews/, April 9, 2015.

Li, Dan and Gina Walejko. 2008. 'Splogs and abandoned blogs: The perils of sampling bloggers and their blogs.' *Information, Communication and Society* 11(2):279–96.

Logelin, Matthew. 2011. *Two Kisses For Maddy: A Memoir of Love and Loss*. New York: Grand Central Publishing.

Lopez, Linda K. 2009. 'The radical act of "mommy blogging": Redefining motherhood through the blogosphere.' *New Media & Society* 11(5):729–47.

Lupton, Deborah 2012. 'Infant embodiment and interembodiment: A review of sociocultural perspectives.' *Childhood* 20(1):37–50.

Lupton, Deborah and Lesley Barclay. 1997. *Constructing Fatherhood*. London: Sage Publications.

MacKay, Steph and Christine Dallaire. 2014. 'Skateboarding women: Building collective identity in cyberspace.' *Journal of Sport and Social Issues* 38(6): 548–66.

Magaraggia, Sveva. 2013. 'Tensions between fatherhood and the social construction of masculinity in Italy.' *Current Sociology* 61(1):76–92.

Marshall, Katherine. 2006. 'Converging gender roles.' *Perspectives on Labour and Income* 7(7):5–17.

Marsiglio, William, Paul Amato, Randall D. Day and Michael E. Lamb. 2000. 'Scholarship on fatherhood in the 1990s and beyond.' *Journal of Marriage and Family* 62(4):1173–91.

Marsiglio, William and Kevin Roy. 2012. *Nurturing Dads: Social Initiatives for Contemporary Fatherhood.* New York: Russell Sage Foundation.

Mauss, Marcel. 1950 (1979). *Sociology and Psychology: Essays.* London: Routledge and Kegan Paul.

———. 1973. 'Techniques of the body.' *Economy and Society* 2(1):70–88.

Maynes, Mary Jo, Jennifer L. Pierce and Barbara Laslett. 2008. *Telling Stories: The Use of Personal Narratives in the Social Sciences and History.* Ithaca: Cornell University Press.

McKay, Lindsey and Andrea Doucet. 2010. '"Without taking away her leave": A Canadian case study of couples' decisions on fathers' use of paid parental leave.' *Fathering* 8(3):300–20.

McNeill, Ted. 2007. 'Fathers of children with a chronic health condition: Beyond gender stereotypes.' *Men and Masculinities* 9(4):409–24.

Merleau-Ponty, Maurice. 1962. *Phenomenology of Perception.* London: Routledge and Kegan Paul Ltd.

Merrill, Barbara and Linden West. 2009. *Using Biographical Methods in Social Research.* Los Angeles: Sage.

Messerschmidt, James W. 1999. 'Making bodies matter: Adolescent masculinities, the body, and varieties of violence.' *Theoretical Criminology* 3(2):175–96.

———. 2012. 'Engendering gendered knowledge: Assessing the academic appropriation of hegemonic masculinity.' *Men and Masculinities* 15(1):56–76.

Messner, Michael A. 1990. 'When bodies are weapons: Masculinity and violence in sport.' *International Review for the Sociology of Sport* 25(3):203–20.

Miller, Edward A. 2010. 'Diagnosis blog: Checking up on health blogs in the blogosphere.' *American Journal of Public Health* 100(8):1514–19.

Miller, Tina. 2010. '"It's a triangle that's difficult to square": Men's intentions and practices around caring, work, and first-time fatherhood.' *Fathering* 8(3):362–78.

———. 2011a. 'Falling back into gender? Men's narratives and practices around first-time fatherhood.' *Sociology* 45(6):1094–109.

———. 2011b. *Making Sense of Fatherhood: Gender, Caring and Work.* Cambridge: Cambridge University Press.

———. 2012. 'Balancing caring and paid work in the UK: Narrating "choices" as first-time parents.' *International Review of Sociology* 22(1):39–52.

Monaghan, Lee. 2002. 'Hard men, shop boys and others: Embodying competence in a masculinist occupation.' *The Sociological Review* 50(3):334–55.

———. 2005. 'Big handsome men, bears and others: Virtual constructions of "fat male embodiment".' *Body & Society* 11(2):81–111.

Mooney, Ann, Julia Brannen, Valerie Wigfall and Violetta Parutis. 2013. 'The impact of employment on fatherhood across family generations in white British, Polish and Irish origin families.' *Community, Work & Family* 16(4): 372–89.

Morgan, David. 1993. 'You too can have a body like mine: Reflections on the male body and masculinities.' In *Body Matters: Essays on the Sociology of the Body*, edited by Sue Scott and David Morgan. London: Falmer Press.

———. 2002. 'You too can have a body like mine.' In *Gender: A Sociological Reader*, edited by Stevi Jackson and Sue Scott. London: Routledge.

Nettleton, Sarah and Jonathan Watson. 1998. 'The body in everyday life: An introduction.' In *The Body in Everyday Life*, edited by Sarah Nettleton and Jonathan Watson. London: Routledge.

Newbold, Ian. 2013. *Parenting With Balls*. London: New Holland Publishers Pty. Ltd.

Norman, Helen, Mark Elliot and Colette Fagan. 2014. 'Which fathers are the most involved in taking care of their toddlers in the UK? An investigation of the predictors of paternal involvement.' *Community, Work and Family* 17(2):163–80.

O'Brien, Margaret. 2009. 'Fathers, parental leave policies, and infant quality of life: International perspectives and policy impact.' *Annals of the American Academy of Political and Social Science* 624:190–213.

O'Brien, Margaret, Berit Brandth and Elin Kvande. 2007. 'Fathers, work and family life: Global perspectives and new insights.' *Community, Work and Family* 10(4):375–86.

Palkovitz, Rob. 1997. 'Reconstructing "involvement": Expanding conceptualizations of men's caring in contemporary families.' In *Generative Fathering: Beyond Deficit Perspectives*, edited by Alan J. Hawkins and David C. Dollahite. Thousand Oaks: Sage.

———. 2002. *Involved Fathering and Men's Adult Development*. Mahwah, NJ: Lawrence Erlbaum Associates.

Paulson, J.F. and S.D. Bazemore. 2010. 'Prenatal and postpartum depression in fathers and its association with maternal depression: A meta-analysis.' *Journal of the American Medical Association* 303(19):1961–69.

Plantin, Lars, Sven-Axel Mansson and Jeremy Kearney. 2003. 'Talking and doing fatherhood: On fatherhood in Sweden and England.' *Fathering* 1(1):3–26.

Pleck, Joseph H. 1987. 'American fathering in historical perspective.' In *Changing Men: New Directions in Research on Men and Masculinity*, edited by Michael S. Kimmel. Newbury Park: Sage.

———. 2013. 'Foreword'. In *Fatherhood in Cultural Context*, edited by David Shwalb, Barbara Shwalb and Michael Lamb. New York: Routledge.

Pleck, Joseph H. and Brian P. Masciadrelli. 2004. 'Paternal involvement by U.S. residential fathers: Levels, sources and consequences.' In *The Role of the Father in Child Development (4th edition)*, edited by Michael E. Lamb. Hoboken, NJ: John Wiley and Sons.

Pleck, Joseph H. and Jeffrey L. Stueve. 2001. 'Time and paternal involvement.' In *Minding the Time in Family Experience: Emerging Perspectives and Issues*, edited by Kerry J. Daly. Amsterdam: JAI.

Plummer, Ken. 2001. *Documents of Life 2: An Invitation to a Critical Humanism*. London: Sage Publications.

Pocock, Barbara. 2005. 'Work/care regimes: Institutions, culture and behaviour and the Australian case.' *Gender, Work and Organization* 12(1):32–49.

Pratt, Michael W., Heather L. Lawford and James W. Allen. 2012. 'Young fatherhood, generativity, and men's development: Travelling a two-way street to maturity.' In *Father Involvement in Canada: Diversity, Renewal and Transformation*, edited by Jessica Ball and Kerry Daly. Vancouver: UBC Press.

Raley, Sara, Suzanne M. Bianchi and Wendy Wang. 2012. 'When do fathers care? Mothers' economic contribution and fathers' involvement in child care.' *American Journal of Sociology* 117(5):1422–59.

Ranson, Gillian. 2001. 'Men at work: Change – or no change? – in the era of the "new father".' *Men and Masculinities* 4(1):3–26.

———. 2010. *Against the Grain: Couples, Gender and the Reframing of Parenting*. Toronto: University of Toronto Press.

———. 2012. 'Men, paid employment and family responsibilities: Conceptualizing the "working father".' *Gender, Work and Organization* 19(6):741–61.

Rehel, Erin M. 2014. 'When Dad stays home too: Paternity leave, gender and parenting.' *Gender & Society* 28(1):110–32.

Rettberg, Jill Walker. 2014. *Blogging (2nd edition)*. Cambridge: Polity Press.

Riach, Kathleen and Leanne Cutcher. 2014. 'Built to last: Ageing, class and the masculine body in a UK hedge fund.' *Work, Employment and Society* 28(5):771–87.

Riessman, Catherine Kohler. 2008. *Narrative Methods for the Human Sciences*. London: Sage Publications.

Risman, Barbara J. 1986. 'Can men "mother"? Life as a single father.' *Family Relations* 35(1):95–102.

———. 1987. 'Intimate relationships from a microstructural perspective: Men who mother.' *Gender & Society* 1(1):6–32.

Robertson, Ben. 2012. *Hear Me Roar: The Story of a Stay-at-home Dad*. St. Lucia: University of Queensland Press.

Rothman, Barbara Katz. 1989. *Recreating Motherhood*. New York: W.W. Norton and Company.

Ruddick, Sara. 1982. 'Maternal thinking.' In *Rethinking the Family: Some Feminist Questions*, edited by Barrie Thorne and Marilyn Yalom. New York: Longman.

———. 1995. *Maternal Thinking: Toward a Politics of Peace*. Boston: Beacon Press.

———. 1997. 'The idea of fatherhood.' In *Feminism and Families*, edited by Hilde Lindemann Nelson. New York: Routledge.

Rummery, Kirstein and Michael Fine. 2012. 'Care: A critical review of theory, policy and practice.' *Social Policy and Administration* 46(3):321–43.

Saiki, Lori S. and Kristin G. Cloyes. 2014. 'Blog text about female incontinence: Presentation of self, disclosure and social risk assessment.' *Nursing Research* 63(2):137–42.

Sayer, Liana, Suzanne M. Bianchi and John P. Robinson. 2004. 'Are parents investing less in children? Trends in mothers' and fathers' time with children.' *American Journal of Sociology* 110(1):1–43.

Schachtner, Christina. 2015. 'Transculturality in the internet: Culture flows and virtual publics.' *Current Sociology Monograph* 63(2):228–43.

Schwartz, Pepper. 1994. *Peer Marriage: How Love Between Equals Really Works*. New York: Free Press.

Seward, Rudy Ray, Dale E. Yeatts, Iftekhar Amin, and Amy DeWitt. 2006a. 'Employment leave and fathers' involvement with children: According to mothers and fathers.' *Men and Masculinities* 8(4):405–27.

———. 2006b. 'Fathers taking parental leave and their involvement with children: An exploratory study.' *Community, Work and Family* 9(1):1–9.

Shilling, Chris. 2003. *The Body and Social Theory*. London: Sage Publications.

Shirani, Fiona, Karen Henwood and Carrie Coltart. 2012a. 'Meeting the challenges of intensive parenting culture: Gender, risk management and the moral parent.' *Sociology* 46(1):25–40.

———. 2012b. '"Why aren't you at work?" Negotiating economic models of fathering identity.' *Fathering* 10(3):362–78.

Shonkwiler, Alison. 2008. 'The selfish-enough father: Gay adoption and the late-capitalist family.' *GLQ: A Journal of Gay and Lesbian Studies* 14(4):537–67.

Shows, Carla and Naomi Gerstel. 2009. 'Fathering, class and gender: A comparison of physicians and emergency medical technicians.' *Gender & Society* 23(2):161–87.

Shwalb, David, Barbara Shwalb and Michael Lamb (eds). 2013. *Fatherhood in Cultural Context*. New York: Routledge.

Silva, Elizabeth B. 2005. 'Gender, home and family in cultural capital theory.' *British Journal of Sociology* 56(1):83–103.

Singley, Susan G. and Hynes, Kathryn. 2005. 'Transitions to parenthood: Work-family policies, gender and the couple context.' *Gender & Society* 19(3):376–97.

Smart, Carol and Bren Neale. 1999. *Family Fragments?* Cambridge: Polity Press.

Smith, Sidonie and Julia Watson. 2010. *Reading Autobiography: A Guide for Interpreting Life Narratives (2nd edition)*. Minneapolis: University of Minnesota Press.

Snarey, John. 1993. *How Fathers Care for the Next Generation: A Four-Decade Study*. Cambridge: Harvard University Press.

Solomon, Catherine R. 2014. '"After months of it, you just want to punch someone in the face": Stay-at-home fathers and masculine identities.' *Michigan Family Review* 18(1):23–38.

Steinmetz, Katy. 2015. 'The Dad 2.0 summit: Making the case for a new kind of manhood'. *Time* magazine online, February 21. Retrieved from http://time.com/3717511/dad-summit-manhood/, April 4, 2015.

Sullivan, Oriel. 2004. 'Changing gender practices within the household: A theoretical perspective.' *Gender & Society* 18:207–22.

———. 2006. *Changing Gender Relations, Changing Families*. Lanham: Rowman and Littlefield.

———. 2010. 'Changing differences by educational attainment in fathers' domestic labour and child care.' *Sociology* 44(4):716–33.

Tahhan, D. 2008. 'Depth and space in sleep: Intimacy, touching and the body in Japanese co-sleeping rituals.' *Body & Society* 14(4):37–56.

Takeda, Atsushi. 2013. 'Weblog narratives of Japanese migrant women in Australia: Consequences of international mobility and migration.' *International Journal of Intercultural Relations* 37:1309–17.

Taylor, Judith. 2009. 'Rich sensitivities: An analysis of conflict among women in feminist memoir.' *Canadian Review of Sociology* 46(2):123–41.

Thiel, Darren. 2007. 'Class in construction: Building workers, dirty work and physical cultures.' *British Journal of Sociology* 58(2):227–51.

Townsend, Nicholas W. 2002. *The Package Deal: Marriage, Work and Fatherhood in Men's Lives*. Philadelphia: Temple University Press.

Tronto, Joan. 1998. 'An ethic of care.' *Generations* 22(3):15–20.

Tucker, Judith S. 2009. 'Foreword.' In *Mothering and Blogging: The Radical Act of the Mommyblog*, edited by May Friedman and Shana L. Calixte. Toronto: Demeter Press.

Turner, Bryan S. 1992. *Regulating Bodies: Essays in Medical Sociology*. London: Routledge.

———. 2012. 'Embodied practice: Martin Heidegger, Pierre Bourdieu and Michel Foucault.' In *Routledge Handbook of Body Studies*, edited by Bryan S. Turner. Abingdon: Routledge.

Twigg, Julia. 2000. *Bathing – the Body and Community Care*. London: Routledge.

Twigg, Julia, Carol Wolkowitz, Rachel Lara Cohen and Sarah Nettleton. 2011. 'Conceptualising body work in health and social care.' *Sociology of Health and Illness* 33(2):171–88.

Ungerson, Clare. 2005. 'Care, work and feeling.' *Sociological Review* 54(1):188–203.

Viner, Brian. 2013. *The Good, the Dad and the Ugly: The Trials of Fatherhood*. London: Simon and Schuster.

Wacquant, Loïc. 1995. 'Pugs at work: Bodily capital and bodily labour among professional boxers.' *Body & Society* 1(1):65–93.

———. 2004. *Body and Soul: Notebooks of an Apprentice Boxer*. Oxford: Oxford University Press.

———. 2014. 'Homines in extremis: What fighting scholars teach us about habitus.' *Body & Society* 20(2):3–17.

Wall, Karin. 2014. 'Fathers on leave alone: Does it make a difference to their lives?' *Fathering* 12(2):196–210.

Watson, Jonathan. 1998. 'Running around like a lunatic: Colin's body and the case of male embodiment.' In *The Body in Everyday Life*, edited by Sarah Nettleton and Jonathan Watson. London: Routledge.

West, Candace and Don Zimmerman. 1987. 'Doing gender.' *Gender & Society* 1:125–51.

Wharton, Amy S. and Rebecca J. Erickson. 1993. 'Managing emotions on the job and at home: Understanding the consequences of multiple emotional roles.' *Academy of Management Review* 18(3):457–86.

Wilkinson, David and Mike Thelwall. 2011. 'Researching personal information on the public web: Methods and ethics.' *Social Science Computer Review* 29(4):387–401.

Williams, Christine L. 1989. *Gender Differences at Work: Women and Men in Nontraditional Occupations*. Berkeley: University of California Press.

———. 1992. 'The glass escalator: Hidden advantages for men in the "female" professions.' *Social Problems* 39(3):253–67.

Williams, Stephen. 2008. 'What is fatherhood? Searching for the reflexive father.' *Sociology* 42(3):487–502.

Wolkowitz, Carol. 2006. *Bodies at Work*. London: Sage.

Young, Kevin, William McTeer and Philip White. 1994. 'Body talk: Male athletes reflect on sport, injury and pain.' *Sociology of Sport Journal* 11:175–94.

Zussman, Robert. 2004. 'People in places.' *Qualitative Sociology* 27:351–63.

# Index

CPSIA information can be obtained at www.ICGtesting.com
Printed in the USA
BVOW08*1240070416

443358BV00002B/2/P